T0366506

Theism and Ultimate Explanation

Theism and Ultimate Explanation

Explanation

The Necessary Shape of Contingency

TIMOTHY O'CONNOR

A John Wiley & Sons, Ltd., Publication

This edition first published 2012
© 2012 Timothy O'Connor

Edition history: Blackwell Publishing Ltd (hardback, 2008)

Blackwell Publishing was acquired by John Wiley & Sons in February 2007. Blackwell's publishing program has been merged with Wiley's global Scientific, Technical, and Medical business to form Wiley-Blackwell.

Registered Office
John Wiley & Sons Ltd, The Atrium, Southern Gate, Chichester, West Sussex, PO19 8SQ, UK

Editorial Offices
350 Main Street, Malden, MA 02148-5020, USA
9600 Garsington Road, Oxford, OX4 2DQ, UK
The Atrium, Southern Gate, Chichester, West Sussex, PO19 8SQ, UK

For details of our global editorial offices, for customer services, and for information about how to apply for permission to reuse the copyright material in this book please see our website at www.wiley.com/wiley-blackwell.

The right of Timothy O'Connor to be identified as the author of this work has been asserted in accordance with the UK Copyright, Designs and Patents Act 1988.

All rights reserved. No part of this publication may be reproduced, stored in a retrieval system, or transmitted, in any form or by any means, electronic, mechanical, photocopying, recording or otherwise, except as permitted by the UK Copyright, Designs and Patents Act 1988, without the prior permission of the publisher.

Wiley also publishes its books in a variety of electronic formats. Some content that appears in print may not be available in electronic books.

Designations used by companies to distinguish their products are often claimed as trademarks. All brand names and product names used in this book are trade names, service marks, trademarks or registered trademarks of their respective owners. The publisher is not associated with any product or vendor mentioned in this book. This publication is designed to provide accurate and authoritative information in regard to the subject matter covered. It is sold on the understanding that the publisher is not engaged in rendering professional services. If professional advice or other expert assistance is required, the services of a competent professional should be sought.

Library of Congress Cataloging-in-Publication Data

O'Connor, Timothy, 1965–
Theism and ultimate explanation : the necessary shape of contingency / Timothy O'Connor.
  p. cm.
Includes bibliographical references (p.) and index.
ISBN 978-1-4051-6969-1 (hardcover : alk. paper) – ISBN 978-1-4443-5088-3 (paperback)
1. Theism.   2. Modality (Logic)
3. Contingency (Philosophy)   I. Title.
BD555.O36 2008
211′.3–dc22
                                        2007032685

A catalogue record for this book is available from the British Library.

This book is published in the following electronic formats: ePDFs 9781444345469; Wiley Online Library 9781444345490; ePub 9781444345476; Mobi 9781444345483

Set in 10 on 12.5 pt Sabon by Toppan Best-set Premedia Limited

1   2012

FOR GAIL
with gratitude and affection

Contents

Preface

This is a book in two parts. In the first part (chapters 1–2), I examine the propriety of beliefs concerning what is (absolutely, or simply) possible and what is necessary: I might have been a roofer, I could not have been a whale, two and two necessarily make four. If such beliefs are rationally justified, as it seems, how do they acquire this status? I contend that such 'modal' beliefs are justified by a process of reflective equilibrium on the jumble of basic and often implicit modal beliefs that we find ourselves with at the outset of theoretical inquiry. At times, this process will lead us to abandon or revise previously foundational beliefs, as we hone and uncover methods for belief systematization and extension, for example, or as we come to see the space of possibility as constrained by necessities, acceptance of which is justified in part by the explanatory role they play within a plausible metaphysical framework. The epistemology of modal belief is a topic of fundamental philosophical importance in its own right, and I hope that what I say concerning it is sufficiently original and well argued to be of interest to the specialist on contemporary discussion of the topic. But these chapters are also meant to lay a foundation for the book's second part (chapters 3–6), in which I consider the traditional metaphysician's quest, nowadays much neglected, for a true *ultimate* explanation of the most general features of the world we inhabit. More accurately, the search is for a metaphysical framework that can be seen to allow for the *possibility* of an ultimate explanation that is correct and complete, even if (as is plausible) significant details must forever remain beyond our ken. Drawing upon my views concerning the role of necessities in ordinary explanations, I defend a version of the 'Leibnizian' cosmological argument from contingency for the existence of transcendent necessary being as the source, and basis for ultimate explanation, of contingent beings and their interconnected histories.

Let me now elaborate on the very general summary of the book I have just given. The motivation behind the first part of the book will not be readily apparent to the philosophically innocent. Many modal claims seem boringly obvious, and the evident justification of our corresponding beliefs seems hardly worth remarking on. Who could doubt that I justifiably believe that it is absolutely possible that I might have been a roofer? But, though we seem to know many such truths (without having to work up a mental sweat), it is unclear on reflection just *how* we know them. We know how to verify at least pedestrian truths about what is *actually* the case through observation and reflection, as when I come to believe that my dog is on the couch by looking in that direction, and that my wife is not nearby by calling her name and receiving no answer. But how do I go about 'verifying' that my dog *might* have been in the yard instead, or that my wife not only is not but *could not* have been simultaneously in this room and upstairs? These truths are not observable, or obviously inferable from what can be observed. Traditional philosophers sometimes spoke of 'seeing' the necessity of certain propositions and the possible truth of others, but, in these sober days of naturalizing the mind, it is hard to credit the idea that there is a primitive capacity to grasp modal facts in a quasi-perceptual fashion. And when we consider that there is some causal story or other to be told concerning how modal beliefs are formed and sustained, the epistemological worry seems to deepen: if the truth in modal matters is independent of the process by which we come to believe them – and it can seem that it must be – then, even if those beliefs are largely correct, this seems accidental, epistemically speaking. And what is in this sense accidentally believed is plausibly not an instance of knowledge.

For reasons such as these, many recent philosophers consider the source of a priori beliefs concerning such matters to be deeply puzzling, enough so that it puts in doubt the traditional status of certain modal propositions as simple and basic truths whose acceptance must underlie our acceptance of other, empirical truths. In Chapter 1, I take a tour of the main strategies for doing away with modality as a realm of fundamental truth. I consider and criticize Quine's modal nihilism; the modal reductionism of Tarski, Armstrong, and Lewis; reductionism's cousin, modal deflationism, as developed by Rosen and Sider; and two varieties of modal anti-realism, Sidelle's conventionalism and Blackburn's expressivism. A common moral running through my critiques is that we simply are unable in our ordinary explanatory projects to do without acceptance of a rich realm of irreducible modal truth.

The next chapter thus assumes that there is such a realm of irreducible fact and tries to outline a plausible epistemology of belief concerning it. The failure of two previous attempts (those of Yablo and Peacocke) underscores the need to integrate our accounts of the justification of modal and nonmodal beliefs and to appreciate the role that necessities sometimes play within explanations. (In much contemporary thought, there is a deeply held but questionable presumption of possibility for nonmodal assertions that leads one to suppose that basic possibility claims are easier to establish than claims that place significant constraints on the scope of possibility. If we are to make headway towards a viable modal epistemology, we must abandon this presumption. (Here, as elsewhere in philosophy, David Hume is the arch-villain.)

I divide modal beliefs into two basic categories. The first concerns highly general – often, but not always, formal – *theoretical* modal judgments. Here, I suggest that, starting from an assortment of basic intuitions, new beliefs acquire and old ones lose epistemic justification through a fallible process of reflective equilibrium. Occasionally, we simply have to weigh the relative strength of conflicting modal intuitions. Our judgments are also refined through many avenues, including the creation and honing of formal methods (especially in mathematics), indirect reflections on other, better-developed disciplines, and the sometimes arduous process of concept development (as with the mathematical concept of continuity). There has been a strong tendency to overplay the significance of revolutions in mathematics, and the rise of non-Euclidean geometry is an overworked example. I try to show how such developments are perfectly congruent with traditional acceptance of the primacy of a priori beliefs in developing our theoretical understanding even of the empirical realm.

My second category is *objectual* modal judgments, concerning ontological categories and individual and kind essences. I argue that the resolution of these vexed matters will turn more on *other* metaphysical issues than is commonly appreciated – in particular, on the nature of causation and the partly empirical question of whether some form of reductionism or a robustly ontological type of emergence is correct, and correct for which high-level kinds. Given particular commitments on these matters, there is a plausible method for resolving questions of essence. (I note that, given the broader metaphysical views I myself hold, it is quite plausible to be conventionalist about some, though not all, high level entities and their ostensible kinds.)

I close the second chapter by suggesting that we think of various "possibilities" in terms of concentric spheres. The outermost layer encompasses all propositions not deemed impossible by purely logical considerations, and inside that is a layer restricted to those that remain consistent once the meanings of nonlogical terms are fixed. But these are not distinct kinds of possibility, just indicators of two groups of necessities that constrain simple possibility. In both science and metaphysics, we uncover further necessities that show the space of possibility to be smaller still. This much is a familiar picture, if controversial. But this way of looking at matters leaves open the question whether there are any constraints on possibility even deeper than those commonly acknowledged, necessities that are invoked in global explanations beyond the reach even of our most fundamental sciences.

The stage is thus set for a consideration of that most fundamental metaphysical question, or set of questions, concerning existence itself. The best form of the question – one that presumes the least – is this: are there contingently existing objects, and if there are, why do those particular contingent objects exist and undergo the events they do? I consider a variety of options for providing an outline of an answer to this question. I argue that the only one that is not beset by fundamental problems is one that accepts the existence of contingent beings and maintains that they are the causal product of a purposive, transcendent necessary being, one for whom existence and essence are inseparable, one that simply *must* be. Ever since our nemesis Hume, it has been argued by many that the concept of necessary being is either incoherent or devoid of meaning; I argue that there is no basis for either of these claims along the lines that are commonly given. It has been further argued, especially in recent discussion, that the claim that contingency is the product of necessity, if followed consistently, will lead to 'modal collapse': all is necessary, right down to the fingerprint presently on my keyboard. I argue that this judgment is mistaken, by presenting a schema of contingent explanation that is not forced to accept *brutely* contingent facts.

In defending the acceptability of this view, I consider and reject several alternatives. In a rather hard-scrabble metaphysical excursion, I argue that broadly Spinozistic views that deem the universe itself or its fundamental constituents to be necessary are not sustainable, given only minimal assumptions concerning the character of the universe. I then consider versions of a 'Chaos' model of transcendent necessary being as an impersonal alternative to the purposive 'Logos' model. I draw upon the contemporary 'fine-tuning' design argument – one that in my judgment is not probative as a stand-alone argument for theism – to defeat the most probable version of Chaos.

In Chapter 5, I revisit the question of the scope of contingency given the foregoing claims. I contend that, if we identify our purposive necessary being with the absolutely perfect being of traditional philosophical theology (something I do not argue here), there is quite strong reason to suppose that there must be an infinity (at least aleph-null) of universes, ordered without finite upper bound by their intrinsic goodness. If this is correct, there could not have been, for example, just one universe, or none at all. I note that this thesis has some relevance to the problem of evil. Finally, I suggest that there is reason to take seriously Leibniz's seemingly outlandish view that the ontological ground of the most fundamental modal truths is the cognitive activity of the one being that is necessary in itself.

In a final chapter, directed as much to academic theologians as to philosophers, I reflect on the relationship of natural or philosophical theology to the revealed theology of the Bible. Natural theology is highly unfashionable among theologians, on both epistemological and metaphysical grounds. The latter have to do with the alleged incompatibility of certain unfamiliar attributes posited in natural theology (e.g., timelessness and immutability) with the God of the Bible, who is portrayed as engaged with and responsive to His people. I give reason for agreeing that *some* contentions made by natural theologians do not cohere with the Biblical portrayal of God, at least given the assumption that human beings have free will. However, I also go on to argue that the denial of the central natural theological thesis I have argued in this work – that the source of contingent things must be conceived to be a necessary being – is flatly inconsistent with the Biblical conception of God's sovereignty over Creation. Do away with 'onto-theology' altogether, and you'll have done away with theism altogether.

My thinking on the topics of this book has been informed by conversation and written comments from a wide range of individuals. The book grew out of a series of public lectures that I delivered at the University of St Andrews while I was a Gifford Research Fellow in the Department of Logic and Metaphysics during the 1996–7 academic year. There I received helpful feedback from philosophers John Haldane, Crispin Wright, and Tim Kenyon, and theologians Richard Bauckham and Trevor Hart. Since then, I have given papers on related material at Wheaton and Franklin and Marshall Colleges and at the following universities: Free (Amsterdam), Notre Dame, Seattle Pacific, Western Washington, Beijing, Oxford, Colorado at Boulder, Central European (Budapest), St Louis, Soochow (Taipei), Azusa Pacific, and Trinity College, Dublin. I thank all these audiences for their discussion, and in particular Dan Howard-Snyder, Hud Hudson, Jon Jacobs, Rob Koons, Brian Leftow, Scott MacDonald, Michael Murray, Ted Sider, Richard Swinburne, Michael Tooley, Peter van Inwagen, Ed Wierenga, Hong Yu Wong, Rene van Woudenberg, and Dean Zimmerman. I have also benefited from excellent criticisms and suggestions from three anonymous Blackwell referees.

Chapters 4 and 5 of this book incorporate material from two articles of mine that were previously published (2004; 2008) respective. I am grateful to the editors and to Oxford University Press for permission to reprint modified versions of this material.

Part I | The Explanatory Role of Necessity

1 | Modality and Explanation

Some of our assertions ascribe properties of "necessity," "possibility," "impossibility," "essence," and the like to propositions or individuals. These *modal* statements go beyond simple assertions about what is the case – *you are sitting in a chair now, wondering if your decision to open this book was a wise one* – and make claims about how things could not possibly be, or could be, or must be – *you could not be listening to Mozart on Neptune, yet you could be lounging in a comfortable chair in your home listening to Mozart, and in any case you must be mad to have freely chosen to read the reflections of a philosopher instead.*[1] Or again, and more relevant to theoretical concerns, *it is impossible for there to be true contradictions, cows are essentially mammals, it is impossible for humans to survive the ingestion of large doses of cyanide,* and (closer to home) *it might have happened (it was once possible) that I was kidnapped at birth by a band of gypsies related to some of my less distinguished Bohemian forebears and joined in their adventures rather than pursuing the far less exciting life of a philosopher.*

As these examples suggest, the specific meanings of modal terms such as "necessity" and "possibility" varies with context. (But note that these properties are interdefinable within a given context: To say that a proposition expresses a possibility, in some particular sense, is just to say that it is not necessary in that same sense. Or to say that it is necessary is to say that it is not possible that it be false.)

Relative and Absolute Necessity

The central distinction to notice is that between absolute and (merely) relative kinds of necessity/possibility (cf. Hale 1996: 93–117; 1997: 487–514).

Many familiar modal claims are clearly made against some set of background assumptions, as when a detective says that Professor Plum could not have been the murderer, or when I say that I cannot run a 4-minute mile. When making such claims, we hold fixed certain background truths (vaguely understood), and intend to call attention to the fact that the 'necessity' in question is an invariable consequence of those truths. (In the examples given, such background truths include, in the one case, perhaps facts about the Professor's location around the time of the murder, together with facts about time limits on travel across the requisite distance given available means of transport. *Given* these and a few other unquestioned facts, the Professor could not have been the murderer. In the second case, the background facts include my current level of physiological stamina and biological facts about the consequence of this when I set out to run a mile as fast as I can.) If we dignify such homely examples by taking them to implicitly express a general form of necessity, then details aside, it is clear that the kind in question would be merely relative or conditional: relative to some basic facts at least some of which need not have been the case, the proposition in question is necessary because a direct consequence of those facts. (One might say that the fact that I cannot run a 4-minute mile represents a 'biological necessity' for me at the present time. And perhaps it is a biological necessity for human beings generally that none of us can run a 2-minute mile.)

Notice that our understanding of such relative necessities rests on a prior grasp of absolute necessity, or necessity *tout court*. To say that it is biologically impossible for a human being to run a 2-minute mile is to say that certain facts about human biology are strictly inconsistent with their achieving such a feat: it is flat-out impossible that such facts and feat co-obtain. Similarly, consider what philosophers term 'the law of noncontradiction': For any statement p, it is not the case that both p and not-p. (That is, there are no true contradictions.) This proposition does not, it seems, just happen to be true, as if it would be intelligible to suppose that tomorrow I should go into my office and discover, contrary to the principle, that my desk both is and is not there at one and the same time. Rather, we recognize that it must be true, entirely independent of engaging in any kind of empirical inquiry, as all such inquiry presupposes it. Contrast the necessity of such a logical truth with the example of biological necessity just given. It is not absolutely necessary that I cannot run a 4-minute mile. Presumably, I can or could have so trained myself that this would have been possible. Likewise, even the physically unalterable fact that none of us can run a 2-minute mile is not obviously absolutely necessary. Imagine there having been different basic physical forces such that the power generated when our feet make contact with the ground is greater than is the case as things actually stand.

Scientifically Established Necessities

Ordinary explanations of particular phenomena that draw upon scientific theories are replete with modal concepts. Human beings cannot survive more than 5 days without water; matter-energy must be conserved; it is possible that this atom of radium will decay within its half-life, and possible that it will not; all physical structures conforming to the molecular structure of H_2O and within a certain range of temperature must exhibit the characteristic properties of liquidity.

Now some philosophers and even the occasional scientist will interpret all this as loose talk. The strict truth, on at least one view, is that a physical theory simply identifies measurable qualities and describes a model of their dynamical co-variation. The theory predicts (and retrodicts) that the distribution of qualities in the world conforms to the model. It does not imply that the world *must* conform to the model.

This sort of view is plausible to the following extent: a well-trained scientist who refuses to assert anything beyond this minimalist claim for a theory he embraces can hardly be accused of misunderstanding the theory. Grasping a scientific theory and engaging in the process of refining it in the light of new evidence surely does not involve taking a contentious stand on the philosophical question of what explanation entails by way of metaphysical commitment. By the same token, this minimalist core that is common ground to all competent theorists, regardless of their philosophical views, cannot simply be presumed to suffice of itself for explanatory purposes. And prima facie, it does not. Given simply a range of observations in which F-ness is linked to G-ness either invariably or by some high statistical measure, and a model that links together this and other observed regularities in an elegant fashion, what reason could we have for presuming that unobserved past and future occurrences of F-ness likewise are accompanied by G-ness? When probed, our strong inclination to think the pattern will hold quickly reveals a deeper assumption that it must hold. 'That is the way nature *works*.' Something's being F naturally gives rise, or has a measurable tendency to give rise, to (a suitably placed) something's being G. The property of F-ness, in other words, is somehow assumed to be bound up with a G-ness promoting *tendency*. How precisely we should think about this is a subject we will consider below. For now, I just note that some such partly developed assumption underlies our pervasive tendency to generalize observed results. And it is not just the vulgar who speak and think this way, but ever so many of the learned as well. Consider these randomly selected snippets from discussion in recent issues of *Nature*:

> Injury to the adult central nervous system (CNS) is devastating because of the inability of central neurons to regenerate correct axonal and dendritic conne ctions. . . . The inability of the adult neurons to regrow after injury cannot be entirely attributed to intrinsic differences between adult CNS and all other neurons. As reported by Ramón y Cajal in 1928, Tello showed in 1911 that adult CNS neurons could regrow if they were provided access to the permissive environment of a conditioned sciatic nerve. Seventy years passed before Aguayo and colleagues replicated these studies with new methods that definitively confirmed that adult CNS neurons have regenerative capabilities. This finding revealed that the failure of CNS neurons to regenerate was not an intrinsic deficit of the neuron, but rather a characteristic feature of the damaged environment that either did not support or prevented regeneration. (Horner & Gage 2000: 963–70)

> It has long been known that stable BECs can exist in an infinite homogeneous gas with repulsive interatomic interactions (that is, positive A), but cannot exist in a gas with attractive interactions (negative A). (Burnett, Julienne, Lett, Tiesinga, and Williams 2002: 225–32)

> The amino acid phenylalanine is yet another. Without it, the body cannot function. It is heavily involved in neuron-to-neuron communication and it controls the release of some sleep-, and appetite-regulating hormones. Too much of it, however, damages the brain.
>   The biological catalyst phenylalanine hydroxylase (PH) fine-tunes phenylalanine levels by converting excess amounts into another amino acid, tyrosine. Faulty PH, therefore, can lead to a build-up of phenylalanine in the blood and hence to mental retardation.
>   This is exactly what happens in the genetic condition known as phenylketonuria. All babies are tested for this PH disorder soon after birth since, if present, brain damage can only be averted by stringently controlling a sufferer's dietary intake of phenylalanine. (Moderation in all things 1999)

> Motor proteins are essential to life: without them, all cellular transport would grind to a halt. (Geeves 2002: 129–31)

> These low-Mg# amphiboles are also able to cause the greatest fractionation between Nb/La and Zr/Sm (Fig. 2b). In contrast, amphiboles with Mg# > 80 cannot impart low Nb/Ta to coexisting melts, nor can they cause low Nb/La. (Foley, Tiepolo, and Vannucci 2002: 837–40)

Necessity plays a yet deeper role in the practice of *formulating* scientific theories. Alongside the ever increasing constraints of accumulating empirical evidence, theories are always held to the constraint of logical and mathematical consistency. Possible models that embody formal contradictions are never (knowingly) given consideration. Why not? Let us not be ashamed to consider the obvious: contradictory theories cannot be true. Reality, whatever its particular character, must conform to fundamental logical constraints. It is a rightfully controversial matter exactly which candidate formal constraints are real ones. Surely not *all* those of first-order logic? The vagueness of most of our concepts, the useful invocation of the notion of property indeterminacy (perhaps conceived along the lines of value intervals for the possession of a property) in describing quantum phenomena, and other considerations all raise legitimate issues concerning the normative character of first-order logic with identity. These controversies of detail may be set aside at present, since it remains plausible that whatever we might think about them, a minimum core of pretheoretic formal constraint including, for example, the law of noncontradiction is inevitable. How we are to decide which logical system best captures the necessary structure of reality is a matter to be considered in the next chapter.

The last few paragraphs express common philosophical claims concerning the place of modality in scientific explanations that have nonetheless been heavily challenged, especially in the twentieth century. Various thinkers have sought to reject, deflate, or reconstrue such claims in ways designed to show how the world might be wholly devoid of primitive modal features. Let us call the view these thinkers oppose "robust modal realism."[2] In doing so, we risk confusing it with David Lewis's notorious identification of possible ways things might be with an enormous array of concrete totalities ('worlds') disconnected to the one we inhabit. But Lewis has misappropriated that title (as will become clear below) and so in the interests of clarity it is fitting that we should claim it back. I will consider and criticize a range of views that stand opposed to robust modal realism shortly. But let us first note an important, perhaps central, motivation for pursuing such revisionary stances.

An Epistemological Worry about Modality: Causal Contact with Modal Facts

Assume for the moment that there are irreducible, objective truths involving necessity, such as *Necessarily, there are no true contradictions*. How could we come to know such a truth? Apparently not by anything even generally like the process whereby we come to know truths about our physical environment.[3] In paradigm cases of environmental knowledge, such as my knowing that there is now a computer screen before me, there is a fairly direct causal signal from the circumstance that grounds the truth to my sensory apparatus, giving rise in turn to my belief. In other cases, such as when I come to learn about the world through the testimony of others, there remains a causal connection between the circumstance and my believing it, albeit one that is rather more circuitous. Finally, even in cases of generalizations, my knowledge is typically based in part on causal acquaintance (direct or via testimony) with some of its instances. But, of course, even if I based my acceptance of *Necessarily, there are no true contradictions* on my repeated failure to observe any 'contradictory scenarios', this sort of evidence would provide (meager) evidence only in favor of the embedded, nonmodal generalization. It gives me no reason to accept that such a proposition is *necessarily* true.

Underlying this 'causal contact' challenge to the modal realist is a thesis that all true propositions are in some way 'grounded' in reality, such that one can sensibly ask for a given case whether there is a causal connection between the grounds and an instance of believing the proposition so grounded. In the previous paragraph, I used the vague term "circumstance" to preserve neutrality between two different views about the general nature of such grounds. On the view I favor, for every truth, there is some *entity* or collection of entities that is its grounds, in the sense that the obtaining of those entities metaphysically necessitates the truth of the proposition. This is the 'truthmaker' doctrine, promulgated in recent times by David Armstrong (most recently, 1997: 115–19). Armstrong's version of the doctrine posits that every truthmaker consists in a *state of affairs*, a structured fact (in the Tractarian sense) that helps to constitute the fabric of the world and that consists in an object or objects having properties and/or standing in relations. (Where the cat is on the mat, there is the cat, the mat, the being-on relation, and a further entity, the-cat's-being-on-the-mat, into which the cat, the mat, and the being-on relation enter as constituents.) A less demanding view of grounds maintains that truth does not supervenes on entities alone – on *whether* things are – but on objects and 'how things are' with respect to those objects. According to this view, objects have properties and stand in relations without their being entities which are their having those properties or standing in those relations (see Dodd 2001: 215–20). Defenders of this minimalist view find mysterious the nonmereological composition of Armstrongian states of affairs. They also point out that Armstrong is forced posit a strange global fact (that delimits the totality of facts) to handle seeming counterexamples such as negative truths and is in any case forced to acknowledge that some truths resist grounding in Tractarian facts – e.g., the truth that redness is a property, not an individual.[4]

One need not commit to a view on this matter to see the problem facing the modal realist. Whatever the metaphysical character of the 'grounds' of irreducible modal truths, they wouldn't seem at first glance to be capable of triggering a causal chain that ultimately impacts our cognitive system. The felt immediacy of our grasp of certain elementary necessary truths makes it natural instead to speak of our directly 'seeing' or 'recognizing' their truth. But when such a perceptual metaphor is taken as some kind of analogy, it becomes obscure. It suggests we have a modal-property-detecting capacity in our cognitive architecture, one that is unmediated by anything like sensory organs, such that modal facts impress themselves *directly* on our minds. The problem here is that such a view is wholly implausible on empirical grounds.[5]

Let us be clear about what a causal/perceptual model of knowledge of modal truths requires.[6] Alvin Plantinga (1993) construes the challenge as simply that of showing how a subject has a causal connection to the *proposition* that is believed to be necessary. On his reading, the root worry for Benacerraf and others concerning a priori knowledge (which includes much of our modal knowledge) is that I cannot so much as believe or even entertain the proposition in question without such a state's having the proposition itself in its causal ancestry. In response to this worry, he suggests that it might suffice that we have ordinary perceptual acquaintance with instances of properties that enter into the relevant modal propositions. (e.g., the greenness and redness that appear in *Nothing can simultaneously be green and red all over*). In virtue of this fact, we might be said to be indirectly acquainted with the proposition itself. But, contra Plantinga, the problem is not merely one of showing how I can be causally affected by an abstract object (a proposition). It is rather to show how my belief is a causal consequence, in part, of the proposition's ground, or truthmaker. And the suggestion is that acceptances of (what we are assuming to be) primitive modal truths resist any such subsumption under familiar causal processes such as sensory perception. Causal acquaintance with the nonmodal features of redness and greenness doesn't explain how I come to know that nothing *can be* simultaneously green and red all over. It is the necessity of these properties' mutual exclusion that apparently fails to play a role in my forming this belief. To make matters worse, there surely is *some* kind of true causal explanation for my having such beliefs, in which case my belief will be explained by something other than the modal fact itself. The upshot is that our modal beliefs are at best accidentally true. Were those facts false (*per impossibile*), our beliefs would be just as they are.

Laurence Bonjour advances an outline of a response to the challenge as follows (1998: esp. 101–10, 156–62, 180–6). Using the example of the necessary mutual exclusion of redness and greenness, he suggests that we may intelligibly suppose that the properties themselves (rather than representational surrogates) in some manner enter into the content of the correlated thought. If this is granted, we can then say that we may 'see', by a kind of inspection of these properties' natures, that the relation of mutual exclusion obtains. This is a primitive act of 'rational insight', but, Bonjour contends, there is nothing mysterious about it. It is just what we find it natural to say about such an example, it requires no mysteriously direct contact between a nonspatiotemporal entity and the mind, and it is anyways implicitly presupposed by our practices of rational inquiry, as no alternative view of the justification of such a priori propositions is possible.

However, even if this last claim were correct (something I will challenge in the next chapter), it is doubtful that adopting Bonjour's suggestion would take us very far towards allaying the Benacerraf-inspired worry about a broadly rationalist understanding of modal belief. First, it isn't possible to extend Bonjour's suggestion to cases of highly general propositions that do not reference specific properties or individuals but which instead have a universally quantified form. Second, and more fundamentally, even if Bonjour were right that we have the kind of maximally direct acquaintance with some properties such as redness and greenness, it doesn't become automatically transparent how we might 'see' their necessary mutual exclusion. How exactly does this go beyond our having a disposition to strongly believe the incompatibility to hold when we consider the matter? As best I can see, Bonjour doesn't say anything further that might shed light on this matter.

My ultimate aim is, with Bonjour, to defend the possibility of justified modal belief. Other philosophers, however, have thought that something in the neighborhood of Benacerraf's worry is sufficiently decisive as to warrant a shift to one of the deflationary or anti-realist positions that we will now consider.

Modal Nihilism

The most influential critic of any form of modal realism is W. V. Quine. Quine not only repudiated the modal realist's unabashed acceptance of primitive modal truths and properties but judged modal talk as altogether beyond rehabilitation. His recommendation, then, is stark: purge our theoretical discourse of modal terminology altogether, letting it go the way of other such unsatisfactory notions as phlogiston and the ether. Not only is nature to be purged of causal powers, in Humean fashion, but the formal structure of logic and mathematics is taken to be a body of claims concerning this world alone, of the same status as those traditionally deemed 'empirical'. (One might be tempted to put the matter thus: all truths are contingent truths. But a Quinean would reject this formulation as resting on the very modal distinction he denies.)

Quine is famous for his attack on the concept of analyticity, which concept he takes to be bound up with necessity.[7] I will not explore this very familiar territory here. I want only to sketch out the consequences he draws from this for the metaphysics and epistemology of necessity.

Quine's repudiation of necessary truths leads him to hold that no beliefs are beyond revision, contrary to the traditional view on which logical, mathematical, and other truths are apprehended a priori and have the epistemic status of certainty.[8] Instead, all beliefs receive their justification from being integrated into a 'web' of interconnecting beliefs, in terms of which we account for the continual flood of data from our sense organs. In contemplating changes in this structure of belief, we have to try to maximize agreement with experience while maintaining the greatest simplicity and explanatory power in our theory. Beliefs concerning elementary logic are *unlikely* to be revised owing to their place at the 'core' of the web (meaning that they are implicated in virtually all other beliefs). Surprising new data is most easily accommodated by making revisions nearer to the 'periphery', where beliefs have fewer connections with the rest of the web, as they generally concern particular matters of fact now or in the past. But should a large body of data prove recalcitrant to less drastic revision (such as revising the particular catalogue of fundamental physical qualities posited in the current physics), the most conservative change adequate to the data might be the most drastic one conceivable: revision of fundamental logical and mathematical beliefs.[9]

Quine's overall epistemological views raise several large issues, but considering many of them would constitute a diversion from our present purpose.[10] I will focus solely on Quine's rejection of facts involving possibility and necessity and his resulting views concerning the justification of beliefs concerning elementary logic.

Crispin Wright (1986) has well argued that Quine's view runs into problems when we apply it to conditional logical statements concerning the observational implications (O) of our theories (Ø) in particular experimental circumstances (C): $Ø \rightarrow (C \rightarrow O)$ (see also Wright 1980: 415–20). We draw upon such statements in order to assess how well our theories fare at the tribunal of experience. But note that on Quine's view one option open to us when experiential evidence contradicts the predicted outcome is to replace that very conditional with another – to change our view concerning the logical implications of the theory. But when should we do so? Only when it will lead to a better optimization of fit with experience balanced by theoretical simplicity and power. To judge this matter, we need to know the logical consequences of the different change-in-logic options open to us. And so again we must ask: Which hypothesis concerning the consequences for each such option will achieve the desired optimization? It appears that in adjudicating the original issue of when it is best to change logics we are led to inquire first, and without end, concerning the theoretical virtue of related higher-order principles. Or perhaps we are just led back to the very principles we were intending to adjudicate. Which is to say we are either caught in a vicious regress or reasoning in a circle.

Thus we cannot sensibly consider the possibility of rejecting statements that are themselves bound up with our most basic standards for good theory formation. Now the moral of this for our question of whether we are to accept that such logical statements are objective necessities has yet to be drawn. For one might contend that Wright's argument shows only that our practice of theory formation requires that some principles or other be regarded as beyond revision (an epistemological category), not that they be accepted as necessary truths (a metaphysical category). So let us now ask how the acceptance of such principles is not only required on practical grounds for theory formation, but also is justified, if with Quine we take them to have the same metaphysical status as exceptionless generalizations in physical theory. In asking this, we are asking about the rationality of the theory-forming practice itself. In particular, we need to consider whether that practice implicitly presupposes theses that run contrary to Quine's modal strictures.

Consider the law of noncontradiction. As we have already seen, it differs from an empirical generalization, such as that mass/energy is conserved, in that we presuppose the law in our inquiries. We do not look and see whether or not there are logical contradictions out in the world and then build theories that reflect what we find in this regard; we presuppose there are not and reject out of hand theories that entail that there are. So we cannot claim indirect, theory-mediated evidence. Nor does it seem sensible to hold, as Mill did, that this logical principle is inductively justified by direct experience of the world. For we have no notion of what it would be to observe a counterinstance to the principle. Once I assume that there might, epistemically speaking, be contradictions 'out there', my experience seems powerless to disconfirm this hypothesis. For as best I can judge, my experience as it is might have just the character I should expect in a world where the hypothesis is true.

Graham Priest, the foremost contemporary defender of the claim that there are true contradictions, argues that we do know what it would be to perceive contradictions and that such perception is not typical of ordinary experience. Hence, we have (defeasible) evidence against all sorts of hypotheses concerning contradictory states of affairs (1999: 439–46). His argument rests on the perceptual effects of certain 'impossible figures' – drawings depicting impossible situations, such as one point on a staircase being higher than itself, or a point in a field being both at rest and in motion. But he does not make a case for supposing that contradictions (supposing there could be such) are apt to manifest themselves in the way that impossible figures, which are not themselves impossible objects or situations, do. Priest cannot rightly claim the anti-skeptical high ground by insisting that only a general skepticism would take seriously the (im)possibility that we might have consistent perceptual experience of an inconsistent situation. We must first perceive some real contradictions before we can make claims about what impossibilities it is reasonable to exclude, given our experience.

It is not reasonable to accept a principle that lacks any positive confirmation and that is, in some sense, an 'open question' – given the totality of our cognitive practice and evidence, it might (epistemic) be false. (This is not the skeptic's reasoning. He restricts permissible evidence in a highly controversial way.) If, contrariwise, we justifiably hold that the principle is *necessary*, our acceptance of its *truth* is in good order. Furthermore, even if I am wrong and success in systematizing our experience through reliance on the law of noncontradiction does confer justification on believing *some* such principle, the target principle is likely to be far more limited. At best, such justification would accrue to belief in a version of the noncontradiction principle restricted to the past and present, for the commonsensical reason discussed in the section above, "Scientifically Established Necessities": if the principle does not reflect a fundamental necessity, but is simply a general proposition that has held good up until now in the particular world there happens to be, we have no clear basis to presume that it not only has held true, but will continue to do so. This is of course a variant of the problem of induction – the problem of showing the reasonableness of projecting certain past regularities consistent with the denial of any kind of necessity in their so holding. Its most usual form concerns lawlike regularities concerning specific matters of fact, regularities that are provisionally posited and in some cases confirmed in scientific theorizing. Oddly, many twentieth century metaphysicians (until recently, anyways) have dismissed the problem with a shrug, perhaps accompanied by the astonishing declaration that rationality "just consists," in part, in presupposing the legitimacy of induction quite apart from any metaphysical theses that might serve to ground it.

A better reply claims the problem is insoluble *whatever* one's metaphysics of modality, and so it cannot be wielded against one who would reject necessities, whether causal or logical (Lewis 1986: 117; Loewer 1996: 101–27). But I think that this reply rests on a misunderstanding of the problem – or if one likes, it conflates two problems of induction, one insoluble but resulting from unreasonably high standards of justification, and the other quite sensible and insoluble only for the impoverished metaphysician. The unreasonable problem, posed by the skeptic, is to give non-question-begging proof or evidence that (proper) inductions will mostly pan out in our world. Positing causal necessity here is no good, of course, since it covertly begs the question. The other 'problem' allows that we may reasonably assume induction to be a fundamentally reliable practice, but it goes on to ask what sort of metaphysical conception of the world (as regards its basic dynamics) meshes with – makes sense of – that epistemological assumption. A Humean world that consisted of fundamentally *independent* occurrences that happened to conform, at a deep level of description, to certain fairly simple regularities would be a "cosmic coincidence" (Armstrong 1983: 161; Strawson 1989: 253–77). If each of an enormous class of descriptions of what the future holds are equally possible, metaphysically, then an epistemological principle that permitted one to believe that the actual future will fall within a particular, very narrow subclass of that space of possibilities would be arbitrary. (Note that the problem actually applies to the past as well, once we question the ground of our accepting apparent memories as veridical. Absent the right kind of causal necessity, the assumption that these states have any reliable correspondence to past events is baseless.)

The only kind of metaphysical account we seem to be able to give is modal in character. True causal structure (as against reductive surrogates, involving actual or counterfactual patterns of regularity) alone can make sense of this.[11] If the world's dynamics are an outworking of stable causal necessities or probabilistic propensities, then it follows that inductions that sufficiently track such necessities will be upheld, notwithstanding the trickiness of spelling out that "sufficiently."[12] What I have done here is simply to generalize this lesson to the very extreme skepticism of Quine, which extends beyond causal to absolute necessity.[13] It *is* reasonable for us to believe that fundamental logical principles will govern the flow of future experience. But this does not cohere with our also believing, with Quine, that logical principles are, metaphysically, just a subset of universal generalizations, distinguished only by their degree of generality. Contrariwise, if some logical principles are absolutely necessary, then it follows that our future experiences will perfectly conform to them, and it is reasonable to incorporate such principles into each attempt to revise or replace our going theories.

Modal Reductionism and Deflationism

Quine's view on modality is extreme and not widely shared. But many take themselves to be kindred spirits even while accepting a legitimate role for modal discourse. In this section, I will briefly canvass the ideas of some who, while accepting that many modal statements are true, have sought either to reductively analyze modal statements in terms of the nonmodal or to deflate their 'ideological' or ontological commitments.

Tarski

Alfred Tarski's famous paper "On the Concept of Logical Consequence" (1983 [1936]), presented a now-standard method for defining the intuitive notions of logical consequence and logical truth. The method involves characterizing a class of set-theoretic models, or interpretations, and defining a notion of truth-in-the-model. A sentence A is said to be a logical consequence of a set of sentences B if and only if A is true in every model in which all members of B is true. And A is a logical truth just in case A is true in all models *simpliciter*.

Tarski's method, broadly speaking, undeniably clarifies these notions. Our present concern is not with the details and applications of these methods, either in Tarski's hands or in those of his successors, but with their significance to reductionist ambitions in the philosophy of modality. I think light can be shed on this matter by considering John Etchemendy's (1990) provocative critique of Tarski's analysis.[14] I am not here concerned with whether Etchemendy has got Tarski right or with the details of the alternative account of model-theoretic semantics that he favors. It is the nature of Etchemendy's central criticism that interests me. Some philosophers see Tarski's analysis as achieving a *reduction* of the concepts of logical truth and consequence: logical truth is not merely helpfully represented in terms of truth in all models, constructed in some fashion, it simply *is* truth in all models. If this were right, it would be a large step in favor of general modal reductionism. Etchemendy agrees that analytic reduction is Tarski's ambition, but he argues that the ambition is misguided. Model theory cannot offer a true analysis of logical notions but must, in fact, presuppose them. The core intuition driving his argument seems to me fundamentally right, though Etchemendy himself, I believe, fails to recognize its full import.

Etchemendy's Tarski ("e-Tarski") develops an "interpretational" semantics for the logical notions. To make short a long story, we hold fixed the logical constants of our sentences and construct interpretations which, in a systematically varying fashion, assign each of the remaining terms to actual-world objects falling within the logically appropriate category (objects to singular terms, n-place predicates to n-place properties, etc.). As Etchemendy puts it, we hold fixed the world and vary the interpretation of the sentence in all ways consistent with its logical (syncategorematic) form. A sentence is then deemed a logical truth just in case it is true in every such interpretation. And a sentence A is a logical consequence of a group of sentences B, C, . . . just in case A is true in every such interpretation in which B, C, . . . are true. These, importantly, are intended as reductive definitions, and not merely claimed to be extensionally adequate.

Etchemendy criticizes e-Tarski for grounding logical truth and consequence in *empirical* generalizations – the actual truth of a general class of statements sharing logical form – and thereby missing the essential element of their independent 'guarantee' of truth and validity. What is special about logically valid forms of inference is that we can recognize their truth-preserving character without first knowing the truth values of their many instances. As a result, we can then learn the truth of a conclusion on the basis of the truth of the premises. But if e-Tarski were right, it would need to go the other way around: to determine an argument's validity, we would have to check all the instances and see whether truth is universally preserved in them. But we don't do this, of course. Somehow, we are confident that appropriate model-theoretic accounts of validity are extensionally adequate without checking the associated generalizations. Validity is, therefore, conceptually independent of the analysis and our grasp of it is indeed used in judging the analysis's extensional adequacy.[15]

Etchemendy's criticism of e-Tarski is strikingly similar to the causal realist's critique of a Humean reduction of causation to general patterns, actual or counterfactual, in the distribution of qualities in the world. Supposing there to be no causal necessity which constrains future outcomes, the realist then asks, what gives us a "guarantee or reason to expect" that our inductive generalizations are true, without our having verified each of the instances? That we confidently judge future outcomes based on quite limited evidence shows, the realist argues, that we regard the truth of such outcomes as grounded in something explanatorily prior to the generalizations.

It is natural to assume with respect to logic that the guarantee stems from the necessity of the truth of a logical truth or the truth-preservation of a valid form of inference. But Etchemendy himself is unclear on this point. In the book (1990), he asserts that necessity is a necessary condition on such properties, but says it is unclear whether it is an alethic or epistemic variety, since some necessities are not logically demonstrable. Perhaps the best way to interpret him is as holding that logical truths are necessary truths that meet some further condition of formal provability. However, in the later paper, Etchemendy says that his own explanation of validity "is semantic, not modal": "the logic of [a given] language arises from the meaning of its constituent expressions," and these logic-generating expressions are not limited to those figuring in first-order logic and traditionally termed "logical constants." (Such 'logical' expressions are special only for their ubiquity in language and their sharpness: "The expressions traditionally singled out in the argument forms studied by Aristotle or Boole or Frege or Gentzen are simply expressions whose logic is particularly clear, interesting, and widely applicable." Hence, not just "and," "or," and "not," but also "elephant" and "grey" contribute to fixing the logic of English. This would seem to lead to a muddying of logic with ubiquitous vagueness, worries about identifying the presumably nominal essential features of natural kind terms, and so on. But the particulars of Etchemendy's views on the demarcation of logic is not our concern here.)

Etchemendy may be supposing – his remarks on this point are unclear to me – that the *nonmodal* properties of the meanings or concepts expressed by the terms of a language suffice to fix the logical properties of its sentences, so that no appeal to primitive necessities is needed. If so, we would have a kind of reduction of logic after all. But such a view, whether Etchemendy's or not, will not carry through. Do our concepts have primitively essential properties? If so, we have not avoided appeal to unanalyzed necessities. If not, our view will face much the same objection that Etchemendy presses against e-Tarski. Even granting that concepts are timeless entities, which fact precludes intrinsic change over time, without a way to ground the further suppositions that they are *essentially* timeless (or what here amounts to much the same thing, that what *is* timeless *cannot* become temporal), and that contradictions *cannot* be true, we have no 'guarantee' that whatever is now true of concepts must continue to be true of them, and so no guarantee that the logical properties they now fix are true for all times. (We would be forced to rest the truth of the logic our concepts generate on unverified generalizations over such abstracta, or abilities, or whatever else we take concepts to be.)

Perhaps we might reply to this problem that it is part of the concept of a concept that it is timeless and unchanging.[16] That is to say, we treat concepts as functional roles. It need not be primitively the case that the occupant of the concept *elephant* itself has primitively essential features; instead, it is the case only that we would not classify that occupant as being the concept *elephant* unless it has the relevant features. Our concept of a concept, then, provides the missing guarantee of the requisite stability in the features of our concepts. But the same dilemma as the original one can be posed to this view of the concept of a concept: is it essentially as described or not? Duplicating the strategy of replying by appeal to a still higher-level concept would result in a vicious regress, since the features of a given concept-level appear to depend on those of the concept one level up.

I conclude that Etchemendy's criticism of e-Tarski reductionism about logical notions stands and appears to generalize. If we rely upon the logical notion of consequence (and those interdefinable with it, such as logical truth) in our theorizing, we are implicitly committed to its irreducibility.

Armstrong

Our next proposal for modal reductionism finds its material not in set-theoretic machinery but in the elementary features of the physical world. David Armstrong (1997) defends an ontology on which the world is constituted by an enormous array of states of affairs, or facts, which themselves consist in a particular's having a property (conceived as an 'immanent universal') or a plurality of things' standing in a relation. The sole higher-order structure to this array are contingent nomic connections among certain universal pairings and a totality fact that all the first-order states of affairs there are, plus the contingent nomic states of affairs, are all the facts there are *tout court*.

His first step towards an account of modality is to advocate the thesis of *Independence* for first-order states of affairs: no states of affairs, individually or in conjunction, entail the existence or nonexistence of any wholly independent states of affairs. (Some complex states of affairs are treated as overlapping. To get the basic picture, think of the world on a logical atomist model, though Armstrong is officially neutral on this matter. Here there will be atomic states of affairs that do not admit of further decomposition. Then Independence says that any conjunction of atomic facts are consistent with the existence or nonexistence of any wholly distinct atomic fact.)

Armstrong then treats possibility in terms of consistent combinations from among *actual* states of affairs. Given Independence, the scope of consistency is quite wide. Corresponding to every form-respecting mereological sum of actual states of affairs and their constituent universals and particulars, there is a possibility. Respecting ontological 'form' here means that a particular can only play the role of particular – for example, be instantiated by a universal, not by another particular – and a universal must retain its – adicity – whether it is a one-place property or n-place relation. What of 'alien' possibilities, involving possible particulars or universals that are nowhere instanced in our own world, such as a fundamental force-generating property completely other than any of our mass, charge and the like, known or unknown? These Armstrong handles by indirect specification, using existential generalization: it is possible that there be a particular *A* (or distinct particulars *A* and *B*) that are not any of the actual particulars a, b, c . . . and that have properties p, q, and r . . . and so on.

Such is Armstrong's basic picture. There are several quite basic problems with it, it seems to me, that show it to be wholly untenable. One concerns the truthmaker for possibilities involving 'alien' fundamental properties (ones not instantiated in our world). Armstrong suggests that the sum of actual states of affairs, minus the totality fact, suffice for these possibilities. But I cannot see that they do. These states of affairs are *consistent* with there being a plenitude of alien possibilities, but also with there being none or only some of those that we might have thought there were. Which is to say that the actual facts can be truthmakers for none of these candidates for the truth concerning alien possibilities. Armstrong might here appeal to Independence, which holds that no states of affairs, individually or in conjunction, entail the existence *or nonexistence* of any wholly independent states of affairs. This fact, if it is a fact, when conjoined with the totality of particular actual facts, is capable of generating a plenitude of abstractly characterizable alien possibilities, but at a cost: for then he can no longer maintain (as he wishes – p. 160) that Independence is itself simply an expression of what possibility *is*, not a further fact needing its own ontological basis. Given its crucial role in underwriting a plenitude of alien possibilities (in fact, garden-variety nonactual possibilities as well), it will have to be posited as an ultimate and irreducible modal fact, which result undercuts the attempt to provide a completely reductive analysis.

Armstrong's problems extend beyond a failure to achieve a plausible and complete reduction of modality. In common with all reductive analyses, it appears arbitrary in refusing to allow us to ask certain questions about its basic reducers. In Armstrong's case, it is natural to wonder why, for example, a universal U could not have been a thin particular.[17] Note that we are not asking why something doesn't count as a universal if it doesn't play the role that fixes the meaning (in this context) of "universal." We are, rather, asking of the entity itself, apart from how it may be varyingly described in different contexts, why it could not possess certain higher-order characteristics had in the actual world by those entities we dub "particulars." It appears that Armstrong simply *stipulates* that the space of possibilities is constrained by adherence to this sort of ontological form without such entities having primitively essential features that make true the constraint. That is to say, a modal truth is treated as trivial despite its lacking a truthmaker.

I turn to a couple epistemological criticisms. If Armstrong were able to achieve his reductionist ambition of analyzing what possibility is, it is hard to see why we should feel constrained to believe that truths concerning *this* world are wholly consistent. There would be no fundamentally normative fact underwriting the consistency of the world. The hypothesis that it is so would seem just that: a hypothesis.

Secondly, I suggest that however successful Armstrong is in allowing a place for modal claims consistent with strong actualist scruples, his account makes them insignificant. If these be the facts of which modal discourse speaks, why should we care? Why should we care about combinatorial arrangements of actual stuff? If Armstrong is right, there is a mereological sum of actual stuff that is just what I am referring to when I say that I might have had the more exciting life of a gypsy. But the world's containing such a disconnected sum doesn't seem worth taking notice of, let alone spending long summer days musing about. Reduce (strictly, ontologically) one class of facts to another whole class of facts and you seem to give up on their having any distinctive significance – yet we assume that both practical and theoretical possibilities often have great and distinctive significance. It is the stuff of our dreams – our hopes and fears, our pride and shame. Alas, the deflationary accounts of possibility to be discussed immediately below, while not equally fraught with internal difficulties, give equal cause for the puzzled response: "Is *that* it?"

Lewis

While we will make several criticisms of our next account, let us acknowledge that its author was not without a metaphysician's proper courage. You say your picture of reality is large? Chances are, when compared to the view of David Lewis, your picture is extraordinarily provincial, a mere speck in the galaxy he took himself to inhabit. For while you believe in one all-encompassing connected totality – in short, a great big world – Lewis believed in uncountably many of these. What we call the "actual" world is just (trivially) the one we inhabit. There are ever so many worlds more or less like ours that we properly call "possible, but not actual," but this distinction is merely perspectival, as when we say that our friend is there and not here. (From the perspective of persons engaged in modal discourse within other possible worlds, their world is actual and ours is merely possible.)

Lewis developed this thesis in great detail and used the resulting theory to analyze a number of philosophical concepts beyond modality itself. Here I will merely indicate a few basic elements of the account of modality, since his account should be familiar to most readers of this work – as should be my criticisms of it, which are very general. One familiar criticism that I won't make is the one that Lewis told us he most commonly faced: the Incredulous Stare. I myself should be prepared to accept or at least take seriously his ontology if I thought it could plausibly claim to illuminate modality and other philosophical issues. In fact, as we will see in Chapter 5, I am prepared to take my courage in my hands and give (quite independent) a priori reasons for thinking there to be very many things rather like the things Lewis called "worlds." (Mine differ from his in having a common source.) But even if there were as many as he thought and they were completely disconnected in the way he required, I should deem them to be completely irrelevant to modality, mental content, causation, and other such philosophical notions.

It is possible that I have been kidnapped at birth by a band of gypsies and gone on to live a very different life. Lewisian truthmaker: another world rather like ours in which a person rather like me – the person most like me within that world – has such a history. (Actually, there are an enormous number of such worlds, differing in various details inessential to underwriting this basic scenario.)

More radically: *I might have been a disembodied spirit, subject to constant illusion of embodiment in a world such as ours by a very powerful evil spirit.* Truthmaker: worlds a lot less like ours than the those cited in the previous paragraph, in each of which there is a disembodied person with a psychological history similar to mine (more similar to mine than any other denizen of that forsaken world) who undergoes such deception.

In general, possibilities for me are grounded in ("made true by") the careers of my other-worldly *counterparts*, defined in terms of similarity relations to me, which Lewis said are inconstant and indeterminate, tacitly fixed by the context in which the modal claim is made. Likewise, for possibilities for other actual things. And there are lots of worlds besides that are so unlike ours that none of its objects bear similarity relations to any of our world's objects except under the most liberal and tenuous of standards. Thus, unlike Armstrong, Lewis provided for robust truthmakers for alien possibilities. While the number of worlds must have some transfinite cardinality, whatever that is, they will together constitute a nonarbitrary plenum, corresponding to all the logically possible ways one might suppose things might have been – given a Humean rejection of necessary connections between distinct existences.

Lewis did not suppose that when an ordinary person utters the sentence "I could have been a contender," the person is thereby claiming that there is a world disconnected from this one in which a person much like himself is a contender. But neither does the person have a contrary conception, tacit or explicit, of the truthmaker of his sentence. According to Lewis, pretheoretic commonsense has no opinion on this matter. At the outset of theorizing, therefore, the philosopher has wide latitude in generating an account of modal truthmakers on which (most, uncontroversial) modal statements come out true.[18] His constraints come from outside the target discourse. Apart from empirical information about the nature of our world, these constraints are principally the general theoretical virtues of theoretical conservatism, unity, and explanatory strength. Lewis thought his picture is a good bargain, overall, since it can analyze away abstract entities such as propositions and properties and reduce the stock of conceptual primitives, all by simply coming to believe in more of what we already believe in (concrete worlds).[19]

Lewis was right to describe his ontology as a philosopher's paradise. The main trouble is, it doesn't plausibly do any of the work it is meant to do. Three basic criticisms that we laid at Armstrong's feet apply equally well here. First, the theory seems arbitrary in ruling out of bounds questions we naturally want to ask about its reducers, questions that betray a dogged refusal to recognize the acceptability of the proposed reduction. (Hence, Lewis's claim that we have no pretheoretic commitments concerning the truthmakers of modal claims seems mistaken. We may not be committed to a *theory* of modal ontology, but dissatisfaction with certain kinds of answers betrays intuitions concerning the direction in which the truth lies.)[20] When we ask, "why could not world A have failed to exist?" or "why could there not have been nothing at all?" we are not given satisfying answers. Instead, we are told "world A necessarily exists," even though there is nothing *about* it or anything external to it that accounts for why this is so. (It is not, e.g., taken on as an ontologically primitive feature of worlds.) Possibilities just are worlds, according to the reductive analysis, and it is a trivial consequence of ordinary modal thinking (and so reflected in Lewis's theory) that whatever is possible is necessarily possible. But even when one entertains Lewis's ontology and sees how he exploits it to do modal theory, it is hard to resist thinking that the question "why must *that* world exist?" is sensible and does not receive an appropriate answer in Lewis's theory. One might say that Lewis's theory, despite its grandiosity, doesn't take modality seriously enough. Being a realist about modality means one can ask for substantive accounts – ones not simply stipulated by the formal apparatus of the theory – of the modal properties of any entities.

And as with Armstrong's reductionist account, we are presented with a theory that underwrites modal claims but undercuts their practical and theoretical significance. It is mysterious that so much of our practical reflection on our lives should concern a realm of objects utterly disconnected from the world in which those lives are carried out. And it is equally puzzling why we should be rational to conform our theories about *this* world to truths about patterns among all worlds, which is just what we are doing according to Lewis when we constrain our theories by logical principles.

Rosen and Sider

Many philosophers balk at Lewis's account of possible worlds because they find the thesis of countless concrete worlds incredible. But most find talk of possible worlds useful, even essential, for systematizing modal beliefs. They take such talk heuristically, rather than literally. Gideon Rosen (1990) suggests that modal thinking is guided by something like Lewis's account *regarded as a fiction*. When I say, "Gandalf is powerful and mysterious," I am not actually asserting the existence of a large wizard having such features. Instead, my remark should be taken along the lines of, *according to the fiction of J. R. R. Tolkien, Gandalf is powerful and mysterious*. Similarly, says Rosen, we might look to Lewis's theory of possible worlds as indicating a large fiction. On Lewis's theory, the modal assertion that there might have been wizards is analyzed as 'in some possible world there are wizards.' The fictionalist likes the form of the analysis, but not its substantive commitment. So he suggests, alternatively, that the assertion be analyzed as *according to the possible worlds theory, in some possible world there are wizards*.

Of course, Lewis did not explicitly state the alleged facts about any of the possible worlds, let alone all of them. Instead, he put forward various principles that he believed governs truths across the worlds, giving us some general indication about what he took the worlds to be like. And this is all well for Lewis, since he straightforwardly believed the modal facts to outstrip anything he might say about them, much as the physicist believes there are ever so many particular physical facts that he has not directly described. But the matter is more delicate for the fictionalist. He does not believe there are any modal facts beyond what is (in some way) indicated by the statements of Lewis's theory. Hence, the fictionalist must suppose that many of these truths are merely *implicit* in the theory. Just as we may assume that

Gandalf's having ten fingers is implicit in *The Lord of the Rings*, despite the fact that Tolkien never explicitly tells us this and it is not a strict logical consequence of anything he does tell us, so we may assume many facts are implicit within possible worlds theory, despite the fact that neither Lewis nor anyone else has enumerated or logically implied them.

Notice that Rosen's "according to the fiction of possible worlds..." operator is *modal* in character, similar to an entailment relation. Hence, Rosen's fictionalism (as he recognizes) cannot be taken as a complete reduction of modality, as with Lewis's own account. Its goal is the more modest one of *paring down* the ontological commitment of one who makes ordinary modal assertions, consistent with the minimum corresponding increase in conceptual primitives. For Rosen, a primitive notion of truth-in-fiction isn't too high a price to pay for rejecting Lewis's worlds.

But notice that there is an awful *lot* of modal truth that Lewis's general theory neither tells us about nor strictly implies. Ted Sider (2002) convincingly shows that Rosen's "according to the fiction of possible worlds..." operator will have to carry a lot of weight beyond not just strict entailment, but also the more liberal (and vaguer) *ordinary* notion of implied truth-in-fiction. For instance, it is impossible for a compact machinery of some fundamental principles plus a generative recombination principle to entail all the mathematical and conceptual necessities there are, let alone truths involving 'alien' fundamental properties (2002: 279–315; see also Sider 2003: 180–208). So the fictionalist will have to contend rather implausibly that these are nonetheless implicit in the basic possible worlds account. One might indeed deem Rosen's notion to be tantamount to simply taking the interdefinable notions of absolute possibility, necessity, and (broadly) logical consequence as primitive.

Sider recommends an alternative account which identifies an ersatz "pluriverse" as the truthmaker for modal assertions about possible worlds and their denizens. On his favored account of this, it is a set-theoretic linguistic construction.[21] By positing such a sentence, we are not limited to a sketchy human account of the nature of possible worlds, and dubious claims about what the account implicitly asserts. Instead, we stipulate the pluriverse sentence to strictly entail *all* the facts about all the possibilities. Sider shows how to do this starting from a primitive modal notion of necessity (and possibility) that guides our construction of the surrogates for individual worlds within the single pluriverse. We then analyze the claim that there might have been wizards as *according to the pluriverse sentence, there is a possible world in which there are wizards.*

For my purposes, the differences between the positions of Rosen and Sider are not germane.[22] Common to their approaches is a primitive modal concept and a story-like construction built upon it. There are no primitive modal properties of things, no modal truthmakers *in rebus*. I believe there is reason to be dissatisfied with any deflationary stance of this sort, as well as a reason to think it is not stably deflated. I will frame the objections in relation to Sider's account, since I accept his argument that he gets more bang for his buck than Rosen does.

The first objection we've already seen, as it is equally telling for all reductive and deflationary accounts of modality. If facts about my possible histories are just facts about the content of Sider's sentence, there seems to be no good reason why I should care about them as I do. Suppose it is true according to the pluriverse sentence that a person with characteristics like I actually have works as a roofer in a world a lot like the actual world, and that the person thereby counts as a 'counterpart' of me. Why should I care about that fact at all, let alone care about it more than I care about an analogous feature of the sentence involving the counterpart of Sider? Sider cavalierly dismisses an objection similar to this ("We're not talking about *that*!") by asserting that our modal concepts are purely structural. But the intuitive indifference one feels in response to Sider's truthmaker is *evidence* that a structuralist view is implausible. Rosen (1990), by contrast, recognizes the intuitive force of the worry without attempting a conclusive response to it. His main suggestion – that perhaps our response to the fictionalist's deflationary analysis of possible worlds should be to change our view of what we should care about – strikes me as simply implausible on its face.

My second criticism is specific to the accounts of Sider and Rosen. I begin with the observation that they follow Lewis in claiming that none of us has pretheoretic views on the truthmakers for our modal claims. The man on the street goes around saying "Possibly, *this*" and "Necessarily, *that*," but is rather clueless when it comes to what his statement is about, from the ultimate, metaphysical standpoint. (If you ask him, are you talking about basic features of the universe and its occupants themselves, or disconnected concrete totalities, or a complex abstract object, he will have no inclinations towards any of them. "I just know it is possible that I have been a roofer, and there's an end on it!") It is not clear to me, though, why a theorist of this stripe should strive (as each of them do) to accommodate a great deal of commonsense modal judgment. Perhaps commonsense opinion has a general grasp, for example, on some main features of Sider's pluriverse sentence, but goes badly wrong on other main features.

This thought, in turn, leads to an objection to Sider and Rosen: their accounts invite a skeptical response to the fact that theorists have stubbornly diverging opinions about substantive modal matters. If all of our modal disagreement is, in the end, directed at the content of a pluriverse sentence, a set-theoretic structure with which we have no causal contact, why suppose we are all trying to get at that *same* sentence? That is, why suppose there is a single, common truthmaker for our modal assertions? There are ever so many set-theoretic structures of comparable scope, differing in detail, among Sider's abstracta. These are all unimaginably complex and, for any one of them, there is a large number of barely distinct others. They won't all count as "pluriverse sentences," since Sider stipulates that such a sentence includes all the *de dicto* modal facts that flow from the *one*, primitive modal concept of necessity. But the truth value of many disputed modal statements (e.g., possibly, there are talking donkeys) are of no consequence for most other modal assertions. Alongside Sider's single modal concept of necessity are ever so many other related concepts that consistently imply different truth values for certain such arcana. So why suppose a common object of our modal discourse built on a single modal concept, rather than a plurality of sentences built on highly similar, but distinct concepts?

Insistence that we are all arguing about precisely the same thing in a subtle and complex subject matter makes sense where, for example, the facts in question are ones directly connected to the objects of our experience, since there could be but one set of such facts, however difficult they may be to pin down in particular cases. But on Sider's picture, no fact *directly* about ourselves or our environment are in dispute, despite how it superficially appears. So where stubborn disagreement persists, why not suppose we simply have in mind *distinct* pluriverse-like sentences? Sider may appeal to the important role of modal claims in a variety of philosophical contexts, roles that require there to be objective modal facts, even if reducible ones. But for this, all we need to suppose is that the objects of our discourse overlap a great deal, which is consistent with supposing that they are partially distinct.[23] What is more, since none of us could ever conceive a pluriverse sentence in all its totality, nor could we conceive a set of rules that would distinguish it from all others which are quite similar to it, there is perhaps no good reason (assuming Sider's account) for thinking that an *individual* modal theorist is getting at a particular pluriverse sentence with his modal assertions.

What this criticism makes plain is that coupling deflationary ontology with continued commitment to a robust objectivity for modal discourse is unmotivated. In Sider's and Rosen's hands, disagreement about the modal 'facts' should give way to a recognition of a somewhat fragmented discourse, in just the way that we (ought to) recognize the lack of an objective answer to disputes about traits of a fictional character on which the text is not definitive.

Modal Anti-Realism and Quasi-Realism

We've seen two general forms of opposition to a robust realism about modality. One denies the meaningfulness of modal language altogether (Quine). The other seeks to tame modality by reducing modal statements and properties (in whole or in objectionable part) to more favored elements of an ontology. A third type of strategy accepts the legitimacy of modal discourse but denies that it aims to make objective claims about reality. Instead, our modal claims reflect facts about certain of our *own* propensities as thinkers and language-users. Given our discussion of other approaches, brief critical remarks on two versions of this anti-realist strategy will suffice.

Conventionalism

Our first strategy holds that nonanalytic modal claims are *conventional*. These thinkers agree with the modal realist that the simple act of reference to an object commits one to supposing persistence conditions for that object, conditions that are modal. But, they hold, the realist errs in his view of the *basis* of such modal truths. According to the conventionalist, Fido the dog could not have been a dolphin because of a tacit convention regarding the use of "dog" and how objects so identified are to be 'tracked' in counterfactual scenarios. These are not facts about objects independent of our language intentions, since there *are* no individuated objects 'there' totally independent of our conceptual scheme. Through language, we carve up the world stuff into certain categories, imposing in the process modal identity conditions. The fount of all varieties of necessity, then, is analytic, in logic and linguistic convention. A view of this sort is defended at length by Alan Sidelle (1989).[24]

One problem discussed in another connection applies here as well. Since the conventionalist denies the existence of a privileged ontology, he cannot be a realist regarding causality. And so, like the Humean, he has no basis for supposing that the 'world-stuff' will continue to be describable in terms of the laws that have adequately described the world through the present.[25]

But the conventionalist's problems do not end with an implausible epistemology. There is a central internal difficulty as well. The individuation of objects is supposed to rest entirely on our linguistic conventions. But we ourselves are among those real-world objects. What should the conventionalist say about us? One possibility is a sharp *dualism*, on which we ourselves are wholly distinct from the stuff of the physical world and exist as an objective matter of fact, prior to all convention. But if this were so, we should want a story on why this cannot be true for at least some physical objects as well. The more principled route for the conventionalist is to say instead that thinkers, too, exist as a matter of convention. But the principled route lands us in paradox. Do human beings not have to exist 'first' in order to do something as complicated as laying down conventions? No bootstrapping metaphor should persuade us that we can bring ourselves into existence.[26]

A conventionalist might respond (cf. remarks by Sidelle on 76–7) that this problem rests on a confusion, at least by the conventionalist's lights. From the fact that we might have failed to conceive reality as including ourselves, it infers that there might have been world-stuff in some sense arranged just like the stuff of our world, but in which it was false that we existed. In so supposing, the critic smuggles in realist convictions. To see this, consider what the conventionalist says about possible worlds containing no thinkers. Such worlds are possible and are characterized in terms of *the categories we use in the actual world.* That is, we hold fixed the conceptual scheme implicit in our actual conventions in determining what the possibilities are, whether or not they contain thinkers such as ourselves endorsing such conventions. It might have been that there were no humans, or thinkers generally, but it is *impossible* that actual human categories fail to apply altogether: necessity-fixing conventions are themselves necessary. In particular, it might have been that there were humans who failed to use conventions specifying human persistence conditions, but this is still a world in which there are humans. (What *they* would say about the denizens of the world would in this respect be *wrong.*)

The logic of modality implicit in this response warrants further discussion.[27] We may leave that aside, however, since, even granting the logic of the conventionalist's picture, the response itself fails to alleviate the problem originally posed. That problem concerned not the seeming contingency of the convention-making that generates necessity. Rather, it points to the unassailable fact that the existence of convention-makers is logically prior, as a conceptual matter, to the activity of convention-making. If, as it appears, our modal conventionalist is committed to denying this fact, we must judge his position a failure.

Blackburn's quasi-realism

Finally, another view that locates the source of necessity within ourselves is *expressivist.* Unlike conventionalism, it is unrestricted, applying to formal truths of logic and arithmetic as much as to claims about essential properties of objects in the physical world. As Simon Blackburn (1986) puts the view, when we say that p is necessary, we are expressing our inability to 'make anything of' p's denial:

> We cannot see our failure to make anything of them as the result of a contingent limitation in our own experience, nor of a misapprehension making us think that their truth should be open to display in a way in which it need not be. We express ourselves by saying that they cannot be true – that their negations are necessary. (136)[28]

Many of the problems of explanatory adequacy for views discussed above also apply here, I believe. But as with conventionalism, there is a decisive internal difficulty. In this case, it centers around the expressivist's core notion, "we can make nothing of p's denial." On its face, this is itself a modal notion. It will not do to say that we are analyzing one type of modality (absolute necessity) in terms of another (causal necessity), since the latter in turn requires the former for *its* explication. The causal realist's appeal to primitive dispositions implicitly makes use of the notion of (absolute) impossibility. ("Under circumstances C, F-ness necessarily gives rise to G-ness, or is necessarily disposed to producing G-ness with probability n.") The same is true, however, for a reductionist account of causality. By way of illustration, the reigning reductionist account, Lewis's, appeals to counterfactuals that treat modal facts as objective, even if reducible to facts about the array of worlds.

Let us examine this in a bit more detail. Impossibilities, for the expressivist, are those propositions we 'cannot make anything of.' We grant the expressivist, for the sake of argument, a reductionist view of causation. He must then tell us how to understand the idea of causal necessity so that it does not rely on an objective conception of logical consequence. Perhaps the best the expressivist can do here is to analyze logical consequence in terms of proof procedures, involving chains of reasoning and the distinctive expressivist attitude towards each move from one step to the next. Plugging that result back into a reductionist account of causation, we will end up with something such as this:

> causal necessities are general 'lawlike' propositions satisfying formal methodological criteria of empirical adequacy, simplicity, explanatory power, etc. – these are the basic causal necessities – together with the vast number of propositions at the ends of chains of reasoning from the basic necessities and true observational propositions, such that 'we can't make anything of' a denial of any step when conjoined with the previous step.

But now we still have that unanalyzed modal residue at the end ("we can't make anything of") and in the idea of "chains of reasoning," which doesn't refer to any *actual* pieces of reasoning.

Furthermore, for the reductionist, the facts about causality supervene on the total distribution of noncausal, 'local matters of fact,' including future facts. So if I am expressing an inability in making a modal utterance, and we go reductionist on this causal notion of inability, then I am in part expressing a conviction about the contingent distribution of psychological facts. (There are ever so many Lewisian worlds like ours up through the present, time t, that radically diverge in different ways from what we now expect. In those worlds, the facts about human inabilities *at t* differ from one another.) What business have I in expressing such a conviction even now? Many of my counterparts *turn out* to be able to make something of the counterpossibles eventually, even if they are hopelessly muddled in so doing. The expressivist cannot retort that it is simply *impossible* to make something of a contradiction, as that retort in the present context is available to the modal realist only. (Nor can he – unlike the realist – reasonably dispute one's making something of the scenario in which a person makes something of a contradiction. Easy as pie: I imagine a person going through a subtle process of reasoning, the outcome of which is that the law of non-contradiction is false.)

Finally, the expressivist allows that we occasionally err in our judgments of necessity, as did earlier thinkers who deemed Euclidean geometry to necessarily describe any physical space. These are, Blackburn says, simply "failures of imagination" (1986: 136). But the expressivist who relies on a deflationary account of causality has no resources to distinguish forever *unrectified* failures of imagination – unbroken failures of human beings to make something of particular claims, throughout their history, as a result of an imaginative block – from true *inabilities*, corresponding to true necessities.

Perhaps more might be said on behalf the conventionalist or the expressivist – though I'm unaware of any place where anything more *has* been said concerning the above difficulties.[29] I submit that we have seen enough to conclude that the modal anti-realist enterprise is fraught with difficulty.

Conclusion

Many of the critical remarks above on this or that deflationary strategy regarding modality are familiar ones, and various contemporary theorists will endorse select criticisms. Less common, however, is to trot out all of them with the purpose of drawing the general moral that deflationism is a hopeless project, which has been my aim here. A great many contemporary metaphysicians have been captivated by the modally denuded Humean picture of the physical world and our interaction with it to an extent that they can scarcely contemplate abandoning a general deflationist conviction, despite the hopeless state of extant proposals. It is time we address head on, then, the epistemological problem many see as confronting the modal realist. I believe we will see that it is far less formidable than has been advertised.

2 | Modal Knowledge

Modal beliefs are woven into the fabric of our conception of the world. Still, despite our inveterate modalizing, it is not obvious how our opinions about the possible and the necessary are justified. Claims about how some part of the world actually is are made true by looking at and theorizing about it. But (1) how do we rationally discern the *possible* truth of some claim that is actually false, or the *necessary* truth of some claim that is actually true? And (2) what, ideally, is the overall structure of our modal beliefs, and how do they inferentially connect with other beliefs?

I seek to offer an answer to these questions that, while highly sketchy and incomplete, is more plausible than the going alternatives. While it has various elements in common with other accounts, traditional and contemporary, their combination is perhaps original. My point of departure is Stephen Yablo's "Is Conceivability a Guide to Possibility?" (1993). Yablo's account is designed to answer the first of our questions, and when we consider that question in isolation from the second it can easily seem appealing. But when we do consider our second question, the appeal of Yablo's picture diminishes. I then consider a more recent attempt by Christopher Peacocke to provide the needed comprehensive perspective without relying upon the broadly Aristotelian view of the metaphysics of modality that I hinted at in the previous chapter. After arguing that Peacocke's theory is fundamentally unsatisfactory, I develop some of the elements of a neo-Aristotelian metaphysical view and then suggest a more *au currant* view of the epistemology of our modal beliefs.

Conceivability As Our Guide?

Yablo begins by claiming the indispensability of Hume's maxim that whatever is conceivable is possible – or rather, of a more modest variant, that conceivability is evidence of possibility, that it provides prima facie justification for accepting the possibility thesis in question. Later, we will ask whether this maxim is worthy of the confidence Yablo and many others place in it. We need first to ask just what its central notion of conceivability comes to. Yablo nicely distinguishes several ideas (1993: 26):

p is conceivable just in case

- it is believable that p
- it is believable that possibly, p
- one can imagine justifiably believing that p
- one can imagine believing p truly
- one can imagine believing something true with one's actual p-thought.

He then identifies his own notion ("philosophical conceivability"), not with any of these, but thus:

p is conceivable for me if I can imagine a world that I take to verify p.

Yablo elucidates the analysans by saying that the content of one's imagining will be highly detailed (though not of course fully determinate) with respect to a specific situation within the world that bears directly on the truth or falsity of p, "while leaving matters visibly irrelevant to p's truth value unspecified" (29). That is, I try to imagine a coherent, connected totality, most of whose matters, though taken to *be* determinate, are not determinately represented in my imagining; and this totality contains a situation I represent with sufficient determinacy to verify that p is true of it. If I can do so, p is conceivable for me, and I am prima facie justified in believing that p is possible.

Philosophers often do use something like this procedure in judging possibility claims, yet their results are sometimes at odds. (Descartes was able to conceive himself existing without his body, but Hobbes could not. Hume conceived an event occurring without a cause; not so, Leibniz.) *Other* basic methods of belief formation, such as perception and memory, yield conflicting results, but we have some theoretical understanding of how they go wrong when they do. One reason some doubt the legitimacy of many or all *modal* beliefs is the apparent lack of a plausible account of how modal error arises when one uses the ostensibly proper method. Yablo contends, however, that a natural account (for most cases) is in fact ready to hand: I wrongly conceive that p – that is, I conceive that p when p is in fact impossible – when there is a proposition q such that

(a) q;
(b)   if q, then necessarily not-p; and
(c)   that I find p conceivable is explained by my unawareness or outright denial that a, and/or my unawareness or outright denial that b. (34)

Consider, for example, a chemist of a bygone era who, accepting an erroneous account of water's molecular structure, finds it conceivable that water exists in the absence of oxygen molecules. His use of the method of conceivability leads him astray because of his factual error in disbelieving that water is partly constituted by oxygen molecules. Or consider a counterpart who accepts the correct account, but still conceives that there might be water in an oxygen-less world because he denies that water has its structure essentially. Here, his error is rooted in a failure to recognize a theoretical claim about essence (corresponding to the schema given in clause b of Yablo's model).

Yablo further claims that we may explain erroneous verdicts of *in*conceivability in precisely parallel fashion. There is a proposition q such that:

(a) q;
(b)   if q, then possibly p; and
(c)   that I find p inconceivable is explained by my unawareness or outright denial that a, and/or my unawareness or outright denial that b. (39, n. 73)

Sticking with our previous sort of example, suppose this time a chemist who wrongly judges it inconceivable that water exist in the absence of carbon (p). He might do so because he disbelieves that water is H_2O (our q), or because, despite his acceptance of this identity, he thinks any world having hydrogen and oxygen must also have carbon (and so denies that if q, then possibly p).

Let us agree that no account of the justification of modal beliefs, including Yablo's, will or need satisfy the skeptical demand for external proof of reliability; nor need one suppose perfect reliability in the modal sphere. Still, there is reason to be unsatisfied with Yablo's account of both the justification of modal beliefs and of how error arises. Consider first his account of modal error. Despite the examples Yablo presses, it is not typically misinformation about nonmodal fact (his a condition), such as the chemical structure of water molecules, that leads to conflicting judgments. Instead, the typical disputes are of two other types:

1. Disagreement over the modal implications of nonmodal facts (the b conditionals in Yablo's error schemas): Could Socrates, who is actually an embodied human, have been an alligator, or disembodied? Are his origins essential to him? Could the property of unit negative charge have played the causal role actually played by unit positive charge?

2. More general, theoretical disagreements where the role of imagination is far from clear: Could an event occur without any causal antecedent whatsoever? Is time travel possible?

Yablo does not illuminate why disagreements of the first sort occur while failing to even take account of the second sort. Central to Yablo's picture of how we determine modal truth and falsity is an act of imagining. However, in neither of these typical sorts of cases where philosophers obtain conflicting results is the problem a failure of imagination. Even when imagination of a *p*-verifying totality is employed, what may be in dispute is whether a situation that is more or less determinately represented in one's imagination is *possible*. (So says the mind–body identity theorist in response to Yablo's imagining himself in a disembodied state.) Alternatively, thinkers may reasonably dispute the possibility of the *wider* totality that an imagining conceives as embedding a determinate situation – that is, one may dispute that one is truly imagining a possible world.[1] One can hardly *see* that it is, given that almost all of its details are not represented. It may be that unrepresented matters Yablo himself would judge to be "visibly irrelevant" to *p*'s possibility are not so in fact. (So say Leibniz and Spinoza, but also theorists who are less extreme in their embrace of a more organic conception of whole possibilities.) Such disputes do not turn on empirical matters or imaginative failures or confusions, but are instead theoretical in nature, concerning the truth or falsity of candidate necessity principles.

The persistence of such disagreements engender a reasonable worry about our access to, or the very existence of, modal facts in the absence of any theoretical perspective on how some of us, at least, go wrong in these ways. Yablo fails to shed any light here. Why do our judgments fall out as they do, even when we are correctly apprised of the nonmodal facts and are sensitized to differences between conceivability in Yablo's sense and, for example, believability? Theorists disagree on certain alleged necessities that constrain possibility – necessities of identity, of origin, and of constitution, for example. What prompts these differing judgments? How might I go about seeking to improve my own judgments? And note further Yablo's blithe acceptance (admittedly, he has plenty of company nowadays) that many wider matters about a totality's overall structure and content are "visibly irrelevant" to the possibility of some localized scenario. This clearly presumes the correctness of some sort or other of Humean 'recombination' or 'duplication' principle, on which, roughly, anything can coexist with anything else.[2] Rationalist philosophers of various stripes deny such principles. Even supposing the Hume crowd were right on this score, we'd like to be able to see why one might think so. How does giving a wide scope to possibility hook up with our other theoretical beliefs? Yablo does nothing beyond inviting us to accept that that's the way it is with possibility, and those who think otherwise are simply mistaken.

Finally, let us return to Yablo's central thesis: conceiving that *p* is prima facie *justification* for believing that *p* is possible. He does not tell his readers what, in his view, epistemic justification consists in. But it is hard to resist supposing that he has something like a deontological conception in mind, on which believing that *p* is justified just in case it is within one's epistemic rights, or one is epistemically without fault or blame. Now the believings of Yabloesque modalizers may well be blameless in this way, while still leaving us without answers to the questions worrying the modal skeptics: what are the truthmakers for modal facts, and what accounts for our (presumed) rough reliability in ascertaining them?[3]

Modality a Matter of Principle?

Before setting out my own view, I will consider one other account of the epistemology of modality currently on offer. Christopher Peacocke advances a novel approach in an intricate, lengthy chapter of his recent monograph, *Being Known* (1999: ch. 4).[4] Peacocke believes it enables him to forge a transparent link between the metaphysics and epistemology of modal theses – something he takes to require eschewing primitive modality as a basic feature of the world – without falling prey to the temptation of thinker-dependent strategies. On what he terms a "principle-based conception," the understanding of modal concepts involves an implicit grasp of certain principles of possibility, which principles specify the truth conditions for modal statements in terms of nonmodal properties of our concepts and of the properties and objects in the world. (These are the Modal Extension Principle, a family of Constitutive Principles, and a Constrained Recombination Principle.) To the extent that I correctly judge the content of these principles and grasp all relevant concepts, I am immediately in a position to judge the truth or falsity of specific modal statements. None of this involves positing or 'receiving an impression of' primitive necessity in the world.

Peacocke's Principles seek to elucidate the concept of possibility in terms of a notion of *admissible assignment*. Ignoring various points of detail, an assignment accords each atomic concept a semantic value of the appropriate category (e.g., an object to a singular concept). Assignments, then, will be total specifications conforming only to broad, categorematic norms. As a result, some such assignments will assign, for example, married men to the concept *bachelor*. The crucial question, then, is how to spell out the class of *admissible* assignments (excluding ones such as those just noted) in a way that does not simply presuppose an intuitive notion of what is possible.

Peacocke assumes that the actual extension of a given concept is determined by a rule. The rule for the concept *bachelor*, for example, is that it is the intersection of the actual extensions of the concepts *man* and *unmarried*. The Modal Extension Principle (1999: 134–6) has the same rules constrain admissible assignments in one of two ways, depending on whether the concept is, in Kripke's terminology, *de jure* rigid (such as those associated with proper names and natural kind terms):

> For concepts which are *not* de jure rigid – An assignment *s* is admissible for concept C only if the semantic value of C according to *s* is the result of applying the same rule as is applied in the determination of the actual semantic value of C.
>
> For concepts which are de jure rigid – Where the actual semantic value of concept C is A, an assignment *s* is admissible only if the semantic value of C is A.

So, assuming Kripke is right on the *de jure* rigidity of natural kinds, the semantic value of the concept *water* is H_2O on *all* admissible assignments. For the non-*de jure*-rigid concept *bachelor*, the semantic value on all admissible assignments will vary, as a function of the values of its constituent concepts of *man* and *unmarried*, where these likewise conform to the same rule governing their applicability in the actual world.

A second set of constraints on admissibility are given by a family of Constitutive Principles. These require that an assignment respect "what is constitutive of the objects, properties, and relations it mentions" (Peacocke 1999: 144). For objects and properties, these will include kind-essential features; for individual objects, these will also concern actual origins. Peacocke does not advance a definitive set of such principles. He instead contends that our very notion of possibility is bound up with the idea that some such principles constrain admissibility, and deems it a matter of difficult *metaphysical* research – not conceptual analysis – that such principles are true.

Finally, the Constrained Recombination Principle asserts that any assignment respecting the above principles is admissible. (149) A proposition is possible, then, if and only if it is true according to some admissible assignment, and a proposition is necessary if and only if it is true according to every admissible assignment. (150)

Will positing principles that are bound up with our grasp of the concepts of possibility and necessity suffice for Peacocke's aim? Note that what Peacocke is trying to do is walk a fine line between thinker-dependency and primitive modality. He wants to ground *objective* modal truths in facts about the *actual world*, on a fully nonmodal conception. (Modal truths could then be a 'conservative extension' of the nonmodal. I say that this is Peacocke's intent, but he wavers here, claiming that even if our concept of the actual is partly modal, his approach will still do its intended job. I will defer discussion of this claim until later.) These facts are the rules determining the actual extension of concepts and the fundamental principles that determine what an object, property, or relation is. The crucial issues are whether ascertaining these facts can be explanatorily prior to our understanding of modal concepts and independent of an acceptance of primitively modal features, such as are posited by a traditional realist conception of causality.[5]

Let us consider first, and very briefly, the rules that are said to determine concepts. We will assume that this is the correct picture of the nature of concepts and ask: What does this picture imply or presuppose, by way of modality? One might worry that talk of rules involves, inter alia, some notion of what it is to conform to a rule, and this appears to be a modal notion. But Peacocke contends that there are plausible available accounts of what it is to follow a semantic rule (and so to employ a concept), and of the identity of a rule or concept, that do not presuppose any modal claims (159). As he notes, one might suppose the actual extension of the concept *diamond-shaped* to be precisely those objects "which, as they actually are, would produce a certain kind of experience in a properly perceiving subject" (135). Accordingly, a subject might be said to be employing the concept *diamond-shaped* just in case they are, for example, disposed to employ certain terms under these circumstances.[6] Here, I wish only to note the crucial role of counterfactual claims in justifying our attributing such a disposition. As we will now see, counterfactuals likewise play an important role in the other half of Peacocke's actualist determination of modal properties – the consideration of the identity of objects and properties.

Peacocke's Constitutive Principles determine the identities of objects and properties (conceived realistically) in terms of select actual properties, those that make them to be the entities they are. These principles are not a reflection of our concepts or categorizing proclivities, or in any other way something that is determined by human cognitive activity. Instead, they reflect metaphysical truths about the entities themselves – though not primitively essential properties. About ascertaining such principles, he says only that they involve difficult metaphysical research, hinting that we settle on them for broadly theoretical reasons. But, *given a nonmodal conception of the actual*, what basis could there be for making an objective distinction between feature F as constitutive of the x's and F as merely accidentally present in all the x's? The constitutive truths, it seems, could be operative only in our counterfactual reasoning.[7] An urgent question, therefore, with respect to the constitutive principles as well as the rules governing concepts, is the status and nature of counterfactual reasoning. Peacocke himself seems to recognize this, when he suggests that the central point of having a concept of necessity is just its connection to counterfactuals within theoretical and practical reasoning (172–3). If this suggestion is correct, one had better not go on to explain, even in part, the nature of our practical and theoretical interests in counterfactual matters in terms of an interest in the genuine absolute possibilities (or relative possibilities that require definition in terms of absolute possibilities). But, the needs of Peacock's own approach aside, it seems natural to do just that. In theoretical contexts, for example, we sometimes explore an assumption whose truth is uncertain for the purpose of deciding whether it has impossible implications. We do so because we believe that anything that implies a contradiction cannot be true, and so is not true. In a more practical vein, I wonder about what might have happened had I chosen a different profession just because I believe that alternative course to have been a real possibility for me, and I care about the possible value, whether a net gain or loss, that I relinquished. Whether theoretical or practical, counterfactual reasoning is significant because the possibilities (and impossibilities) have direct significance for our understanding of, and engagement with, the actual.

A further problem arises for Peacocke's view when we consider the modal status of the principles of possibility themselves, which are said to map facts about the (allegedly nonmodal) actual into truths about the possible and the necessary. Peacocke draws our attention to the recursive nature of the Modal Extension Principle. The Principle (in conjunction with the others) specifies the rule for determining the *actual* extension of the concept of an admissible assignment. This concept, in turn, helps to specify the rule for determining the actual extension of the concept of necessity: a proposition is necessary if and only if it is true according to all admissible assignments. When we then apply the modal extension principle to this last rule fixing the concept of necessity, it returns that in *any* admissible assignment, the rule for fixing the concept of necessity will be the very one just noted. Peacocke concludes, "Hence, according to any admissible assignment, the above Characterization of Necessity will be true. But this is precisely what it is for it to be necessary, under the principle-based conception" (152).

But surely this is an illegitimate kind of bootstrapping. What such a self-subsuming principle lacks is a truthmaker – an independent ground of its truth. Suppose we delineate several rival sets of candidate principles of possibility, each possessing a recursive element, and ask, in virtue of what is Peacocke's the correct set and the others wrong? I take it that Peacocke's answer will be simply that his set captures our modal concepts and the others (to varying degrees) do not: "The theorist of the principle-based conception will say, though, that if something is counted as true by an admissible assignment, that is all there is to its being possible. Nothing more is required" (181). But this, surely, undercuts the significance of true modal statements. Yes, they are, on the proffered account, determined *in part* by independent features of the world – features of our other concepts and of 'constitutive' facts about objects and their properties. These facts, however, do nothing to ground their own extension into truths of possibility and necessity; *that* work is done solely by the principles of possibility. These principles do not answer to any further facts, but simply specify the modal concepts. So we are led to wonder, as we did in the previous chapter when considering deflationary accounts of modality, what difference modal concepts could make to our understanding of the world if Peacocke's account of them were true.[8]

That Peacocke indeed presents, in the end, a radically deflationary account of modality can be seen by his remarks on the implications of a 'partially modal conception of the actual' itself. Would the vindication of such a conception undermine his principle-based account of necessity, or his theory of understanding? Not at all, he contends – all that a partially modal conception would establish is a kind of 'local [meaning] holism', such that modal and other concepts are interlinked (175). It will remain that the principles of possibility are ungrounded determiners of modal statements.

But, contrary to Peacocke, a modally tinged conception of actuality is not fundamentally about our conceptualizations but about the nature of the world – the character of its constituents objects, properties, and (thereby) causality itself. Such a conception is guided by the conviction that only an enriched metaphysics of the actual (one encompassing primitively modal features) can adequately sustain the work our concepts of causation and of object and property identity are called upon to do, including within contexts of counterfactual reasoning. The interlinking of modal and nonmodal concepts is a reflection of the fact that the concepts are meant to link to the world by doing explanatory work. Again, without underlying truthmakers, this work is negated and the project becomes deflationary.[9]

Peacocke's project was to account for the epistemology of modal belief by tying our very grasp of modal concepts to an acceptance of principles specifying modal truth conditions in nonmodal terms. Its central failing is the deflationary character of its metaphysics, on account of which it falls prey to criticisms much like those of the metaphysical views given in the previous chapter.

The Theoretical Roles of Modal Claims: Towards a Modal Epistemology

Reflection on the failed attempts by Yablo and Peacocke underscores the need to show how modal and nonmodal beliefs and methods of belief formation may be integrated while not retreating from the evident fact that modal beliefs play a unique role within our theoretical understanding of things, which fact apparently requires that at least some modal truths are metaphysically primitive. To determine how to go from there in outlining a plausible account of modal truth and modal knowledge (or at any rate a robust degree of warrant or rational justification), let us review the core 'data' that an integrated theory of modality ought to illuminate:

General level

We have a strong propensity to accept certain very general (*sometimes* formal) propositions and to regard them as obvious and yet transcending obvious empirical truths about the world. And our *explanatory* schemes appear to be built on such general propositions, so that theoretical rationality is attainable for us only if our modal notions are fundamentally legitimate.

Object level

The notion of necessity is bound up with our grasp of things, properties, and causation. Thus, there is no *perception of the actual* that is not imbued with an implicit grasp and acceptance of a modal character to reality.[10]

We should do justice to these data while also:

1. Allowing that in ordinary contexts, people reliably track the instantiation of modal features in the world – in a very rough and ready way –

without attempting to develop or draw upon a theoretical perspective on modality that would enable them to correct their judgments or set them within a coherent explanatory framework. Sound theoretical perspective is surely capable of improving the reliability of modal judgment, but theoreticians and ordinary folk alike work from much the same base of basic modal judgments.

2. Explaining how there can be rough yet reliable tracking of modal features at a 'commonsense' level that nonetheless is matched by systematic error at a more 'theoretical' level. (Faulty theoretical perspectives are capable of *worsening* the reliability of modal judgment.)

3. Responding to the contention that nonaccidental belief requires perceptual or causal contact with the facts believed, in application to both object-based and general modal judgments.

Theoretical modal judgments

Let us first consider the epistemology of general theoretical modal judgments. As I argued in considering Quine's skeptical position, some judgments concerning formal necessities are necessarily at work at the very outset of theoretical inquiry. So, assuming that rational theoretical belief is attainable at all, there must be rational or warranted a priori beliefs concerning these necessities.[11] Such prima facie warrant extends to virtually every competent thinker, as even the theoretically unsophisticated are dimly aware of the role of logical and mathematical necessities within explanation – that of structuring the space of possibilities to be considered in formulating empirical theories in response to experience.

For such unsophisticated thinkers, however, this awareness is commonly accompanied by an ignorance of rigorous procedures for precisely determining the facts so necessitated. The *honing and extending and occasional creation of formal methods*, as frequently occurs in the history of mathematics, allows errors to be corrected and judgments to be refined. Judgments are also properly modified by a wide variety of types of *indirect reflection*. One variety involves taking into account work that sets within a more general framework what hitherto had been seen as a largely complete and independent formal domain. Consider, for example, the impact of Riemann's celebrated 1854 lecture that generalized the very conception of geometry to the study of n-dimensional manifolds in any kind of space.[12] This allows one to probe the source of previously foundational convictions, and on occasion come to see them as having been confused or conflated with true propositions that previous theorists lacked the resources to correctly identify. Here again, developments in geometry provide an unusually dramatic instance of this with Hilbert's insight, itself building on the creative work of Riemann and others, that geometry is properly understood to be a formal or axiomatic discipline dealing with abstract relational structures rather than an a priori theory of the nature of physical space. In another kind of case, much the same improvement of perspective is provided by simple analogy with better-developed disciplines. Philosophy is rife with instances of creative thought being spurred in this way through reflections on scientific models, leading to a better grasp on possibilities of philosophical concern. A modest example of this is the range of 'Chaos' models in Chapter 4 of this book.

Finally, attention to the history of mathematics shows that revision of a priori beliefs is not always a simple matter of shifting from one set of beliefs to another. The development of key concepts has often been a long and arduous process, one littered with proposals that proved unfruitful or incoherent and were quickly abandoned. One salient example of this was the long process of attempting to clarify the notion of continuity, which eventually moved from geometric to algebraic characterizations, culminating in Dedekind's work in the nineteenth century. The long constructive phase was carried forward through a mixture of strongly and weakly justified a priori beliefs, confused notions used as guides, hunches, and the like. But the later mathematician can study its completed product, with distinctions properly drawn, and have as a result a rich, stable set of strongly justified a priori beliefs.[13]

The procedure of refinement and development of theoretical modal judgments is thus one of reflective equilibrium, much emphasized in other contexts, but here at work within the a priori realm. This immediately implies fallibilism, of course, which is contrary to what most philosophers of tradition have held.[14] That older view seemed inevitable for those taking at face value the metaphor of 'directly seeing the necessity' of at least some elementary truths. But once we suppose that the sober truth of the matter is that there is but a strong disposition to believe of certain propositions that they are not just true but necessary, and that this disposition is fed by an often hidden, underlying commitment to the explanatory role of such necessities (or of related claims), the notion that we sometimes err is no more disturbing in the a priori realm than in the a posteriori – unless one is still plumping for the heroic, skepticism-slaying project of the classical foundationalist.[15]

It is striking how few traditional proponents of the a priori as a rich source of important truths seem to appreciate, much less squarely acknowledge, that our a priori judgments come with varying degrees of confidence, and rightly so.[16] We all believe that *if Derrida is wise, then Derrida is wise* is necessarily true with near maximal confidence (despite the considerable doubts of many of us about the truth of its antecedent). Likewise with 2 + 2 = 4, *for any positive integers x, y, and z, if x is greater than y and y is greater than z, then x is greater than z,* and *if an object is red, then it is colored.* Many of us also believe in the necessary truth of *it is possible for there to be a disembodied thinker, there are universals,* and *W. V. Quine exists in more than one possible world,* but appropriately not with the same degree of confidence. Much of our philosophical theorizing consists in weighing the relative confidence we have in apparently conflicting a priori judgments in order to retain only those that we deem to be more likely. It would be unreasonably dogmatic, then, not to allow that I might – it is *epistemically* possible that I – be warranted in the future in revising some of my present a priori beliefs. (Note that in some cases, such as when we set certain beliefs into a newly developed and more comprehensive mathematical framework, the result could be a proper *increase* in our confidence in them.) This fallibilism is wholly consistent with my believing, at any given stage, that sundry propositions that I believe with less than maximal confidence nevertheless are unconditionally *necessary.*

Some who proclaim the downfall of the a priori upon clearer recognition of fallibility in the target domains are simply failing to distinguish the idea that the warrant for these beliefs is in some sense not essentially dependent on empirical information or experience – apart from whatever experience may be necessary for thinkers like us to form the relevant concepts – from the traditional, but here rejected theory that the underlying belief-forming mechanism is an unmediated, direct accessing of truths. Other critics of the a priori point to the fact that revisions in formal domains often occur in the course of *empirical* theory formation – or even, apparently, in direct response to empirical data.[17] It is one thing, such critics will say, to allow that purely a priori reflection might occasion adjustments in some of our a priori beliefs. But once we recognize that reflection on empirical evidence has done so, we have effectively gutted the idea that the truth of such claims is independent of contingent, empirical facts, and so the *necessary* status of even those logical and mathematical propositions that withstand empirical theorizing is rendered implausible.

In responding to this challenge, it is important to separate cases. I have repeatedly emphasized the importance of what we might term 'core' a priori beliefs. While the borders of this notion are not sharp, the core will certainly include at least the validity of some central rules of inference (and necessary truth of their associated propositions) in first-order logic with identity, elementary arithmetic, and some methodological truisms guiding any form of empirical inquiry. *Pace* Quine, it is not conceivable that empirical evidence could lead us to abandon any of these beliefs, and for two reasons. First, each of these beliefs are rationally warranted to a greater degree than could be the plausibility of any complicated argument from a conjunction of experience and well-supported theory to their falsity. When faced with an incongruence (contradiction being the limiting case), the rational course is to give up the less certain. Secondly, and most decisively, our 'core' a priori beliefs are essential to our understanding of empirical theoretical confirmation. Demonstrating a tension, incongruence, or contradiction between a core belief and a theoretical framework that has empirical support requires tacit acceptance of that very core belief.

But what of slightly less entrenched formal beliefs? Haven't there already been instances where experience have led us either to discount or at least to question beliefs that were held with nearly the same degree of confidence as, for example, the Law of Noncontradiction? I suggest that a careful look at the cases typically cited in fact reveals that empirical evidence per se does not (properly) lead to the revision, or contemplation of revision, of putatively a priori beliefs. Instead, the empirical enterprise occasions continued reflection on the formal tools it uses, leading to developments sparked by purely a priori advancements. Rather than trying to argue the point at length here, I will just make a couple of particular observations that the reader, hopefully, will recognize as sensible, despite being overlooked by the more cavalier critics of the a priori.

The first observation concerns everyone's favorite example of geometry. We are reminded that Kant was just the latest in a long line of the best mathematical thinkers who championed the a priority and necessity of Euclid's flat, three-dimensional geometry (though for Kant this necessity attached to human thought rather than a mind-independent external space). But Kant and the rest were wrong, and we now have a well-confirmed empirical theory that shows that it likely isn't even a contingent truth. But naysayers who trumpet this example curiously fail to highlight the obvious fact that the pre-nineteenth-century tendency to overproject necessity within geometry was fundamentally a result of failure of a priori imagination – a failure to grasp possibilities afforded in part by the independence of the parallel postulate from the other axioms of Euclidean geometry. (And note that even before the development of other systems of geometry based on many-parallels and no-parallels postulates – developments unprompted by physical evidence or theorizing – theorists regarded Euclid's one-parallel postulate as less evident than his other axioms and sought to derive it from them.[18])

My second point is that much of the impetus to reconsider certain parts of classical logic comes from a priori reflections on, for example, the nature of concepts and their relationship to natural properties. (For more on this relationship, see the following section.) So some are led to reconsider the Law of Excluded Middle on the grounds that most of our concepts are vague – even if this is not so, or could not be so, for fundamental natural properties in the world.[19]

Finally, we come to the proposal of Putnam (1965: 75–101) and others (following the mathematician Neumann) that adequately characterizing surprising quantum phenomena requires us to adopt a 'quantum logic' that rejects the classical laws of distributivity for conjunction and disjunction. This claim is bound up not only with highly technical issues within the physical theory but also with the question of scientific realism with respect to quantum mechanics under one's favored interpretation. It would take us too far afield to consider these matters – and needlessly, since the "science has uncovered the need for a revision of our logic" suggestion has not received widespread support. Here a fundamental procedural point suffices: insofar as this goes beyond the mere suggestion that one might usefully employ nonclassical algebras for modeling certain phenomena to the contention that these 'odd' data (within the context of a well-supported theoretical framework) ought to lead us to change our pattern of *reasoning*[20] in accordance with a nonclassical logic, it seems indefensible on *nonempirical* grounds. The proponent must make his case for such a revision either in classical logical terms – reasoning classically both in showing the supposed 'incongruence' of classical logic and certain quantum phenomena and in defining the quantum logical connectives and rules of inference – or in terms of the new logic. If the former, he hasn't really repudiated the normative status of classical reasoning. If the latter, he fails to persuade us, as pointing out that there are difficulties with our system of reasoning if one accepts another system of reasoning is necessarily underwhelming.[21]

These points notwithstanding, I grant that broadly empirical considerations could lead one to give up an a priori belief somewhere outside the core, but in a way that will not do much to advance the case of the Quinean vision that all beliefs ultimately stand before the tribunal of experience. Plantinga (1993: 112) plausibly suggests the following simple case: I believe a sophisticated mathematical claim upon a priori reflection, but I am a little out of my depth. (His example is a person's coming to the belief that a function cannot be everywhere continuous and nowhere differentiable.) I am told by a trustworthy mathematician that there are such functions, though he does not provide the proof. In such a case, I will (or ought) abandon my belief, and for a clearly empirical reason. However, my warrant for abandoning the claim here derives from the superior a priori warrant the mathematician has for its denial. What if the mathematician is sincerely mistaken or even pulling my leg, and there is no such proof? Of course, in that case, I may not be warranted in affirming the denial of my original belief, but I am surely warranted in abandoning the original belief. Here, we must grant there is no a priori judgment of anyone that is the basis of my rational revision of my a priori belief. My sole basis is the (reasonable but mistaken) a posteriori belief that there *is* an a priori basis in the community of inquirers for thinking my belief is mistaken. But it also seems that this is a special kind of case that cannot do the work of showing that significant a priori beliefs are subject to the possibility of direct disconfirmation by future scientific developments. It admittedly highlights the large and complicating role of shared knowledge, though, regrettably, I cannot delve into its implications for a priori justification here.[22]

I want to consider briefly a final, original suggestion concerning the nature of a priori justification and its role in empirical inquiry. Michael Friedman has argued in sophisticated detail for a "relativized and dynamical" conception of the a priori insofar as it bears on scientific theorizing (2001). This view is based on a careful reading (from a perspective steeped in the logical empiricist tradition) of the revolutionary changes in physics from the Aristotelian paradigm to Newton's mathematical physics and the latter to general relativity and quantum mechanics. Friedman argues that we must replace a two-place picture of formal apparatus plus empirical theory with a tripartite structure (35–8):

1. Formal mathematical structures (Euclidean geometry, calculus, and tensor calculus, or the general theory of manifolds)
2. Coordinating principles (Newton's laws of motion, Einstein's constancy and source independence of the velocity of light)
3. Empirical laws (Newton's law of gravitation, Einstein's field equations)

The mathematical structures define a space of purely logical possibility. But in similar fashion, Friedman argues, the coordinating principles function to define a space of 'empirical' or 'real' possibility. There simply can be no empirical testing of the empirical laws unless the coordinating principles are assumed, or treated as justified a priori. This is not for the Quine–Duhem thesis that one cannot test one branch of a theory in total independence of the other parts (as reflected in the fact that testing the influence of gravity on the trajectory of a beam of light requires one to assume the theory of optics underlying your use of telescopes). Rather, and more strongly, this is because the coordinating principles, by serving to connect the formal apparatus needed to make precise predictions to the empirical concepts and laws, are necessary conditions on the meaningfulness of the latter. Without these principles, the empirical laws "are empirically meaningless," having no empirically defined consequences. Contra Quine, there is an asymmetrical epistemological dependency of empirical laws on the coordinating principles. (Friedman 2001: ch. 2)

At the same time, the status of these coordinating principles differs from what tradition assigns to propositions justified a priori. While they cannot "become empirically false" by disconfirmation in a crucial test or experiment with respect to their theoretical alternatives, at a later stage of empirical progress involving a changed overall structure they can be so tested and indeed in some cases disconfirmed. Hence, they require a relativized and dynamical conception of the a priori (86–7).

Now, this is all as may be as an account of the structure of mathematical theories and how their *empirical* parts (coordinating principles and dynamical laws) are subject to (dis)confirmation. But for the purpose of evaluating the place of a priori beliefs *in the ordinary sense* in the practice of forming and assessing empirical theories, the real action is at the top level of mathematical structures. Does Friedman believe that formal mathematical and logical beliefs, too, have only a relativized and (indirectly) empirical justification? It is hard to say with confidence. He makes the usual nod to the demise of Euclidean geometry as an account of the necessary structure of space. He emphasizes that the calculus and tensor calculus were "controversial," not "part of mainstream mathematics" when Newton and Einstein, respectively, introduced them – *just as* the associated coordinating principles were revolutionary in the then-current physics (39–40). And he looks favorably on Neumann's quantum logic proposal, whatever its ultimate merits, as "[indicating] a way in which the idea of a relativized and dynamical a priori can even extend to fundamental principles of logic" (123). All of these contentions suggest that Friedman *is* thinking of at least much of mathematics as but relatively a priori. On the other hand, he speaks at one point of the theorems and principles of the abstract theory of Riemann manifolds as being "justified purely mathematically" (80). And further complicating matters is the obscure talk in one place of the field equations of relativity theory being "logically possible *as soon as* we have Riemann manifolds within pure mathematics" (84). (Were they not always possible, with the mathematical innovation simply making it possible for us to *appreciate* their possibility?)

So, it is not clear how radical a thesis lies behind Friedman's picture of a "relativized and dynamic" a priori. In the light of our earlier discussion, however, what is clear is that the remarks just noted that might indicate a thoroughgoing commitment to the relativity of the a priori make for an uncompelling case. Nothing about Friedman's description of theory development and revision in basic physics supports the claim that even core principles of logic and mathematics are (properly) taken as given only provisionally (within the context of Kuhn's 'normal' as opposed to 'revolutionary' science). Nor does he give reason to suppose that reflection on data in the light of our best going theories of the empirical world might directly induce, or rationally require, change even in our defeasible a priori beliefs (outside the core). Friedman's picture of a relativized and dynamical a priori is at best a correct (albeit misleadingly termed) account of the nature of theoretical confirmation and revision in physical science proper.

There is a good deal more to be said about the particular examples noted above and, more generally, about the relationship of a priori and empirical justification. My aim here is more modest than working out a full-blown picture. In the last chapter, I argued that there is no way to make sense of empirical knowledge of the world that does not rest in part on some metaphysical necessities. My aim here is merely to point out that there is an attractive, broad picture of warranted a priori acceptance of such necessities that differs from the traditional 'rational insight' account. This alternative picture is fallibilist and does not invoke quasi-perceptual rational capacities.

Objectual modal judgments

When we turn from general to specific modal judgments (concerning objects and their kinds), it is natural to begin with Kripkean considerations. Our prescientific ignorance of the underlying nature of things easily leads us to overplay the scope of possibilities – for example, supposing that there might have been water in the absence of hydrogen. (These are instances of Yablo's first condition for faulty conceivings.) Error in this regard is compounded by the subtlety of the distinction between epistemic and metaphysical possibility.[23]

These loci of error in commonsense judgment are well recognized and easily resolved. More difficult to sort out are the consequences of the constantly changing, multilayered approach of modern science for ontology in general, and so modality as one of its aspects. Obviously, changes in the *categories* of our best empirical theories requires corresponding adjustment in modal claims that quantify over those categories. But crucial problems remain even were our theories at various levels to be taken as more or less finished products. First, do we deem only certain scientific kinds to be fully objective, in the sense that any description of the world that fails to quantify over such kinds is necessarily incomplete, failing to recognize certain of Nature's 'basic joints'? If so, by which criteria? Second, how does one distinguish essential features of such natural kinds from those inessential features, if any, which happen to be had by all actual instances of the kind?

As I will now show, our answers to these questions will flow, in part, from our responses to the traditional *metaphysical* problem of universals and the modern problem of reductionism. These problems, in turn, are connected to the analysis of causation. I believe it is most efficient to begin with this last matter, and then work our way back. After our foray through these basic metaphysical topics, we will draw some lessons for modal epistemology.

Causation
Earlier, I contended that induction would lack a rational basis apart from a tacit acceptance of causal and formal necessities as primitive structural features of the world. Those traditional philosophers who agreed with this assessment have cashed out causal necessity in terms of an object's causal powers, which are closely linked to the object's intrinsic properties. Since Hume, however, it has been common to repudiate this account on the grounds that the posited powers are unobservable and mysterious. More recently, David Armstrong has added to the chorus of criticism by charging that in cases where, ex hypothesi, causal powers go unrealized, the dispositions appear to be akin to the absurdity of a one-sided relation: the potential cause tends towards a circumstance that does not exist (1997: 79).[24]

I believe these criticisms of the causal powers account are unfounded. However, Armstrong (1983) and Tooley (1987) suggest that there is a way to have primitive causality without objectionable dispositions. As their approach has gained some currency, it is worth showing that it cannot deliver the goods before turning to defend the traditional account.

Armstrong and Tooley posit a primitive relation of causality, or necessitation, that *contingently* links certain universals. They develop this basic idea in different ways, in part reflecting their differences on the immanence or transcendence of universals. I will confine my attention to Armstrong's account, as I believe his understanding of universals as immanent is the more defensible. (I return to this matter below.) Start by thinking of the world as largely constituted by an enormous array of spatiotemporally related, particular matters of fact, which we may term the 'first-order states of affairs'. We will have particle a's having *spin* $\emptyset$ and *charge* -1, b's having $1/2$ $\emptyset$ and *charge* $+1$, and so on. Suppose we observe a number of occasions in which the instantiation of a structured universal F (a big conjunctive fact about some entity or system of entities) is accompanied by the instantiation of G, and through the usual scientific methods this pattern is taken to reflect a direct causal connection. Here, says Armstrong, we should posit an irreducible *second-order* state of affairs, N (*F*, *G*), where N is a nomic relation. Doing so, he contends, will enable us to *explain* why the F-G pattern is observed, why ever so many particular instances of *F* are accompanied by instances of *G*. In all these instances, there are literally common elements – the universals *F*, *G*, and the linking relation, N. Because of this single, second-order relation, no instance of *F can* occur without *G* (and so none *does* so). The second-order relation provides structure to the world, permitting some first-order state of affairs sequences and precluding others.

Armstrong originally conceived the second-order state of affairs, N (*F*, *G*), as ontologically distinct from particular instances of it: a's being *F* at time t1 *brings about* b's being *G* at time t2, which fact is explained by the logically prior second-order state of affairs. As several have pointed out, however, it is not transparent how a second-order relation among universals such as N (*F*, *G*) constrains the character of particular first-order sequences (van Fraassen 1988: ch. 5; Lewis 1999b: 40). Recognizing the difficulty, Armstrong (1997) now suggests that the second-order necessitation relation among universals is in no way distinct from its instances: causation is a relation among *types* of states of affairs. (So when I experience the causal force, say, that is exerted on my toe by a heavy object, what I am experiencing is nothing particular, but rather causation in general, or nomicity.) This move succeeds in making transparent the relevance of the second-order relation to first-order sequences, but at a steep cost, as the explanatory advantage over the brute conjecture of the Humean regularity theorist has vanished. For each occurrence of *G* is ontologically and so explanatorily prior to the co-occurring N (*F*, *G*) fact. (The existence of a second-order N-relation between *F* and *G* as part of the fabric of the world, multiply instanced, implies but is not implied by the constant conjunction of first-order *F* and *G* instances.) So the posit of the N relation is gratuitous, as it can only be put into the world consequent upon the regularity – unless one makes a stronger claim to the effect that *F*-ness by its very nature is disposed to bring about *G*-ness (bringing the second-order constraint into first-order facts), in which case we are back to the primitive dispositionality thesis Armstrong has sought to avoid.[25]

What our discussion shows, I think, is that the Armstrong–Tooley picture is simply second-order Humeanism, adding a bit more structure to the inert Humean picture of the world at no explanatory gain whatsoever. Therefore, let us return to the causal powers account. It ascribes a fundamental duality to properties: they are qualities that are disposed to produce other qualities in particular circumstances.[26] Since Hume, it has been common to excise the dispositional from the world, leaving only pure, qualitative 'suchness', on the grounds that the posited *powers* are unobservable and mysterious, something we cannot receive a direct 'impression' of. But the claim that the dispositional aspect of things makes no impression on us is question-begging, and the assumption that we can make do without them is dubious. I observe events without, such as rushing water, and am aware of states within, such as my believing that Hume was badly mistaken. Of what am I aware – sequences of purely qualitative and categorical states only, or states that also dispose towards activity? We may take this question two ways: (1) What is the nature of my perceptual and introspective processes and of their objects? (2) How do I conceptualize these processes? As for the first question, if the world is as the anti-Humean claims, then to look at rushing water (or flying birds, or . . .) *is* to perceive dispositionality: I perceive intrinsic characteristics, and these are, on this view, partly dispositional in character. As for the second question of how I *conceive* what is going on in perception, Hume's anti-dispositionalist account of the matter is unconvincing. As William James long ago observed, the Humean picture of a patterned sequence of mental 'snapshots' of independent external states is not how anyone without a tendentious philosophical axe to grind would characterize our perceptual life: "Every examiner of the sensible life in concreto must see that relations of every sort, of time, space, difference, likeness, change, rate, cause, or what not, are just as integral members of the sensational flux as terms are . . ." (1987: 757).

Might we nonetheless, on philosophical grounds, shake ourselves of our actual, dispositionalizing conception of what we experience? Not without emptying our scientific theories of any content concerning the intrinsic character of fundamental kinds, all of which are individuated in functional terms.[27] (The concept of unit negative charge is the concept of a feature that interacts with other fundamental qualities in specified regular ways – for instance, and put intuitively, to repel instances of positive charge.)

Basic properties

I've been exploring the metaphysics of causation for the broader purpose of showing how fundamental natural kinds posited by scientific theories might be objectively basic joints in the physical world and, still further, for developing a plausible recipe for distinguishing the essential from the inessential features of such kinds. We've seen that a satisfactory account of how we are justified in making causal inferences requires a robust realism about causal dispositions, on which properties necessarily confer tendencies to act in specific ways. Hence, our template for how we may come reasonably to form detailed beliefs about the modal properties of things has as a core building block the thesis that modal properties are woven into the basic fabric of the world. But surely these do not include *all* 'properties', on an indiscriminate use of that term. My 'property' of being such that Ron Artest is a tenacious basketball player does no causal work. Nor even does my 'disjunctive property' of being 6 feet tall or being a Martian. And it is unsatisfactory to simply declare that some properties do causal work and others do not.

It is often assumed, quite implausibly, that a single category of entities (properties) serves a variety of disparate functions, from underwriting statements about the structure and dispositions of objects to being the meanings of terms. Causal realists, however, will wish to sharply separate the truth-makers needed for metaphysical and semantic purposes into the categories of property and concept, respectively.[28] Our concepts for things are abundant and can be as useless as you please for explanatory purposes, but properties (as I will use the term) are sparse and earn their keep: they are those aspects of things which ground objective, intrinsic similarity and difference among things and that confer basic capacities to act. Many concepts might truly apply to an object in virtue of a single one of its properties.

Armed with a metaphysics of properties, I will now outline a congruent approach to the essential properties of objects. We should divide our topic into two categories, corresponding to basic and composite individuals. I set aside the difficult question of individual essence and focus exclusively on the essential feature of object kinds.

Basic object kinds

We do not yet know what our world's fundamental kinds of particulars are. Among the posits of present-day particle physics are electrons, quarks, messenger particles, and fields of interaction among them. It identifies these kinds in terms of limited clusters of features that are themselves characterized dispositionally. Electrons, for example, have unit mass, unit negative charge, and spin 1/2. Importantly, it does not just fall out of physical theory that these features happen to co-occur ubiquitously at the subatomic level. Rather, these features are treated as *constitutive* of the (possibly fundamental) kind, *electron*. It is quite plausible to suppose more generally that all universally shared features of the fundamental object kinds (whatever these might turn out to be) are essential to that kind. Granted, we could perhaps imagine epistemic circumstances in which this supposition would not be well founded. (Imagine that the roles of distinct fundamental particle kinds overlapped a great deal, and that for each kind, there were some properties had by nearly, but not quite, all of its instances.) But given our actual circumstances, in which physical theory take certain property-clusters of fundamental particle kinds as basic units of explanation, and does so with great success across a wide spectrum of experimental circumstance, the hypothesis that universally shared features of the basic object kinds are alike essential is a reasonable, if defeasible, one.

Composite object kinds

I said earlier that our theory of properties should be sparse, countenancing only those candidate kinds that 'earn their keep' by doing nonredundant causal work. Just how many properties are there? And – what is a related question – how many kinds of object possessing wholly objective persistence conditions are there? Answer to questions concerning essence, alternative possible histories, and the like depend on answers to these more basic questions – and these, in turn, depend on how the properties of composite 'objects' relate to those of their fundamental constituents. So this last matter is where we must begin.

Aristotle supposed, quite commonsensically, that *horse* was a basic natural kind. Horses appear to share numerous salient *and distinctive* characteristics that explain all manner of phenomena. But modern biology clouds this picture considerably. We know that many macroscopic features of living organisms, including horses, are wholly constituted by the enormously complex activity of their parts. It is an open possibility – hardly established, but far more plausible since the mid-twentieth century than it ever was previously – that *every* observable feature of a given horse at a given time has such a microstructural constitution. If this were so, and we were to embrace a parsimonious ontology of universals, we should conclude that, appearances notwithstanding, *horse* is not a true natural kind. There is a concept of *horsehood*, and a useful one at that, but an ontological inventory of the natural world that fails to employ it is not thereby incomplete. It will be ignoring a certain derivative macroscopic pattern running through parts of nature, but not, again, any of its basic joints.[29]

The reductionist program in biology, then – not to mention chemistry and neuroscience – complicates the metaphysician's task of identifying true natural kinds. In my judgment, a plausible criterion will involve the notion of ontological *emergence*. An ontologically emergent property is *structurally simple*, (therefore) *primitively efficacious*, and a *causal consequence* of a composite's having the requisite type of intrinsic and functional complexity. A property is 'nonstructural' if and only if its instantiation does not even partly consist in the instantiation of a plurality of more basic properties by the object or its parts. It is 'primitively efficacious' in that it has a causal tendency that is neither constituted by nor supervenient upon the fundamental causal tendencies of the object's microphysical features, including the relations among its parts. Instead, the emergent state appears as a causal consequence of the object's having a certain complex configuration – one that could not be anticipated through analysis of microphysical dispositions in contexts lacking the required complexity.[30]

If there are any properties that are emergent in this sense, they clearly will make a fundamental difference to how the world works, even from the vantage point of microphysics. Any attempt to give a general account of the world's evolution in purely microphysical terms – an account holding at all regions of space-time, no matter its occupants – would falter in regions where emergent features are instanced. Even a parsimonious ontology would have to quantify over them, and so over the *objects* that have them. Such objects would thus fall under genuine natural kinds, with the holistic features conferring the 'natural unity' that is the hallmark of genuine composites, as against mere aggregates. Furthermore, there is a plausible general criterion for identifying the essential properties of emergent objects: whatever structural features are causally necessary to sustain the persistence of the emergent feature. At any rate, this is a start. (We can imagine lots of complications on this simple emergentist model.)[31]

I will not address the question of whether it is plausible to suppose there are any such emergent properties, although I have done so elsewhere.[32] I note only that it is plausible that questions about the essential properties of composites hang on this prior question. It is important to see that some sort of conventionalism about many or all mid-sized objects is compatible with a robust commitment to nonconventional essentialism about the fundamental entities, whatever they may be. Indeed, conventionalism is extremely plausible for many objects in commonsense ontology, beginning with artifacts, as it is very likely that none of the features of such 'objects' are ontologically emergent.

This completes my very sketchy and incomplete treatment of objectual modal judgments. I hope to have given the reader some sense of the direction I would take a fuller treatment, enough to make claims by modal deflationists about the hopelessness of the realist project appear overblown.

A modal skeptic briefly considered

Peter van Inwagen is a realist about modality who nonetheless is moderately skeptical about claims to modal knowledge (1998: 67–84). He allows that we can know modal truths that are relevant to everyday life ("this table could have been over there") or to well-confirmed theories in science, and even that we can justifiably believe some that are strictly philosophical. But, he thinks, modal claims that are far removed from everyday life ("there could be a three-inch-thick sheet of iron that is transparent to light") or which are controversial and have substantial philosophical implications ("it is possible that I exist and nothing immaterial exists") are simply beyond our ken (69–70). He draws an analogy to judgments of distance made by the naked eye, which are quite reliable within certain limits, but which are wildly unreliable when, say, judging the distance of the sun.

Furthermore, while van Inwagen thinks we do have some modal knowledge, he thinks it is mysterious how we come by much of it. The nonmysterious variety concerns those modal propositions whose truth or falsity can be established by logic, mathematical reasoning, and reflection on the meaning of words. The mysterious variety concerns (or depends upon) knowledge of possibility for claims which are not known to be true or knowledge of necessity for claims that are known to be true.

We know that a table in front of us could have been two feet to our left and that there could not be liquid wine bottles – somehow, but in a way that we do not, at bottom, really understand. That we do not understand how we know these things is seen through reflection on a picture of how basic knowledge of this sort is acquired, a picture which he claims is at least on the right track: Yablo's method of justifying the claim that p is possible by imagining a scenario which one takes to verify p. Even if this is roughly right, says van Inwagen, it doesn't really enable us to see *how* we know the possibility claim. For it requires us to know that the scenario we imagine is itself a possible one (as I noted earlier in criticizing Yablo), and we are not given a way to see how we know that such a scenario is possible, which seems required for us to know *how* we know what we know in this sphere (75–6). Nonetheless, van Inwagen supposes that we do (somehow) know some such possibility claims, and Yablo's method, or something like it, is part of the story. *Skepticism* about knowledge of possibility comes in when we consider the limits on using Yablo's method. We cannot imagine in sufficient detail potentially verifying scenarios involving 'remote' or overly complicated matters (e.g., the transparent iron case), or controversial philosophical possibility claims, which implicate contentious and not fully imaginable factors about the large-scale character of any world in which these alleged possibilities would obtain. As for controversial (nondemonstrable) *necessities*, van Inwagen claims that it is "less clear whether we know of any proposition that it is a necessary truth if it cannot be shown to be true either by reflection on logic and the meaning of words or by mathematical reasoning" (74).

In my judgment, van Inwagen should have pressed further in querying our 'basic knowledge' of possibilities, as it would have revealed its partly theoretical basis. Consider our confident judgment that the table before us might have been two feet to our left. Underlying such a judgment, surely, is the knowledge that this table and various features of its environment are intrinsically like other objects in relevant respects and so (we judge) like them with respect to certain modal *constraints* they induce. Judging there to be no relevant constraints on the possibility of *this* table's occupying a certain location when similar objects have occupied similar locations, we endorse the possibility. In other words, judgments of the kinds and scope of necessity enter into our judgments of possibility, which fact appears to run counter to van Inwagen's suspicion that there is no "very close connection between" knowledge of possibility and knowledge of necessity (74).

In some ways, van Inwagen's most careful statement of the skeptical side of his position on modal knowledge (appearing in a final note) is quite sensible and congenial to my own view. For it merely questions whether we can know truths involving remote and complicated unactualized *possibilities*, on the assumption that Yablo-esque imaginability is the only method available for deciding the matter in question. Even on the present view, which does not share that assumption, it is highly plausible that we are simply not in a position to confidently determine possibilities for kinds of entities, structures, or situations whose properties are not clearly grasped. The (to my mind unwarranted) skepticism in van Inwagen's position really comes in when this statement is conjoined with the strong inclination to deny knowledge of *necessities* beyond demonstrable ones, which inclination is expressed elsewhere in the text (74). As I have argued above, we can have warranted claims about necessity where these play clear explanatory roles in our best overall conception of the world. (I leave aside what we might say about which of our true modal beliefs might be *known* as opposed to possessing a more limited degree of warrant. My interest, again, is not to provide a thorough epistemology of modal beliefs. It is, instead, to sketch a plausible picture of how we reasonably come by modal beliefs in best-case scenarios and to explore important implications of this picture in the chapters that follow.) To be sure, confidence in claims of necessity must be tempered by recognition of the fallibility of our theoretical judgments and the likely need to revise aspects of our current picture of the natural kinds that structure the world's dynamics and are crucial to determining its ontology. And we should always allow for the possibility of our coming to discern motivation for hitherto unrecognized constraints on possibility – something to which I will return in the final section of this chapter.

A causal role for theoretical necessities?

Earlier, I suggested that the justification of *theoretical* modal beliefs increases through a process of complex inference and reflective equilibrium, assuming that our foundational modal convictions are reasonably on track in the first place. But a familiar reflection suggests this can't be the whole story. Surely it matters what the causal origin of these fundamental modal convictions is. Our acceptance of all such claims had better not be 'accidental' from the point of view of evolutionary history, being explained in a manner that is causally independent of the truthmakers of such claims. (Contrast our disposition to accept the deliverances of memory, say, which disposition is presumably explained in part by the fact that memory is usually reliable in the main.) Here we return to the problem raised back in Chapter 1, in the section "An Epistemological Worry about Modality: Causal Contact with Modal Facts," which problem has animated many deflationary and anti-realist theorists of modality.

This problem of accidental truth appears to afflict the position David Lewis staked out in *On the Plurality of Worlds* (1986), for example. Lewis attempted to sidestep it by exploiting the difference between contingent and necessary facts. A causal condition on knowledge, he suggested, is warranted only where it is possible that our beliefs not track the facts – only, to be precise, where we can sensibly ask what we would have believed were the facts believed to have been otherwise. But necessary facts could not be otherwise, and so the idea of 'tracking' the facts cannot apply (111–12). In the modal sphere, he suggests, we are fundamentally guided by a recombination principle (as we saw with Yablo), which we apply to possibilities we already accept to extend our beliefs. We properly modalize when we engage in piecemeal revision, balancing the virtue of theoretical conservatism with the pursuit of theoretical unity. "If we are prepared to expand our existential beliefs for the sake of theoretical unity, and if thereby we come to believe the truth, then we attain knowledge" (109).

Charles Chihara argues that this reply is insufficient in a way analogous to the inadequacy of the justified true belief (JTB) analysis of knowledge (1998: 90–3). So long as our acceptance of modal claims on the basis of theoretical unity considerations is causally independent of the truthmakers of those claims, we will still have something similar to accidental truth that figures in Gettier problems for the JTB analysis. Chihara presses this worry by suggesting we have no reason to accept the truth-conduciveness of accepting modal claims for reasons of theoretical unity. In that, I think, his objection misfires, as all that need be the case for Lewis's position on modal knowledge to be plausible is for it to be *true* that the structure of modal facts is such that using the principle tends towards truth. A better way to cast the worry is the one I give above, in terms of the causal origin of our fundamental modal convictions, including the disposition to believe that theoretical unity conduces towards truth in the modal sphere. Given Lewis's own wider views on modality (the truthmakers for modal truths are worlds causally disconnected from our own), it seems not only possible but unavoidable that our acceptance of all such claims is 'accidental' from the point of view of evolutionary history. There will be a (complex) contingent historical explanation for why we modalize as we do that is causally independent of these truthmakers.

What might one say here? Bear in mind that one need not *demonstrate* the connection of modal beliefs to their truthmakers. It is enough that one tell a just-so story on which they are in fact so connected, a story that is not wildly at odds with settled fact. I will not offer such a story, but will state a story *beginning* that I think is worth considering. It is this: An evolutionary advantage accrued to cognizer-types that readily assent to the *actual* truth of core logical and mathematical principles and that systematize the world in terms of natural kinds; some such cognizers in our ancestral history were selected in part owing to this fact; and *the truthmakers for these actual truths are none other than their modalized counterparts.*

Such are the beginnings of my story. But now what are these truthmakers for highly general modal facts? For now, I leave this as an unanswered challenge for the position I am sketching. I call attention to (without endorsing) a radical answer Robert Koons has recently proposed: in the course of developing an information-flow account of causality in the context of situation theory, he argues that we need logical and mathematical information to play a causal role (2000: ch. 15). This leads him to hold that these formal facts are literally embedded in the natural world, as part of the structure of situations that cause our judgments. If this view could be worked out within an attractive metaphysic, it would both provide a linkage between baseline modal facts and dispositions to modalize and allow for general modal facts literally to give structure to the actual world (as opposed to the one merely corresponding to the other). But can we plausibly integrate this formal structure with the contingent causal structure imposed by actual properties, such that the formal structure is still capable of being realized within possibilities with "alien properties"? I do not know. Even if we adopt this proposal, we still need an account of the epistemology of belief *revision*, such as the one I've sketched above. In any case, Koons's bold proposal may be gratuitous given the case for the unification of modal facts that I will make in the next chapter, a case that leads to a venerable but unfashionable view of their ontology.

The Spheres of Possibility

It is common for contemporary philosophers to think that there *several* distinct kinds of alethic modality, so that we have narrowly logical possibility (consistency with theorems of first-order logic with identity, perhaps); conceptual possibility (logical possibilities that are also consistent with conceptual or 'nominal' definitions); metaphysical possibility (also consistent with a posteriori identities of kind and individual essence); and causal possibility (also consistent with causal and structural laws of the actual world). If the broad conception sketched above is on the right track, then this common view is mistaken.[33] As an alternative, I suggest that we think in terms of concentric spheres (see Figure 1), denoting increasing theoretical constraints on possibility *tout court*, with merely formally consistent statements in the outermost sphere, and genuine possibilities in the innermost sphere.

Looking at things this way leads to the conclusion I have already urged that quick 'recombination' principles are misguided, but it also explains why they are tempting. What a philosopher is able to grasp in suitably constrained 'modal thought experiments' that the present view might deem to involve impossibilities are incomplete possibility-candidates, involving partial considerations which abstract away one or more grounds of their impossibility. There can be reliable reasoning about and with and such incomplete possibility-candidates, provided one is clear about the sphere by which such reasoning is to be constrained.[34]

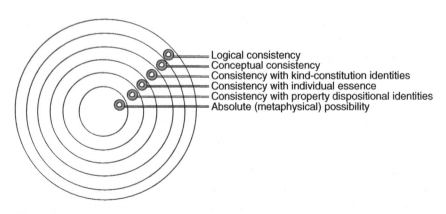

Logical consistency
Conceptual consistency
Consistency with kind-constitution identities
Consistency with individual essence
Consistency with property dispositional identities
Absolute (metaphysical) possibility

Figure 1

I've said that the innermost sphere is distinctively constrained by necessities of nature, pertaining to both kinds and individuals. I now raise the following important question: Are there extrascientific explanatory considerations that should lead us to posit yet further modal structure to the space of genuine possibility?

Part II | The Necessary Shape of Contingency

3 | Ultimate Explanation and Necessary Being: The Existence Stage of the Cosmological Argument

The nearly century-long trend towards a deflationary view of modality has wide philosophical implications, affecting the central aim of metaphysics itself. Traditionally, that aim has been to articulate a theoretical framework that makes possible *ultimate* explanation of reality – that is, a natural or nonarbitrary stopping point (even if only a schematic one) to the nested series of available plausible explanations for increasingly general aspects of the world. The realization of this aim had been thought to require an answer to the most basic of metaphysical questions: *Why is there anything (contingent) at all?* Of course, this question admits distinct formulations of greater precision: What explains the fact that there are contingent things? What explains the fact that *these* contingent things exist? What explains the fact that *these* contingent things exist rather than *those* others that were possible? Why are there contingent things rather than there being nothing contingent at all? I will in due course consider the relevance and appropriateness of certain of these formulations below. For now, we will take our question to be this: *Why do the particular contingent objects there are exist and undergo the events they do?*

The aim of developing and defending such a comprehensive metaphysic has been largely abandoned in the twentieth century, and even when it is occasionally addressed, it is usually not done in a sustained, rigorous fashion. The contemporary philosopher is far more likely to make a passing gesture at the unifying explanatory power of some general metaphysic or other (as the case may be, naturalism or theism) in order to justify an approach to a more localized issue, such as the nature of the intentionality of mental states, of moral values, or of epistemic justification. Such appeals bypass altogether the basic question of explaining the existence of apparently contingent reality. And none of the three most prominent twentieth-century philosophers who have taken this question quite seriously (Heidegger, Wittgenstein, and J. J. C. Smart) has tried to provide an answer to it.

For those sympathetic to the broad historical developments in modern philosophy, there is a plausible explanation for this disregard of the traditional aim of metaphysics and its correlated question concerning existence. And that is that the existence question is widely thought to be unanswerable, and the more general aim, to the extent that it is realizable at all, is held by a good many philosophers to fall within the province of empirical, not philosophical, inquiry. The ways in which the existence question is thought to have been exposed as problematic are various. Setting aside those resting on highly dubious empiricist assumptions about meaningfulness, perhaps the most important of the objections may be summarized thus: If the existence question is pushed hard enough, we will inevitably be forced, as many traditional philosophers have supposed, to posit a relationship of contingent reality (comprising those things that need not have existed) to a 'necessary being', a being whose nature is such that it cannot fail to exist. But when this notion of necessary being is scrutinized, the force of the reasoning that led us there quickly vanishes. For, first of all, is the idea even coherent? (What is supposed to be the relevant notion of necessity? Surely not *formal logical* necessity, as there is no contradiction in the denial that such a being exists. But if we are not talking logical necessity in speaking of 'necessary being,' what is the nature of the weaker type of necessity in question, and why does it not fail to allow for the ultimate explanation sought on account of the very fact that it is held to be weaker than formal logical necessity – would not the supposed necessary being have a kind of brute existence relative to the wider sphere of logical possibility?) Secondly, in what way is the posit of such a being truly explanatory? Third, even supposing we could satisfactorily answer these questions, does not the assumption of necessary being commit us in the end to denying the very *contingency* of mundane things which it is supposed to explain? (If not, if there is at some point a merely contingent link between necessary being and contingent being, so that this contingent world might not have existed, even given the existence and nature of necessary being, does this not call into question the whole program? Isn't one thereby guilty of something analogous to the charge that the nineteenth-century philosopher Schopenhauer raised, in a slightly different context, when he complained of those who treat the "principle of causality . . . as a hired cab which can be dismissed once we have reached our destination"?)

Finally, even if we were to accept the traditional answer involving necessary being to the existence question, its wider significance may be challenged. While it is often incorporated into what has come to be known as the 'cosmological argument from contingency' for the existence of *God*, the bare idea of 'necessary being' seems quite thin: it says nothing about power or knowledge, let alone goodness. Now, it may be that a correct answer to the existence question involves the existence and activity of a necessary being even if traditional monotheism is false. This would be a highly significant result for the metaphysician nevertheless. However, since contributing to the case for theism is among my goals, I regard it as an appropriate further challenge to somehow show that the highly general idea of necessary being has implications that will bring it into the neighborhood of God as traditionally conceived.

Despite the impressive credentials of many who have raised such challenges, I believe that there are good replies available to each of them, replies that at the very least place the onus squarely back on the shoulders of those who would dismiss the appeal to necessary being as discredited metaphysics, of no concern to 'post-Kantian' philosophers. The remainder of this book is devoted to developing what I take to be the most promising of those replies.

The previous two chapters have sought to clarify the nature of necessity in view when speaking of an absolutely necessary being. I argued for this notion's importance and ineliminability in causal-theoretic explanation generally, thereby controverting those contemporary critics of the cosmological argument from contingency who balk either at its conception of absolute (or 'metaphysical') modality or of the role it presumes for modalized statements within explanatory frameworks generally. Perhaps most importantly, we have seen reason to reject 'halfway house' views which hold that the sole intelligible explanatory connection in general is a purely formal logical necessity. Formally provable necessities cannot reasonably be taken to drift without ontological mooring in natures whose existence is not formally demonstrable. And once we are committed to some 'opaque' internal and external relations of necessity (at least 'opaque' to *our* cognitive capacities), we can hardly object *on this ground* to the move that the upholder of necessary being wishes to make.[1]

In this chapter, I begin by exploring the notion of necessary being and defending its explanatory significance. I then reply to three objections to its use in responding to the existence question. In the final section of the chapter, I will try to show how the causal efficacy of a necessary being *could* figure into an explanation of a contingent universe that affirms the universe's contingency – that is, it does not end up implying that this

universe *had* to exist, as, for example, an inevitable emanation of the necessary being – without thereby conceding an ultimate explanatory surd. This
will involve the familiar picture of a transcendent personal being acting
on the basis of reasons. I will sketch the explanatory framework required
by such a picture, modeled on one conception of human agents acting
on reasons.

It will be evident to anyone familiar with the extensive medieval discussions bearing on this matter, particularly the work of the brilliant thirteenth
century philosopher-theologians Thomas Aquinas and John Duns Scotus,
that much of what I will say here and in Chapter 4 carries echoes of that
material. (I would be remiss not to mention also the later contributions of
Leibniz and Samuel Clarke, though their work has less directly impacted my
own thinking.) Indeed, what follows is in part a modern restatement and in
remainder a development and updated defense of older ideas, dressed in the
more familiar garb of analytical philosophical terminology. However,
Aquinas and Scotus press too hard on certain plausible implications concerning the unity of a necessary being, and in consequence they are vulnerable
(their avowals notwithstanding) to objections that their metaphysics has
no room for contingency.[2] I draw a map enabling one comfortably to steer
clear of their necessitarian excesses even while retaining Schopenhauer's
cab as a permanent mode of transportation on the way to a philosopher's
paradise.

Necessary Being

> One need only shut oneself in a closet and begin to think of the fact of one's
> being there, of one's queer bodily shape in the darkness . . . of one's fantastic
> character and all, to have the wonder steal over the detail as much as over
> the general fact of being, and to see that it is only familiarity that blunts it.
> Not only that *anything* should be, but that *this* very thing should be, is mys-
> terious! (James 1998: 415–18)

> For me the question "Why is there something rather than nothing?" has
> become a bit like what Zen Buddhists call a *koan*. It is a constant niggling
> question that has worried and goaded me (often, I think, against my will) into
> a different level of understanding, a different vision, of the world and our
> place in it. (Williams 2002: 30, quoted in Netland 2004: 503–18)

The puzzle of existence may not captivate every reader to the extent it
gripped William James or more recently Paul Williams, but there is undeniably a powerful impetus in human beings to ask the question (while waving

one's hands all about) "Why is there *this* – why, indeed, is there anything at all?" Reflections on the immense nature of the physical universe as seen by science at the start of the twenty-first century do nothing to dispel the sense that there is no 'must' about the existence of it or any part thereof. Considered in itself, it would seem entirely inexplicable that this particular totality happens to exist. Noting the unity of dynamical laws underlying macroscopic phenomena – even to the point of conceiving the possibility of *one* fundamental physical law underlying all the vast array of observable and unobservable goings on – is clearly of no help here. And of no help either (despite the overexuberance of the occasional theoretical physicist) is the possibility that the 'visible' universe arose by a 'quantum fluctuation' from 'a quantum vacuum,' as suggested in highly speculative contemporary cosmological models. For both of these considerations merely invite the further questions, so why should the universe proceed in accordance with such a law or laws, or why should there have been such vacuum conditions (misleadingly labeled 'nothing' in some popular accounts) predating the expansion of the universe and possessing a propensity to give rise to it in the manner proposed?

Clearly, none of the properties that physicists do or potentially might ascribe to any aspect of physical reality will provide us with the materials for a final resolution to our question. Perhaps a naturalistic *metaphysician* inspired by Spinoza may wish to ascribe to the universe a further feature or set of features beyond those relevant to science, one(s) in virtue of which our question may have an answer without appeal to any *transcendent* being. I will give this response a full hearing in the next chapter; for the moment, I merely note that this has seemed deeply implausible to most who have con-sidered the matter, including most naturalists. My present concern is to address those who hold that any explanatory appeal to nonempirical features (whether immanent to *or* transcendent of the physical universe) is otiose, confused, vacuous, or in some other way impertinent or at the very least unseemly, coming from the lips of a modern thinker. Bas van Fraassen gives a comparatively gentle expression to this common disdain, when he remarks, "I . . . lack sympathy for metaphysics, though not in general: only for pre-Kantian metaphysics – and then only if practiced after Kant" (1988: viii).

Now, prima facie, it seems unreasonable to say that the question is a perfectly coherent one, and that it correctly presupposes that the universe and everything therein need not have existed – that is to say, its existence is entirely contingent – and nonetheless hold that there is no answer to it: hold that the universe's existence is simply a brute, unexplain*able* fact. It seems even more unreasonable, then, to deny that, other things being equal, given two metaphysics such that one of them provides a final, nonarbitrary answer to the existence question and one of which leaves it unanswerable, we should prefer the one that answers it on account of its greater explanatory power. If the main line of argument of the first two chapters is correct, if we are to explain certain highly general observable features of reality, we inevitably will posit modal structure as part of the explanatory apparatus. That we do so in attempting to explain that most general fact of contingent existence itself, then, should not be ruled out of bounds absent some compelling reason to think that in this context modalized explanations cannot succeed. But *could* there really be a metaphysic that provides the outlines of a reasonable answer to our question without deeply untoward consequences?

Well, let us begin to consider the matter. In its barest form, the traditional answer that I will defend is this: The reason that any contingent thing exists at all (and, in particular, the world of which we are part) is that it is a contingent causal consequence of an absolutely necessary being, a being which itself could not have failed to exist, since *that* it is is inseparable from *what* it is. I will consider below how we might conceive this causal dependency of contingent on necessary reality. But first, I will explore the very notion of *necessary existence* itself, which many philosophers contend is incoherent or otherwise radically defective.

The claim that there is a necessary being is the claim that there is a being whose nature entails existence, so that *any* possible world would involve the existence of such an entity. Such a being, we might say, is absolutely invulnerable to nonexistence. By way of relevant contrast, were there a being which was causally immune from destruction (no existing thing or collection of things have the capacity indirectly or directly to destroy it), but whose existence was contingent, it would still, in the end, just *happen* to exist. Were such a being conscious, it could sensibly feel *fortunate* that it exists, even though it owes its existence to no existing thing.

One should not be misled by an injudicious acceptance of the authority of Immanuel Kant into thinking that accepting the thesis that there is necessary being as part of an answer to the existence question implicitly commits one to the probity of some form of *ontological* argument as a means of settling the question of the existence of such a being. (Since it is widely affirmed that that there is *something* deeply wrong with all forms of ontological argument, Kant's aim here is to provide a rather complicated *reductio ad absurdum* of the cosmological argument.) I am not here arguing from a claim that it is possible that there is some (perhaps uninstantiated) nature that includes existence, and so (since whatever is possibly necessary is actually necessary, on standard modal semantics) there must actually exist such a being. For such an argument gives no reason to think that the nature in question is genuinely possible, and not merely logically consistent. Rather, in the present context, the assumption that there *can* be such a being is made in part on *explanatory* grounds: only if there is (and therefore can be) an entity with such a nature can there be ultimate explanation of existence. It is reasonable to believe that such an explanation is there to be had (whether or not we can know it in any detail), so it is reasonable to believe that there can be such a being. This prima facie reasoning, I will argue, is not overturned by any good argument to the conclusions that the existence of such a being is incoherent or could not serve the explanatory role described.[3]

Having (wrongly) reduced the cosmological argument to the ontological argument, Kant famously responded to the latter with the objection that "existence is not a predicate." Since both arguments employ the concept of necessary being, it is worth responding to this complaint here. Kant's idea is that existence is not another quality or property on a par with extension, shape, or mass. If I contemplate two similar objects A and B in my mind, and add to the idea of A alone that it has existence, I am not thereby making it an idea of something different from, let alone greater than B. Whether Kant is right or not on the propertyhood of existence, however, is beside the point. For what is distinctive of necessary being is not the fact of its existing, but that it enjoys *necessary existence*. And this very much is a substantial, distinctive property, involving a superior mode of existing. The natures of other things (whether instanced or not) will include the property, *being a contingent being* – that is, existing contingently, if at all. And the difference between these two classes of things is evidently intrinsic and fundamental. The one class will include natures that are self-existing, whereas those in the other class are ontologically and explanatorily incomplete, existing, if at all, in dependency on other things.

I conclude that widespread claims that the notion of a necessary being is incoherent are groundless. Our second challenge to its invocation concerns its explanatory potential. Some contend that we have no firm grasp on the alleged property of necessary existence, so explanatory appeal to it is vacuous, affording no true insight. It is putting a label on a mystery. I assume the idea's legitimacy (says the critic) because it appears vaguely to answer to an explanatory gap at the limits of *genuine* human understanding of the workings of nature. I thereby display an arrogant tendency of human beings to assume that reality must fully conform to our explanatory goals. (This is where the moral vituperations I alluded to above come in.) But against this, three things may be said.

First, it is overstating the shortcomings of the explanatory appeal to necessary being to say that we have no understanding at all what 'necessary existence' is supposed to be. If that were the case, then appeal to it truly would be vacuous, as it would amount to no more than the claim that there is a being in whom the mystery of existence has its answer! We clearly do understand the rudimentary concept of necessary existence, even those philosophers under the baleful influence of Quine who have skeptical doubts about necessity claims quite generally. What we lack is a deep understanding of what the instantiation of such a property would involve. (Better: we lack an understanding of what the concrete reality that manifests necessary existence would be like thereby.) We do not have a direct acquaintance with such a reality, at least not in a way that discloses this primal feature in qualitative terms as sense perception discloses the shape of a middle-sized object. (In the case at hand, such an acquaintance would involve an immediate *recognition* that such a being simply *must* exist.) And neither, clearly, can we close the gap in any exercise of imagination. But there is another way of understanding, the way of functional definition. We grasp the constituent concepts of necessity and existence, and understanding *necessary existence* as a property that directly grounds its possessor's own existence and serves as a ground for the possibility of contingent things, which fact is presupposed but not explained by our theorizing concerning the contingent world.[4]

The second point I wish to make is that charges of hubris and the like fit equally well those who *deny* that any aspect of reality manifests a property which we grasp only superficially, even where we see that it alone can play an explanatory role crucial to the coherence of our overall scheme. Or perhaps the cognitive vice lurking within such a rejection is better expressed as one of undue fastidiousness: "hang on to concepts that are neat and clean, and sweep their unruly congeners into the bin." One would have thought that a gesture at twentieth-century science suffices to show the folly of such an attitude.

Finally, there is a further respect in which the objector's display of intellectual caution and modesty is a sham: if our world is not ultimately intelligible ("intelligible through and through," as the critic John Mackie has put it), then ultimate intelligibility doesn't just happen to be absent from our world, as it happens to be the case that there are no unicorns; it is *impossible*. For it cannot be that while there is no necessary being, there might have been. (The concept of a necessary being is of one that could not have failed to exist, absolutely speaking. For such a being to be possible, it must be such that it would exist in every possible circumstance, including the actual one.)[5] Thus, in opposing our 'rationalist' commitment to the ultimate intelligibility of our world, our critic is thereby advancing an equally strong thesis, implicitly held as a *necessary* truth. Given that our natural, intuitive assent is towards our world's being ultimately intelligible (as the pervasive tendency to raise the Existence Question reveals), why should we retreat when we see where it leads us? One gets the impression that what moves at least some modern philosophers is simply a dislike of the intelligibility thesis, or of the broad conclusion to which it appears to lead, more than any philosophical/explanatory consideration connected to working it out in systematic fashion. And consider in this regard that we may sharply distinguish two such 'rationalist' theses:

1. Reality is intelligible "through and through."
2. Human beings are capable of laying bare the full intelligibility of reality.

Attacks on rationalism are quite plausible when directed at 2, a thesis held by very few philosophers, and certainly not by any medieval philosopher-theologians. What we seek here is not a comprehensive answer to the Existence Question, but the outline of an answer (or range of possible answers, if there is more than one). Schematic answers may suffice for very significant constraints on general metaphysics. Anti-rationalist attacks are far less plausible when directed at 1, once we see what its repudiation commits us to and we further recognize that it is entirely independent of the inflated optimism embodied in 2.

Two Objections to the Traditional Answer

From the possibility of a beginningless sequence of causes

The traditional answer to the existence question maintains that there is a true explanation that involves a contingent explanatory connection between a necessary being and all of contingent reality. In Part 9 of his masterful *Dialogues Concerning Natural Religion*, David Hume argues that explanatory appeal to something outside the realm of contingent beings is *unnecessary*. This objection clearly misfires, but I want to discuss it because the proper reply to it is not always appreciated. Hume's character Philo speaks (1935: Part IX, 190):

> In such a chain, too, or succession of objects, each part is caused by that which preceded it, and causes that which succeeds it. Where then is the difficulty? But the *whole*, you say, wants a cause. I answer that the uniting of these parts into a whole, like the uniting of several distinct countries into one kingdom, or several distinct members into one body, is performed merely by

an arbitrary act of the mind, and has no influence on the nature of things. Did I show you the particular causes of each individual in a collection of twenty particles of matter, I should think it very unreasonable should you afterwards ask me what was the cause of the whole twenty. This is sufficiently explained in explaining the cause of the parts.

Hume assumes that the universe is a beginningless, unbroken causal chain of objects/events, so that there is no first event lacking a causal explanation in terms of what preceded it. This assumption initially appears to be at odds with modern finite Big Bang cosmology, in contrast with the infinite Newtonian cosmology of Hume's day. Whether contemporary models of the universe as finite but unbounded would suffice for Hume's purposes is a subtle matter we needn't settle here.[6] The more speculative, recent idea that the universe we inhabit may be the product (perhaps one of many) of a primordial 'quantum vacuum' surely could be formulated in a way congenial to Hume's basic thesis. In any case, I will regard Hume's empirical assumption as an open question to which he may rightly appeal in rebutting the cosmological argument.

Hume contends that a beginningless sequence of events may admit of a complete, purely internal explanation – even if each of its constituent objects is a contingent being. All that is needed is that each stage of the sequence has a causal explanation in terms of what preceded it. That there can be immanent, stepwise explanations for particular events in terms of prior causes is hardly news. The crucial claim here, it seems to me, is that this form of explanation can be *complete*, leaving nothing further to be explained, *even when the explanandum is a single event of short duration*. This claim is simply mistaken.[7] A complete explanation would be *unconditional* – it would not appeal to factors that are themselves left unexplained. This requirement evidently is not met for local, sequential explanations where one event is explained in terms of another *which itself is an unexplained given* in terms of the explanation at hand. (This is not to say that there is anything wrong with conditional scientific explanations. I am merely pointing out that such explanations do not *aspire* to what would be required for Hume's objection to go through.) The point generalizes to other forms of scientific explanation familiar from contemporary theorizing. Explanations of large-scale patterns in the distribution of matter in the universe that point to early conditions and dynamical patterns treat these latter facts as simply given. Explanations cannot be unconditional if the terms are themselves all contingent. We can reduce the *number* of contingent facts lacking explanation when we seek to explain the enormous macroscopic diversity of things in terms of a very small number of elements and their dynamical propensities, together with basic features of the universe's topological structure. But in the end, what we get is conditional in character.

Alex Pruss (2006: 44) gives the following nice example that illustrates the essential explanatory incompleteness of simply noting the stepwise dependence within a beginningless sequence of events. Suppose a cannon is fired at time t_0 and the cannonball lands at t_1. Now consider the infinite sequence of momentary events spanning all times between the two events, excluding t_0 and including t_1. There is no first event in this sequence, as there is no first temporal instant after t_0. Thus, though the entire sequence has a finite duration, it still meets Hume's envisioned scenario of a beginningless infinite sequence of events, each causally dependent on events that precede it. Hume should conclude that this series is explanatorily complete, but this is evidently false: the entire sequence of events has a partial explanation in terms of the firing of the cannon at t_0.[8]

It might be thought that my contention that there cannot be an internal, complete explanation of a beginningless sequence of contingent events rests on the thought that if our universe were that way, we would still want to know why contingent reality was that way rather than another way, or no way at all. The contention would thereby be exposed as resting on an assumption that complete explanations are always fully contrastive, so that if E explains P, it must also provide an explanation for why P rather Q, for any alternative Q. And, the objection goes, demanding a fully contrastive explanation for every contingent event or state of affairs has the disastrous consequence that there are no contingent events, that all is necessity.

I will consider further this question of contrastive explanation in the section to follow. I agree with the objector that requiring fully contrastive explanation for every contingent event has the charged implication, and that this result is unacceptable. But my rejection of Hume's claim that a beginningless and contingent causal chain (a "Hume world") would permit an immanent and complete explanation for the chain does not and need not assume that complete explanations are fully contrastive. We can see this by considering a Hume-world that is causally deterministic. In such a world, an event E_1 will have a fully contrastive explanation in terms of a finite number of prior events in the noninfinite past (together, perhaps, with the laws of nature). That is, it will have a fully contrastive explanation of the sort that science standardly provides – a sort that I claim is necessarily incomplete. *Even so*, it will not be a *complete* contrastive explanation, since, determinism notwithstanding, that world might not have obtained at all, and so we clearly would not have the makings of an explanation for why this sort of (deterministic) world obtained rather than some other. And if not a complete and *contrastive* explanation, then plausibly not a complete explanation *simpliciter*. For, as we'll see in the next section, what is lacking here could, in principle, be filled by a transcendent-cause explanation that itself is noncontrastive.

If our universe truly is contingent, the obtaining of certain fundamental facts or other will be unexplained within empirical theory, whatever the topological structure of contingent reality. An infinite regress of beings in or outside the spatiotemporal universe cannot forestall such a result. If there is to be an ultimate, or complete, explanation, it will have to ground in some way the most fundamental, contingent facts of the universe in a necessary being, something which has the reason for its existence within its own nature. It bears emphasis that such an unconditional explanation need not in any way compete with conditional, empirical explanations. Indeed, it is natural to suppose that empirical explanations will be subsumed within the larger structure of the complete explanation.

From the availability of alternative, principle-based explanations

A second objection to the argument is that there are alternative answers to the Existence Question that do not invoke the existence of necessary being, and these answers are at least as viable as ones that do. John Leslie's alternative is that the world exists *because it should* (1979, 1989).[9] There are Platonic facts about the existence of some things and the absence of others being ethically required. These facts, says Leslie, are not existing things such as agents, but they are *realities*. The existence of our world is objectively better than nothing, and also better than many on-the-whole-bad worlds. Leslie's postulation is that facts about what is ethically required can be creative without any agent. The postulation's justification is that only in this way can the Existence Question adequately be answered.

Derek Parfit accepts the formal adequacy of Leslie's approach, but holds that there are still other possibilities (1998: 418–27). Here are some important 'global possibilities': this universe alone exists; every conceivable universe exists; no universe exists; the best possible universe exists; all universes above some threshold of overall goodness exist. Each of these possibilities, he claims, *could* obtain for no reason. It could be just a coincidence, for example, that the best possible universe alone exists. So the Random Hypothesis is that whatever global possibility obtains, even if an 'interesting' one, its obtaining has no explanation. Nonrandom Hypotheses, by contrast, claim that there is a Selector, a feature had by the actual global possibility and such that its obtaining is no coincidence – it is explained by some true principle. So, for example, if the best global possibility is one having our universe alone, and that is what obtains, the hypothesis will be that this possibility obtains *because* it is best. (Or it might be that the best possibility has all universes that are on-balance good, and *that* is what obtains.) While it could have obtained for no reason, it is more plausible to suppose that it obtains just because it is best. Supposing this to be a coincidence, says our hypothesizer, would be unreasonable.

Now Parfit does not endorse a particular explanatory thesis, whether appealing to an Axiarchic Principle, such as Leslie's, or a Plenitude Principle. All are formally open, he claims, and while the empirical facts may make unlikely the claim, for example, that this is best possible universe, they are unlikely to significantly constrain the range of admissible answers.

Here I can confess only that I am not able to make sense of the form of explanation considered by Leslie and Parfit. What sort of 'because' is involved in asserting that a global possibility obtains because P, for some nonagential principle P? Evidently, it is not causal in the efficient-causal sense. (If it were, we should go on to ask about the nature of this peculiar causal entity. In particular, we can ask whether it is a necessary being, and whether its causality is structurally analogous to nonpersonal causal agents in the universe. It will not do to ward off further inquiries by saying it is an 'abstract' entity.[10]) But if the explanation is not causal, we are left with a truth without a truthmaker. And not just any old truth, but the most fundamental truth of all. And that does not seem like any answer at all.

We can better appreciate the position of Leslie and Parfit by asking why they both reject appeals to necessary being as, for example, a transcendent cause of this and any other universe that may exist. Neither is explicit on this matter. But it is fairly clear in Parfit (1998: 421), at least, that his view rests on a conception of absolute possibility as corresponding to whatever is fully conceivable, a view we've seen to be untenable. Taking this view has two consequences for one seeking an answer to the Existence Question. One consequence is that posits of a nonconceptual, 'opaque' necessity is a nonstarter. The other is that any answer we give will not be a natural stopping point to inquiry, as it will itself be a brute contingency from a higher vantage point. Parfit recognizes and embraces this consequence (425–7). If we suppose, for example, that our universe exists because it is the best possible universe, there will be no ready answer to the further question, why is that the operative Selector, rather than the Plenitude Principle – and why is there a Selector at all? It is conceivable that other Selectors should have obtained, so it is contingent that this one did obtain in fact. Or if there is some further explanation, involving a hard to imagine meta-Selector, as to why that base Selector obtains, *it* will be unexplained. Contingent explanation must end somewhere in brute fact.

By contrast, our own hypothesis that the universe is a causal consequence of an absolutely necessary being is not subject to further substantive questions. It is true that a necessary being is *necessarily* necessary, but this is not an explanatorily prior fact about it that leads to an infinite regress of more ultimate truths. Precisely the reverse: Because it is a necessary being, it is (trivially) true that its necessary existence is itself necessary. Such metafacts supervene on and are explained by its nature, the truthmaker for them all.

Furthermore, if our hypothesis is correct, the null hypothesis (nothing exists) turns out to be impossible. This is a consequence of our insistence that possibility claims require truthmakers.[11] (Had there been nothing, that could not have been a contingent fact, since then there would be no basis for the possibility that there have been something. So nothingness is necessary, if possible at all. But it is not actual, and so is not necessary, and so is not possible.) Note that this result also falls out of Lewis's account of possibilities as concrete totalities (possible worlds). While reductive, Lewis's account is equally emphatic on there being truthmakers for possibilities.

I have contended that the Existence Question is meaningful and one that we ought to suppose admits an answer. While we may not be able to give the answer with any detail, we can explore what broad sort of metaphysics are and are not consistent with there being such an answer. Thus far, I have tried to make plausible that any adequate answer will use the concept of necessary being. The significance of this concept is made clear by the reflections of the first two chapters. Absolute necessity is not restricted to purely formal logical axioms (or even to an enriched notion of conceptual necessity), but encompasses propositions grounded in a necessity of natures. And *which* such propositions are to be accepted, while always controversial, is a matter best decided on the basis of theoretical explanatory considerations. The admission of a nature describable as 'necessary being' well fits this criteria, on the assumption common among ordinary folk that the existence question is meaningful and connected to the general goal of a unified, complete theoretical explanation of our world. For that reason, it confers a significant advantage on the metaphysic that uses the concept in this way.

However, one may say this much without making any very strong claim about the *self-evidence* or *demonstrability* of the theses constituting such a position. Though such claims have been common enough in the history of natural theology (and indeed of philosophy generally), they are hardly necessary when recommending a philosophical position. A curious vestige of that older history is that, while philosophers nowadays rarely claim that arguments on behalf their favored views can meet such an inflated standard, critics of any form of natural theology invariably raise it in reply. It is as if the very mention of such arguments, given their history, triggers a latent tendency towards hyperrationalism that is buried deep within the philosopher's breast. But this whole business is clearly a red herring. The argument from contingency to the existence of a necessary being has intuitive force and concerns a matter that goes right to the heart of the explanatory enterprise. Hence, restricting one's conception of ultimate reality in accordance with the strongly empiricist scruples favored by modern-day philosophical naturalists appears to come at a significant theoretical cost. It is up to the naturalist to try to show otherwise.

Necessary Being As the Explanatory Ground of Contingency?

An important and persistent objection to this type of argument is that it proves too much. If it were true that contingent actuality and all absolute possibilities require necessary being, ultimately, for their basis, then further reflection should lead us to the absurd conclusion that there is no contingency at all: the only genuine possibilities are those that are actualized. This is argued without assumptions concerning the nature of necessary being: it might be immanent to the natural world in Spinozistic fashion, or transcendent, as on Leibniz's picture. Either way, it is claimed, the consequences are the same for mundane contingency.

Such a damaging consequence is generally drawn from an argument at least superficially different from the one I have developed, an argument most commonly identified with Leibniz. The essentials of this no-contingency argument may be put thus:

> The proponent of the cosmological argument from contingency holds that for any truth whatever – truths about the existence of particular objects, truths about the nonexistence of others, truths about the pattern of events in the world, etc. – there must be a sufficient reason why it is thus and not otherwise. (This is the "Principle of Sufficient Reason.") The existence of the natural world in all its particularities is one such (albeit very complicated) truth. But without pausing to consider which of its component truths might most plausibly be thought to be contingent and which (if any) necessary, let us consider that truth which is the conjunction of all merely contingent truths, whatever they may be, and let us call that truth "C." By hypothesis, C might have been otherwise. Clearly, no reason as to why C holds is to be found within C itself, i.e., among the contingent truths. But by the Principle of Sufficient Reason, there must be a reason for C's holding. Hence, the reason for C must be some necessary truth, N. The explanatory *link* between N and C, whatever its basis,

cannot be a contingent one, since in that case the truth about it would be contained *within* C, and so could not serve as part of the explanatory grounding of C. So it must be necessary. But necessary consequences of necessary truths are themselves necessary, and so our original assumption that C is contingent is shown to be false.[12]

This argument from the Principle of Sufficient Reason (PSR) to the necessity of all truths is, I believe, unanswerable.[13] (And I follow the objector in taking this conclusion to constitute a *reductio* of any thesis that implies it.) In point of fact, though, *my* argument for the existence of a necessary being made no mention of PSR or anything superficially like it.

However, some will claim that the persuasiveness of that appeal, such as it is, rests on a *covert* assumption of this Principle.[14] For if the physical universe is held to be causally dependent on necessary being, and yet there are features of the universe for which there is no sufficient reason within the nature of necessary being, then (it is argued) we have not really succeeded in indicating the basis for an explanation of *this universe's* existence, where "this universe" picks out the concrete totality of contingent things, in all its detail. An explanation that appeals to a factor that does not uniquely determine the existence of this universe *ipso facto* fails to explain why this universe obtains rather than any other possibility not ruled out by the explanans – and so, it is suggested, does not explain why this universe obtains *simpliciter*.

This objection, I will argue, founders on wrongly assuming that giving a fully adequate explanation of some state of affairs involves explaining why it obtains rather than any competing possibility. Explanation need not be *contrastive*. Rather than trying to establish this point via a highly general exploration of the nature of explanation, I will instead focus on *one* form that a noncontrastive explanation of the universe could take, a form that is consistent with the denial of anything like PSR. (In the next chapter, I argue that there is reason to think this is the *only* way in which an adequate answer to the existence question can be given.)

The form of explanation I want to outline is a variety of *intentional* explanation in terms of the desires, intentions, and beliefs of a purposive agent. The issues involved here are numerous and difficult. Accordingly, I claim only to show that there appears to be a way in which this might go, the details of which must be developed elsewhere. It is widely thought that the form of intentional explanation that is needed here has been discredited as an account of human action. I think that this has been a mistake,[15] but in any case the most pressing problems for the application of the account to human action are empirical, not conceptual, and stem from assumptions concerning human beings and the wider natural order that need not be made in relation to a transcendent necessary being.

Our model characterizes the necessary being as a personal agent, with a capacity to conceive possible courses of causal activity and to choose from among them. This, in turn, presupposes the applicability of a notion of preference or desire, construed broadly. However, we need make no assumptions concerning the substantive nature of such a being's valuations (in particular, we make no assumptions concerning its apprehension and expression in action of objective moral or metaphysical goodness). Bold metaphysician I may be, but I do not claim to discern the mind of God a priori. Our model is schematic, laying bare the form that such an intentional explanation would take, while being silent on its specific content.

Nor do I assume (as the medievals commonly did in this context) that such being would have to be metaphysically simple in a very strong sense. I will eventually argue that the sort of consideration typically appealed to on behalf of the simplicity thesis does indicate that a necessary being would have a highly unified nature, to the extent that it provides a strong reason to reject the identification of necessary being with the physical universe. But it does not necessitate robust simplicity – an important consequence, because the compatibility of simplicity with the account of intentional action that I discuss here is far from clear.[16]

Now, Leibniz held that the necessary being that provides ultimate explanation *must* choose what is the *best* of all possible arrangements, where 'best' here has a metaphysical sense broader than that of 'morally best'. If it were otherwise, if there were a range of alternatives any one of which might have been chosen (for different reasons in each case), then there would not be a sufficient reason for the choice that was actually made, and so really no explanation at all. More generally, he held, an agent's action is explained by some reason(s) only on the supposition that given this reason in that context, it was inevitable that the particular action ensue. (Leibniz himself, of course, would not have used unqualified language of 'inevitability' or 'necessity' here, but his demurral on this point is famously unconvincing.)

Why suppose that intentional explanation of action must show it to have been necessary in the circumstances? One such reason (though not Leibniz's, it is commonly held among contemporary philosophers) stems from treating a 'causal theory' of human action as a conceptual truth about acting for reasons. Broadly speaking, the causal theory holds that some bodily behavior of mine is an action only if it is a causal consequence, in an appropriate manner, of factors prominently including my having a reason to do so. Bodily movements that are not a causal consequence of reasons are mere (unintentional) movements. Thus, an agent's *control* over his activity is taken to reside in the causal efficacy of his reasons. A defender of such a view *might* add (what is controversial among causal theorists of action) that for such reasons truly to explain the action, the link must be deterministic.

But this causal account of intentional agency is not the sole, nor even the most intuitive, option. One would ordinarily suppose that I myself settle the matter of how I will act by freely *forming* the intention that results in the action while having been free to form competing intentions that are motivated by other reasons. I experience this control, not as the joint efficacy of states of belief and desire, but as a direct, distinctively personal form of control *guided* by reasons. The 'agent-causal' account of *human* activity suggested by our experience as agents is hardly popular among contemporary philosophers. But here we presume only the conceptual point that this alternative to the causal theory is coherent. We now show that it permits *contingent* reasons explanations of actions and their effects.

I claimed in the last chapter that a satisfactory account of causation takes the notion of causal capacities as ontologically basic. Once one recognizes that this is so, there is no conceptual bar to the thought that the way in which capacities are manifested or exercised may differ in important and general respects. We have come successfully to treat impersonal objects and systems of objects "mechanistically," that is, to understand them as having the basis of their capacities in their underlying natures – their chemical, physical, or genetic constitutions and dynamical structures – and as manifesting these powers in observable effects *as a matter of course* in suitable circumstances. On this broad conception, circumstances prompt the exercise of such a power either by stimulating a latent mechanism to action or by removing inhibitors to the activity of a mechanism already in a state of readiness to act.

How might a contrasting, nonmechanistic picture of the agency of a transcendent necessary being go? There are various complicating issues here, and thus my treatment will have to be quite sketchy. A personal necessary being's activity in generating a contingent order is to be thought of, in the first instance, as the direct causing of an internal state(s) of intention that a particular determinate state of affairs obtain. This is not, importantly, to be treated as an elliptical expression for there being some prior state of the agent that brings about, in *mechanistic* fashion, the agent's coming to have the intention. Rather, the intention is irreducibly a product of the agent *qua* agent. This implies as a corollary that the causal power that is manifested in such a case is of a different sort from the mechanistic variety describable by mathematical functions from circumstances to effects (or from circumstances to ranges of effects, in cases of probabilistic, rather than deterministic, causation).

When we apply this generic picture to the creative activity of a transcendent necessary being, the explanatory framework it will engender is roughly this: Let it be supposed that our necessary being has some purpose whose content is P and recognizes that creating contingent order C would satisfy P. Suppose further that he generates an intention whose content is *that C obtain* in order to attain P, and that *C's* obtaining is itself an immediate product of that intention. In such a circumstance, I claim, the core activity and its product are perfectly well explained by reference to the agent's purpose and his belief that C would satisfy it, without any Leibnizian assumption that the activity was *necessary* given the explaining purpose and belief, or even that they made it probable. In the context of an agent who exercises a capacity to freely act for a purpose, explanation is grounded in an internal similarity relation of the content of the prior purpose to that of the effective intention. To understand why an intention is freely generated, one need only identify its reasons-bearing content.[17] This contrasts, of course, with a mechanistic model of intentional action on which an agent's purposes or desires and beliefs explain the choice, or formation of an intention, solely in terms of an external, causal relationship to it. But it is readily understandable in its own terms.

Our present goal is to give a schematic account of intentional explanation that allows for a robust contingency to many aspects of the natural order without being forced to admit brutely inexplicable phenomena. We suppose that a necessary being *might* have sustained any of a very wide range of possible orders answering to competing motivations, none of which came decisively weighted, as it were, above any of the rest. What is it that would remain unexplained? Not the enormously complex range of connected *events* involving the existence and interactions of concrete objects and systems, which totality I earlier dubbed "C." For I have already argued that the occurrence of such phenomena and the existence of their constituent entities would be adequately explained by reference to the reasons *actually* guiding the necessary being at their origin. (The *having* of such reasons is part of the essential nature of such a being, and so these states are themselves necessary, even though it is not necessary that they be the reasons acted upon.) Neither is it plausible that the necessary being's own activity is unexplained. The action's constitutive intention is a direct product of the being itself, explicitly guided by specific motivating factors. And it would be a confusion to suppose that we need a further explanation of the *generation* of the intention – for that just is the agent's exercise of control over his state of intention and its product.

The most likely target for an explanatory loose end within the present picture will be '*contrastive* facts' of the form *C's obtaining rather than C**, where C* is a possible but rejected alternative to C. I have been silent until now about the explanatory status of such contrastive facts – or as I should prefer to say, 'contrastive truths'. (Recall the motivation noted in the last chapter for a 'sparse' ontology of properties. We'll want to distinguish the sum total of instantiations of fundamental properties and relations – which is none other than concrete reality itself – from the many propositions thereby made true. On my usage, at least when I am being careful about basic ontology, this distinction is captured by the terms "facts" and "true propositions," respectively.) Let us suppose, then, that there is no explanation for many such contrastive truths. That is, there is an explanation for why C obtained, a reason that *ultimately* involves the necessary being's causal activity as guided by particular reasons, but there is no explanation for why C obtained *rather than* C*, a possible state of affairs for which there also were motivating considerations. On a natural reading of the question "Why did C obtain rather than C*?" what is being asked for is a factor that 'tipped the scales' in favor of C, a factor the obtaining of which ruled out the occurrence of C*. But once we analyze the question in this way, we see that it amounts to little more than a demand for an account that renders the actual state of affairs inevitable. But that there is no such account to be given, owing to its contingent origins, does not entail that explanation is absent for what has actually obtained: the *concrete* reality of persisting particulars interacting and undergoing change through time.

Some contend, contrary to the view I am defending, that the fundamental objects of explanation just are contrastive facts, not concrete entities such as objects and the processes they undergo.[18] Suppose this is correct. One could still press the Existence Question in a principled manner by urging that one should seek explanation for *every fact other than those for which there is an explanation of why there can be no explanation of those facts*. If an event is an outcome of a nondeterministic causal system, there will be no explanation of why it occurred rather than any of the other possible outcomes of the system (at least in many cases). But there *is* an explanation for why we cannot explain such contrastive facts that involves the character of the system in question. By contrast, the philosopher who maintains that the existence of the universe is a brute, inexplicable fact cannot, by the very nature of his position, explain why such a fact is unexplain*able*.[19] (Even if the universe has no explanation, it could have had one, as there could have been an equally contingently being that caused it to be.)

The point I am making is not restricted to the model of agency being explored here. It applies to indeterministic mechanistic causal processes in the natural world, and the kinds of scientific explanations that may be given for them. Tertiary syphilis, when untreated by penicillin, leads to paresis, a form of motor paralysis, about 28 percent of the time.[20] Furthermore, paresis arises only in syphilitics. Assuming for the sake of the example that this statistical fact is a result of a fundamentally 'chancy', indeterministic process, we can explain a given occurrence of paresis, nonetheless, by pointing to the presence of the untreated syphilis. (And this, despite the fact that the explanandum was not even made likely by the explaining factor cited.) For the latter, ex hypothesi, caused the former in an indeterministic fashion. It may well be that in such a case we cannot explain why the paresis occurred *rather than not*, given that it was causally possible (and indeed likely) that it not occur under just those circumstances. But why is it not enough for a *noncontrastive* explanation of what actually occurred that we point to the causal mechanism (however chancy) that produced it?

Though the manner of activity is quite different within the model of personal agency sketched here, the moral is the same. On this view of things, the existence of each natural particular and the events in which they participate admit, in principle, of a fully adequate explanation in terms ultimately involving their causal dependency on a necessary being, whose activity was guided but not determined by some goal(s) that the actual order of things were seen to satisfy. Which is to say, there is an account of why there is anything at all and why the natural order has the character it has. And by understanding schematically the nature and characteristic activity of the being on whom all possibilities and actualities ultimately depend, we can see, too, why these dependent entities exist *only* contingently.

4 | The Identification Stage

In the last chapter, I argued that it is reasonable to assume that the Existence Question has an answer and that a formally adequate answer to it must posit a necessary being as the explanatory ground of contingency. I also defended the coherence of the transcendent, personal-creator model of necessary being. In this chapter, I consider whether it is preferable to apparent alternatives. I think that there is reason to think that it is, bearing in mind again that we should not hold ourselves to the absurdly high traditional standard of *demonstrating* that such a picture follows from the core attribute of necessary existence. What follows is a line of 'probable reasoning', inspired in part by argumentative strands set out by John Duns Scotus in his dense and original (and alternately intriguing and obscure) cosmological-ontological argument.[1] It argues that the transcendent-creator model best comports with a rigorous understanding of the role necessary being plays in excising brute existences and circumstances from our account of what there is. In calling it 'probable reasoning', I do not mean to give the impression that I regard it as fairly unimpressive or trifling. Quite the contrary. I am simply acknowledging that I rely at one point on what is involved in our general conceptual grasp of the very idea of impersonal or mechanistic causation. Consequently, we must always leave it as an open possibility, epistemically speaking, that a sufficiently ingenious metaphysician will persuade us to broaden our conception in a way congenial to possibilities my argument purports to exclude.

From Necessary Being to God, I: Transcendent, Not Immanent

It is natural to begin with the most economical response to the conclusion that contingent existence is founded in necessary being. This is the response of Spinoza (in very broad terms, as the details of Spinoza's particular account will not concern us here): deny the premise that there *is* contingent being by maintaining that the universe itself, in all its totality, is necessary being. Let us be brave and not balk outright at the striking implication that our world is the only possible world that there could possibly have been (*modulo* some modest degree of variation that we, unlike Spinoza himself, might permit in conformity to any indeterministic processes at work in the actual world). For the friend of the broadly Spinozistic metaphysic might with some justice point out that accepting the existence of a necessary being is already to exclude some offhand intuitions about what is metaphysically possible. It implies, for instance, that there simply could not have been nothing, nor any world that does not include necessary being.

But though the friend of Spinoza deserves a hearing, his position appears untenable. I argue thus: The Spinozist believes the universe has necessary existence *of itself*, as the medievals liked to say, rather than being a necessary emanation of something existing of itself. But the universe is a complicated thing, and a necessary being *a se* (NB) must have a nature characterized by a kind of unity that is incompatible with the complexity manifestly had by our universe.

As a first step towards seeing this, consider the following question: Is the property of necessary existence something that *results from* the rest of its essential nature, or from some part of its nature? Apparently, neither of these can be the case, because then there being, 'in the first place', so to speak, a thing having the 'base' set of properties giving rise to necessary existence would itself be a contingent fact, which contradicts the assumption that NB is truly necessary. That is, there would be a problematic explanatory/ontological priority of these base properties relative to the property of necessary existence – the problem being that the existence of the putatively necessary being would be only *conditionally* necessary on the instantiation of some more basic features. So, the logic of the concept pushes us to conclude that necessary existence is not a derivative or emergent property of NB, but a basic one.

Might it be that, while necessary existence (N), and certain other properties (call their conjunction 'E') are alike essential *to* NB, nonetheless N could have been conjoined to some other nature and not to E, as it actually is? (That is, might N be only contingently connected to E?) It seems not. Were this so, there would be no explanation for the fact that N is *actually* connected to E. N is by hypothesis a final, ultimate locus of explanation. There is no getting behind it to explain any purely contingent connections it has with other features.

So, it seems, there must be an internal, necessary connection between N and the correlated nature, E. Which way or ways might the entailment go? Might E entail N, but not vice versa, leaving open the possibility that there are two or more natures, E_1, E_2, ... E_{20}, each of which entails N while N entails none of them?[2] Again, were this possible, E_1 and E_2 would be explanatorily prior to N. If we asked, Why do the natures E_1 and E_2 necessarily exist, and not some others (E_{20}, say)? the answer would be, Because E_1 and E_2 – apart from N – are the sorts of nature that simply must be (whereas E_{20} is not). But this (contrary to intention) can only allow for the entities' existing by a kind of conditional necessity: *given* that there *is* an E_1, it exists 'of necessity'. And this is inconsistent with the claim that the necessity is absolute. So, we conclude, N entails the nature E.

I will pause for a few comments on this. First, most medieval philosopher-theologians such as Aquinas went so far as to assert that this internal necessary connection among attributes must be that of identity. (Necessary existence just *is* omnipotence, just is omniscience – and indeed, just is the necessary being Himself.) True to his title of 'The Subtle Doctor', Scotus himself placed the most exquisitely subtle qualification on such an identity, connected to his famous notion of the 'formal distinction'. We will not consider that doctrine here, in part because, as intriguing as subsequent commentators have found this idea, it is very hard to be sure just what it is supposed to come to.[3] In any case, prima facie it is possible to stop short of asserting the simplicity-identity thesis, and suppose instead only that there is an intimate internal connectedness short of identity. (And if it is possible, it is highly desirable, as the doctrine of absolute simplicity is a very hard saying, bringing all sorts of conceptual problems in its train.)

I cannot make plain the interconnectedness of distinct attributes here inferred, as our grasp on the property of necessary existence is tenuous. But here is a quick example of how one might come to see subtle entailment relations between properties that at first seem mutually independent. In philosophical theology, God is often conceived as being perfectly powerful, perfectly free, and perfectly knowledgeable (where perfection entails maximality). One might think these are simply three impressive attributes that have no deep connection. After all, the corresponding attributes of more limited agents often fail to covary: powerful people are not always the most knowledgeable, nor the most free. We can plausibly argue, however, that perfect power entails perfect knowledge. Extent of power seems to be a function of at least two variables: the amount of work that can be performed in a single task and the range of tasks one is able to perform in a given circumstance. Corresponding to any total circumstance, an impersonal causal agent is disposed to generate a single effect, or perhaps any of an indeterministic range of effects along some scale of magnitude. The range of possibilities for a circumstance is thus narrow. A personal agent with freedom of choice, by contrast, is capable of a broader array of actions in a given circumstance. Other things being equal, then, a causal agent endowed with free choice has greater power than one lacking it. So a perfectly powerful agent would also be free, indeed perfectly free. Further, freedom of choice requires knowledge of the possibilities and how they are to be achieved. Perfect power and freedom would require an essentially unlimited knowledge, corresponding to the unlimited range of possibilities. So ends my quick little argument, whose point was merely to convey a more concrete mental 'fix' on what might be meant by saying that a range of properties are distinct and yet internally connected.

When suggesting that we resist the identity thesis of simplicity, I spoke of an internal connection between necessary existence and the other *essential* attributes of NB. Contrary to Aquinas and other simplicity theorists, I believe that we may legitimately distinguish between those properties of a necessary being essential to it and those that are not – those that are "accidental," in the Aristotelian/scholastic jargon. I will not argue this point until Chapter 6. So when I develop arguments here concerning the implications of necessary existence for an entity's *nature*, the reader is encouraged to mentally 'bracket' the question of whether it is consistent with those arguments that the entity might have accidental properties, and indeed be subject to change.

One final comment before returning to our main line of argument. Some may wonder whether I might not have improperly foreclosed one avenue to understanding how the universe could be a necessary being by the very manner in which I set out the challenge (the challenge of understanding the relationship of necessary existence to the rest of an NB's essential nature). In some recent philosophical-cum-scientific cosmological speculation, some theorists apparently have entertained the idea that the causal laws governing our world might be the only logically *consistent* set of comprehensive laws.[4] If this were to prove correct, then, contrary to initial, offhand impression, there simply could not be a consistent *conception* of a physical universe that differs from ours in its causal structure. (I say "apparently," because I strongly suspect that this way of putting the matter, as some do, is a result of a confusion, and that what is meant is something such as "consistency relative to some base set of assumptions, themselves contingent." But let us ignore that.) The suggestion, then, is that we might have a kind of explanation of why this world exists that differs from the familiar causal/intrinsic feature sort of explanation, a kind that is analogous to purely *geometrical* forms of explanation. However, even if it were true that there is only one *consistent* set of comprehensive laws (and of course we have at present no reason at all to think that it is), this would not provide a means of evading the assumption that necessary existence must be a basic, intrinsic property of a necessary being. The putative logical explanation entertained would only circumscribe fundamental aspects of the *character* had by any universe there is; it would not explain why there *is* anything in the first place to which such a law would apply. (Compare the analogous cases of geometrical explanation.)

Let us now return to the main line of inquiry. Thus far, I have argued that there must be an internal connection between necessary existence, N, and any other essential features of NB. Now apply this to the hypothesis that the physical universe is NB. How can N be a basic property of the universe, given that it has enormous mereological complexity? Apart from topological features, its other basic properties are properties of its parts (the elementary particles and fields), not the thing as a whole. And we can't say that it *emerges* from the organizational structure of the whole, given the previous reasoning that necessary existence must have explanatory/causal priority to other properties of NB, on pain of its turning out to be only conditionally, rather than absolutely, necessary.[5]

Perhaps we should consider a substantial modification of our hypothesis. Rather than supposing that N is a basic feature of the entire universe, we may conjecture that each elementary particle/field is an NB. We have already argued that there can only be one *kind* of correlated nature connected to N. So we must hold that there is only one kind of *fundamental* physical particular. (String theory to the rescue?)

To take our reflections further, we must consider the properties of this supposed fundamental kind of particular. Philosophers dispute whether these are best conceived as *universals* (which can be wholly present at any number of places at a given time, present in such a way as to enter into the metaphysical makeup of various particular things) or *tropes* (particular entities which generally don't stand alone but come bundled together to form individual substances such as electrons). I should not like my argument to have to hang on so controversial a matter as the proper philosophical account of properties. So let us consider the broadly Spinozist position on necessary being from the vantage point of each of these alternatives.

Suppose first that properties are universals: entities wholly instantiated in distinct particular objects. Since no particular object could *entirely* consist in a collection of literally shared (or shareable) features, objects must also have some individualizing aspect, something in virtue of which the object is *this* thing, and not some other, possibly qualitatively identical thing.[6] If our modified Spinozist adopts this metaphysic of universals plus individuating elements, he faces an argument that there can only be one *individual* that is NB on grounds parallel to those given for there being only one *kind* of thing that is NB: Otherwise, *per impossibile*, there would be no explanation of why the individualizers, the thisnesses, of all those entities that are NB instantiate necessary existence, N. We may grant that universals cannot exist in the absence of individualizing aspects, and vice versa. (Universals and thisnesses are always 'immanent to' their instances, each incapable of existing on their own.) Even so, there will be no accounting for the union of the thisness of this particle (say) and the universal feature of necessary existence *a se*, literally shared by the others.[7] For contingent particulars, this union is explained by the activity of an external causal factor in giving being to the new individual. But this form of explanation is obviously unavailable in the present context. As I stressed earlier, necessary being is the locus of *ultimate* explanation. And it does not seem coherent to suppose that there is an internal relation between a universal, of whatever sort, and an intrinsically property-less individual aspect or thisness. There's nothing *about* the latter that could ground the connection: it is just *this* (and not *that* or *that other* or . . .). So what can we say here, whatever our view (whether Spinozist or not) of necessary being? Just this: necessary existence *is* NB's thisness. That is, necessary existence is not a shareable property – not a universal. If, then, there are a plurality of NBs, as the view we are exploring maintains, each one will have its own N, an unshareable individuating feature of necessary existence.

It seems our modified Spinozist has been cornered into embracing the trope alternative to the universals/particularizers metaphysic. On it, again, properties are not literally shared or shareable by more than one particular, but are instead abstract particulars, or 'tropes' (such as "this bit of unit negative charge"), which are constituents of concrete particulars, such as electrons. Each NB would have an exactly resembling trope of the N-type. Obviously, our Spinozist won't make any further headway if he supposes with some trope theorists that, in addition to a bunch of tropes, each object has a nonqualitative, individualizing aspect (Martin 1980: 1–10; Molnar 2003: 47–51). So let us take our trope theory to be instead a 'bundle' view, on which particular objects such as electrons just are bundles of tropes related by some special relation of 'compresence', as trope theorists like to say, whose nature we needn't consider here. Each of the fundamental particles or fields in our world is simply a bundle of tropes, perhaps including charge, mass, and spin tropes alongside necessary existence. It is not implausible to suppose that tropes are essentially had by their actual bearers, in the weak sense that a given trope could not have been had by some other concrete object. Let us accept this assumption, which helps the Spinozist cause, as we thereby sidestep the problem posed for the universals version of his view.

Recall that it is not enough for something to be necessary being *of itself* that it necessarily exists. It also cannot be causally dependent for its existence, even by way of a kind of metaphysically necessary emanation, on any other thing. Now, the view under consideration has it that the 10^{80} or so elementary particles constituting the universe are severally necessary beings in this way. Consequently, none of the fundamental tropes that are necessary features of those particles has been caused to exist. The only place for causal dependency is in the spatiotemporal distribution of the particles and any inessential tropes they may have. Each particle exists of itself, but it occupies the location it does and has certain of its features because of the causal activity of the other particles.

But, on second look, we cannot say even this much. For the fact that the particles are spatiotemporally distributed as they are would be, in the final analysis, a brutely contingent fact. The Spinozist in fact faces a fatal dilemma: maintain that a particle's position is externally determined or hold that it is (somehow) an essential feature of it. If the former, then the fact that the structure unfolds just as it does (with the particles occupying their respective places) is an ultimate contingent fact. To concede this is to abandon the explanatory quest that made him a Spinozist in the first place. However, the second alternative is not viable either, for we have already argued that all necessary beings (if there are a plurality) must have the very same essential nature.

The conclusion to which the foregoing argumentation points is that, owing to the mereological complexity/diversity of the natural world, on the one hand, and the constraints implied by the very notion of necessary being, on the other, a necessary being cannot be right in the thicket of natural-worldly things, as the friend of Spinoza would have it. It must be transcendent. Although some of the details of the route we've pursued are novel, the upshot should not be entirely surprising, given the tradition of metaphysical reflection stemming all the way back to Parmenides. For when necessary being has been conceived as immanent to the universe, it has invariably involved the supposition that the natural world is radically different from that which it appears to be. I have argued that this move cannot be sustained, given only the minimal assumption of the compositional and causal nature of the universe. (And what can be said against the philosopher who would deny this assumption? For my part, it is enough to note that neither he nor anyone else could ever maintain such a position without thereby falling into pragmatic inconsistency, denying the truth of a precondition of his making that very denial.)

Two Models of Transcendent Necessary Being: *Logos* and *Chaos*

I have argued that there can be only one kind of necessary being, whose properties are particulars bound up in relations of mutual entailment. Might a similar line of reasoning show that there can be only one such individual? I do not see that it can. As I noted above, on the trope metaphysics of properties, there is some plausibility to the claim that this instance of electric charge, say, could not have been had by another electron. Likewise, if there were 17 necessary beings, NB#1's instance of the property of necessary existence plausibly could not have been had by NB#17. It may seem odd that there are 17 necessary beings, no more and no less. But given that the explanation of the existence of a necessary being is immanent to it, the global fact of how many there are will fall out of those individual facts, however many there are.[8] Nonetheless, the contingency of our own universe does not give us reason to posit more than one transcendent necessary cause of it, and the fact of the universe's tight structural and causal unity (stemming from an initial singularity) seems to be evidence in favor of a singular cause. I will hereafter speak of 'the necessary being', meaning that which lies at the origin of our contingent realm and taking uniqueness as a working hypothesis.

Now, the thesis that there is a unique, transcendent, and highly unified necessary being is compatible, on the face of it, with two very different pictures of the nature of such a being: the familiar model of a personal agent discussed in the previous chapter and an impersonal, 'mechanistic' model. As Peter van Inwagen has put it, we have not yet seen reason to prefer the conception of Arché, the primordial fount of being, as *Logos* to that of *Chaos* (1993: 146).

Varieties of *Chaos*

Chaos admits of several varieties falling under the general categories of single-stage and multistage generation.[9] In the present section, I will discuss each of them and argue that there is at least one significant consideration of a cosmological/causal sort that favors the *Logos* conception over all but one of these varieties.

I begin by considering single-stage models, of which there are three basic varieties. *Immutable Chaos* acts out of a necessity of its own nature in producing the actual dependent order (and it alone). *Abundant Chaos* produces an enormous range of discrete worlds, including our own. *Random Chaos* is a 'chancy', indeterministic mechanism, having the capacity to generate any of a very wide range of worlds. It in fact generated our world, though it need not have done so.

In weighing the comparative advantage of the *Logos* view and versions of *Chaos*, we must consider in a bit more detail (beyond the fact of contingency) what they are intended to explain. When we contemplate our universe as a whole, we cannot help but notice the variety and, especially, the *particularity* of its features. Here I do not have in mind highly specific facts about the location and states of individual objects, many of which may well be a chancy outcome of indeterministic systems within the world. Rather, we may focus on more general facts such as the *nature* and *quantity of matter*, the *size of the universe*, and so forth. Contra *Immutable Chaos*, on which this world is its necessary, unique product, it is difficult to imagine that a nature whose attributes form a tight unity (as we have argued must be true of NB) could be *necessarily* ordered to just such effects, for there would have to be a necessary correspondence between facets of NB's nature and each of the general features (at least) of its effect, the spatiotemporal universe, and this is simply implausible. This consideration of the seeming 'arbitrariness' of a world of just our sort might tempt one to move to *Abundant Chaos*, on which this world is but one of many fruits of *Chaos*. But I cannot see that it helps matters at all on this score. For surely it is no explanation of why the nature of *Chaos* is ordered to *this* effect to say that it is because it is ordered to that entire *range* of effects, and this is one of them. Really, the situation is just made more problematic. How is it that a highly unified source could be causally ordered to just this effect, and *also* to just that one, and . . . ?

The worry with these versions of *Chaos* thus turns, not on a presumption of *uniqueness* of this world as its outcome, but on the 'arbitrary' because variegated *particularity* of it. Perhaps my point will become clearer by considering the Leibnizian version of *Logos* that shares the necessitarian implications of these versions of *Chaos*. On Leibniz's account, the necessary causal connection of the universe to NB's nature is less direct, as it is mediated by a representation of possible scenarios, including the one ultimately selected because there is putatively objective reason to prefer it above all the rest. The basic causal *capacity* out of which our world flows on Leibniz's picture (or any other rendering of *Logos*) is of a much more general, dependent-being-generating sort. That it inevitably gets directed at one highly particular scenario is a result of the controlling function of God's goodness together with His recognition that this world is best. The particularity of the effect is thus not directly tied to the divine nature, or power of that nature, per se, but to the fact that our world, for all its particularity in detail, uniquely fulfills the basic intention to create what is best. And of course, NB is even less directly tied to this world as consequence if we reject Leibniz's assumption that there is a best possible world and suppose that *Logos* could have given rise to any of a wide variety of worlds.

But now if this is so, one will naturally wonder whether a suitable version of *Chaos* could ride piggyback on this alleged advantage of the *Logos* view. And indeed, is this not the case with *Random Chaos*, whose chancy mechanism gives us the desired implication of a causal 'loose fit' between NB and our world, without supposing purposive agency? Perhaps, but consider that it must hold that the selfsame causal capacity that gave rise to our world might have given rise to any of a wide range of different worlds. (If it held instead that corresponding to each possible outcome there was a distinct mechanism in *Chaos* that might have generated it, though it was undetermined which would 'win out', by chance, then it would just be a variation on the multiple-worlds-generating picture and inherit the latter's problem.) And this is puzzling at first glance. How could a very generic generating capacity come to give rise to one particular possibility (differing greatly from many of the others), absent some further factor that focuses it in that way? The natural phenomena from which the view draws its inspiration do not seem to help here. On one reading of apparently indeterministic processes in nature, there are irreducibly 'chancy' mechanisms that have a capacity to generate any of a range of effects, without being determined to bring about any particular one of them. But in such scenarios, the range in question is highly circumscribed, typically having to do with the precise value(s) of a variable(s). A highly specific *type* of effect is determined, but certain quantitative or temporal details are not. Such indeterministic outcomes can be *magnified* so as to have more strikingly different future effects, but that is owing to the subsequent activity of yet further mechanisms. The radically unstructured causal mechanism envisioned on the present version of *Chaos* is quite unlike this. Surely its mechanism has to have more structure, or else be given focus in its activity by some additional factor. That is, it needs to be made to be a more specific capacity *in context* – if you like, the mechanism plus focusing contextual factors would jointly *be* such a more specific capacity.

Consider the *Logos* alternative on this score. *Logos* has, at an abstract level, an equally open-ended creative capacity. But its nonmechanistic capacity is given focus by reasons (intentional states). By hypothesis, *Logos* could realize any of a large range of possibilities, yet in any case of its *doing* so, its generic capacity to act is focused by reasons. Put differently, prior to its actual exercise, *Logos*'s causal capacity is generic, or open ended. But the *exercised* capacity is narrower, being the generic capacity plus the actually guiding reason(s). If *Logos* acts with freedom, there is no inevitability of its acting on this narrowed capacity.

What *Random Chaos* needs, then, is an *internal* factor that likewise focuses its activity in indeterministic fashion. Here a device akin to a (truly) random number generator seems to fit the bill. Just imagine that its outcome determines the values of the basic variables circumscribing its output.[10]

Random Chaos thus appears to be a more defensible version than either of the other two considered thus far. But we cannot yet conclude that it is the sole remaining contender, as we have yet to consider the possibility of a *multistage* approach. I have argued that two of the single-stage generator accounts cannot plausibly bridge the gap (faced by any view) between the unity of essential nature required for NB and the highly variegated character of our world. Perhaps an alternative route for *Chaos* is to cross the gap in several small steps, rather than one giant, randomized leap.[11]

I am able to conceive two versions of the multi-stage generator approach. The first is modeled on a 'rotating tray' assembly, where a product sits on a tray, has a fillip added by one machine then rotates over to a second, which adds a different part, and so on down the line. We might suppose instead a single machine that acts on its product. After the action, the tray spins around (the product changing somewhat in the process) and returns to the original location, at which point the machine acts anew. Analogously, *Chaos* might have a first-stage product, simpler in form and variety than our world, which evolves internally for a spate of time, until *Chaos* acts on it again. Since the evidence we have suggests there is no such systematic external tinkering within our universe, we would naturally posit this activity at limit points. Oscillating universe cosmologies, with their periodic Big Bang/Big Crunch singularities are readily amenable to this idea.[12] The second version does away with the inelegance of periodic tinkering by supposing an incremental series of more complex cosmoi whose development is entirely self-directed, with significant modifications occurring at the limit points. The highly particular complexity of our universe merely suggests it is somewhere down the chain.

I concede that these versions of *Chaos* are harder to dismiss. However, part of the reason for that is simply the obscurity of what occurs at the crucial limit points. If the views are not to collapse into forms of *Abundant Chaos*, which generates distinct cosmoi by independent actions, there must be internal causal continuity between the stages. What seems quite unclear to me is whether overall integrity of the whole is consistent with additions at the singularities either of new fundamental agents (new kinds of particles, perhaps) or new dynamical or topological parameters. Without such additions, you'll not be able to suppose a significant gap in kind between *Chaos* and our universe, and this is the very premise motivating the multistage approach. While not ruling out the eventual workability of such a model, I tentatively judge the multistage approach to be less preferable than either *Random Chaos* or *Logos* owing to its greater obscurity.

Interlude: The Fine-Tuning Argument

It remains to make a case for Logos over *Random Chaos*. To do so, I first turn to a form of theistic argument that has received far greater attention in recent years than the cosmological argument: the 'fine-tuning' version of the argument from design.[13] The arguments are similar in seeking to explain seeming contingencies associated with the physical universe in terms of a transcendent cause. Design arguments differ, however, in that they focus on special contingencies as needing explanation, and they allows that the explanation itself may posit yet other contingencies. They are not, thus, looking for *ultimate* explanation. In the present section, I will briefly sketch the fine-tuning argument and first consider it on its own terms as a stand-alone argument for an intelligent designer. I will argue that, so taken, it is undecisive. In the section below, "From Necessary Being to God, II: *Logos*, Not *Random Chaos*," I will suggest that it nonetheless has significant evidential value when taken as subsidiary to the cosmological argument from contingency I am developing here: given that the existence of our contingent universe has its ultimate explanation in the activity of a transcendent necessary being, the fine-tuning data provide reason to prefer the identification of the latter as *Logos* to that of *Random Chaos*.

The fine-tuning argument in outline

The basis for the modern design argument is a vast range of information from cosmology and fundamental physics, appearing since the mid-1970s. Physicists have documented dozens of fundamental respects in which our universe, according to present theory, is exquisitely 'fine-tuned' for the eventual appearance of biological (and so intelligent and sentient biological) life. What is meant by the neutral term "fine-tuned" is that there are apparently contingent features of the universe, involving such things as ratios of basic particles or forces or the specific value of very large numerical constants in dynamical laws, such that had any one of them differed appreciably, the universe would not have evolved in a way consistent with the appearance of biological life. The details have been documented in several places.[14] Here, I will merely list in qualitative terms a few of the most striking of these features, the fine-tuning of which ranges from one part in 1,000 to one part in 10^{120} for the cosmological constant:[15]

- the precise strength of the weak nuclear force, the strong nuclear force, and the electromagnetic force
- the weakness of the weak nuclear force in relation to the others
- the value of the expansion-driving cosmological constant
- the proton/electron mass ratio
- Pauli's exclusion principle
- the fact that space has exactly three dimensions

It is currently estimated that there are more than thirty examples of fine-tuned features of the universe, many of which appear to be independent of the others. Current physics, of course, is rife with speculation about structures more fundamental than those which current theory treats as basic. Informed opinion appears to be that some of the seemingly arbitrary constants will be explainable in more fundamental terms, but it is quite unlikely that all will be. It is noteworthy that some current speculative models that promise to explain away some fine-tuned features introduce others (as is the case with both chaotic inflationary theory, which has received significant empirical support, and the at present purely speculative string theory, which contemplates a great simplification of the basic ontology of physics).[16] I will here presume that this opinion is justified.

Some have suggested that such apparent fine-tuning is less significant when we contemplate the possibility of exotic life-forms that, unlike biological life, do not have a basis in chemistry. Feinberg and Shapiro (1980) imagine the possibility of strong-force-based life-forms inhabiting neutron stars, for example.[17] But even if these fancies correspond to real possibilities (something which is perhaps highly doubtful), it remains that significant fine-tuning is required even for the development of neutron stars and planets.

What, then, are we to make of all this? According to the defender of the argument from design, we should infer that our universe is fine-tuned because it was created by an intelligent, powerful designer, who created the right elements in just the right initial conditions as to allow for the eventual emergence of intelligent and sentient life. It is not improbable, and perhaps is more probable than not, that such a being would desire a universe containing some form of intelligent life. The alternative hypothesis is that the one universe there happens to be exists as a brutely contingent fact. But this is overwhelmingly *improbable*. Think of all the variations on the above constants as specifying a space of possibility. Those possibilities which are life-sustaining occupy an incredibly tiny portion of this space. That the one realized possibility happens to fall into this tiny, yet highly significant portion calls out for explanation. Assuming that the existence of such an intelligent designer is not as improbable a priori (prior to the consideration of fine tuning) as the existence of the universe itself on the chance hypothesis, the most plausible explanation is in terms of intelligent design.

A version of the argument may be expressed in the formal apparatus of Bayesian confirmation theory as follows:[18]

Let
L = a universe's basic parameters must be finely-tuned for intelligent life to exist in it.
E = Our universe permits intelligent life.
D = There is a supernatural universe designer.

Where "P(A/B)" is to be read as "the probability of A, given that B is true," the argument's proponent contends that

P(E/L & ~D) is *very* low
P(E/L & D) is significant
P(D/L) is significantly greater than P(E/L & ~D)

That is, what we observe (E) is much more likely on the assumption that there is a supernatural designer (D) (given that L is in fact true) than on the denial of that assumption. Bayes's theorem tells us that this should lead us to upgrade the probability we assign to D (and correspondingly downgrade the probability of ~D) proportionate to the strength of the last two conditional probabilities and the weakness of the first. When a bit of evidence is highly unexpected on one theory but not so unexpected on another, the second is to be judged more likely, provided its prior probability is not so low as to swamp the significance of these conditional probability differences.

Three lousy objections

The argument from fine-tuning has evoked quite a range of response. We should begin by noting, and setting aside, some popular responses that are clearly inadequate.[19]

Of course *the universe is of a sort suitable for life. If it were not, no one would be here to ask the question of why it is. So we should not be at all surprised that it is.*

One way of seeing what is wrong with this objection is to see it as an instance of a common modal fallacy. The conditional statement *If there is life in a universe, there must have been conditions capable of generating and sustaining it* is necessary. But from that it does not follow that those conditions were themselves necessary. The necessity attaches to the *consequence*, not the *consequent*. John Leslie offers the following analogy. You are facing a firing squad of expert marksmen. They fire and – incredibly! – you are still alive and well. The captain of the guard lets you go, a lucky reward for the fluke occurrence. Surely you should suppose that the whole scenario was rigged, and you should not be allayed by the comment, "But *of course* they missed; if they hadn't, you wouldn't be here to puzzle over the wonderful fact of your survival!"

All possible lawlike structures are equally improbable on the chance hypothesis – the many that do not sustain life no less than the few that do. Since any non-life-sustaining possibility, were it actual, would not require special explanation, neither should this one which, while life-sustaining, is no more improbable.

We may again counter by analogy. You are playing five-card stud, and the dealer gets an (unsurpassable) royal flush in three straight hands. Suspecting foul play, you reach for your gun. The dealer protests, "Wait! You have no reason to suspect me of foul play. All hands are equally improbable – a lousy hand of unrelated cards no less than a royal flush. Likewise for any sequence of hands." You are not amused. Why? Because it is not merely the extreme improbability of the outcome, but the fact that the improbable outcome is highly significant in a way that favors a purposive explanation over the chance hypothesis. People have a motive to cheat in poker, and some are willing and able to do it well. It is just the sort of outcome that reeks of purposive arrangement. Certainly, it is not *impossible* that a dealer deal himself three unbeatable and highly improbable hands. But the 'design' hypothesis is by far the more reasonable one. Likewise, a universe containing sentient and intelligent life is a valuable sort of universe, one that is apt to be of a sort that would appeal to an intelligent being capable of bringing such a universe into existence. A design hypothesis is indeed more reasonable for *this* of universe than for a universe that lacks this feature.

Why are we so confident that the fine-tuned features are contingent, and so suitable candidates for causal explanation? Has it not been a theme of the present work that the scope of contingency may be vastly narrower than that of imagination?

It is true that the essentialist viewpoint espoused in Chapter 2 will see no room for alternatives concerning, for example, the behavior of a given kind of particle in a given context. Even so, there are plausible contingencies among the fine-tuned features emphasized by proponents of the design argument: the various delicate particle ratios and distribution and their density and distribution in the early stages of the universe; the happy combination of framework features (the three-dimensionality of space, and perhaps Pauli's Exclusion Principle on electron valence) and fundamental forces or laws; and most fundamentally the existence of the whole shebang, with the kinds of particles and fields that act as they do. Causal essentialism is not going to eliminate contingent fine-tuning from current physical theory.

Three better objections

I turn now to consider three related and more substantial objections to the design inference from fine-tuning. All of them question the possibility space the argument invokes or the probability judgments that are drawn.

The first objection is that the argument unjustifiably restricts the range of possible universes against which the probability is assessed to those whose fundamental laws are schematically identical to ours, differing only in the specific value they give to their constants. It is understandable that cosmologists interested in alternative scenarios should restrict their attention to just these universes, as they are the only ones about which firmly grounded judgments concerning life sustainability may be made. For these cases, one who is apprised of the basic chemical preconditions of life may 'crunch the numbers' for alternative initial conditions or force strengths and determine with some confidence how matters would have developed on the large scale, providing just enough detail to determine whether life-friendly environments would have been possible anywhere. But there is no reason to think (assuming our universe's existence is a brutely chance matter) that this even comes close to exhausting the range of what might have been. And who can say what might sustain life (in a suitably broad, functional sense) in worlds with utterly alien basic properties governed by an entirely different form of law? Or sustain minded entities, which many (not least the defender of the fine-tuning argument) suppose could exist in a purely nonphysical reality? What proportion of possibility space does the latter sort of scenario encompass?[20]

We may reply that the fact that the range of possibilities to which our attention is directed – those sharing a generic law structure to our own universe – is plausibly but a small subset of possibility space does not undercut the significance of fine-tuning. It is still a remarkable fact that, given that a universe within this subset happened to obtain, it should be one within the relatively narrow band of those that are suitable for intelligent life. John Leslie again provides an apt analogy (1989: 17–18): Suppose that we encounter a long wall that stretches beyond sight in both directions. The largish portion that we are able to see has only a few flies concentrated in a very small patch, and as we are looking at it, we observe that one of the flies is hit by a bullet. With no further information, we consider two possibilities: the bullet was fired toward the wall more or less randomly or by a marksman who saw the group of flies as a suitable target. If we are initially inclined to suppose that the marksman hypothesis is the more likely one, should we reconsider upon being told that other patches of the wall are known to be covered with flies? It seems not. For all we know, the likelihood of hitting a fly if one aims completely at random is nonnegligible. Nevertheless, the more specific likelihood that one should hit a fly at random while shooting in the direction of this particular stretch is still quite low, much lower than the likelihood of a marksman's doing so while intentionally aiming at the group of flies.

A second criticism of the fine-tuning argument is that, even if the point behind the fly-on-the-wall analogy holds, there is still a problem concerning the 'possibility space' against which we are to assess the probability of specific hypotheses. Physical calculations of the extent to which a particular constant is fine-tuned for life appear to assume a bounded range of values. But (it is urged) this is unmotivated. Doing so may answer to some vague sense of what is reasonable to consider in a context where physicists are reflecting on the detailed content of our actual theories. The fine-tuning argument, however, turns on probability estimates concerning chance outcomes from among wholly objective absolute possibilities. Since we cannot discern a priori any limits that these values may take, we should assume they encompass all the real numbers. Once we lift the limits in this way, we run into a fatal problem: the notion of relative probability breaks down in such a transfinite context.

It is a basic assumption of standard probability theory (countable additivity) that the sum of all pairwise disjoint probabilities is one, which represents certainty. We assign a probability of 1/6 to the possible event of rolling any particular side of a fair die, for example, so that the probability that *one or another* of the sides will land face up on a given roll is 1. Matters are more complicated where there is a continuum of possibilities, but all is well provided that the continuum falls within an interval of finite measure, as is the case with the continuum of reals within the finite interval [0, 1], say. In such a case, we may coherently talk of the probability that a value will fall within a given subinterval, by providing a probability *measure on the set of numbers* [0, 1]. (In a uniform probability measure, the probability that the number falls within the subintervals [0, 0.5] and (0.5, 1] is 1/2 in each case and they sum to 1.) But where the set is (0, ∞) or (−∞, ∞), we have trouble. If we assign a uniform probability measure, so that the likelihood of an outcome's falling within a finite interval of length L is the same for every such interval, additivity must fail: either such intervals are given a small real value, in which case the infinitely many such intervals sum to infinity, or they are given the value of 0, in which case they sum to 0. But as we've noted, on classical probability theory, the sum must be 1, which represents the certainty that one of the total set of possibilities will occur. The objector concludes that the notion of probability is simply inapplicable to such a context.[21]

Here the objector makes an unassailable point, one that forces the argument's proponent to retreat from the formal characterization of the reasoning. Nonetheless, it is doubtful that that this shows the inference from fine-tuning to be baseless. As is well known, similar objections can be made to forms of reasoning structurally analogous to the argument from fine-tuning that it would be folly to dismiss. For example, suppose there were a fair lottery (it would need to be administered by God!) in which there were an infinite number of entries. You would reasonably conclude that it is effectively certain that your entry will not be being picked. We may not be able to capture the sense of likelihood here in terms of classical probability theory (and no one has an idea of how to extend classical theory in a way that would capture such infinite scenarios), but the soundness of the inference seems beyond challenge. Consider it as the limit case of lotteries of increasing size: if there are a million entries, your chance is small; if a billion, smaller still. If the set of entries is infinite (aleph-null cardinality) – well, now you really should set aside any notion that you might win and get back to something more productive![22] It may be unsatisfying to have to rely on an informal, intuitive judgment in place of the precise notion of classical probability in order to capture the appropriate response in such unbounded scenarios, but doing so in this particular case seems perfectly in order nonetheless.

The critic is not easily assuaged, however. To those who persist in thinking that there is a sense in which the existence of a fine-tuned world is improbable against the backdrop of an unbounded set of alternatives, McGrew, McGrew, and Vestrup (2003: 204) reply with a *reductio ad absurdum*: surely one would not judge a constant to be fine-tuned, requiring special explanation, if it could take a value within several billion orders of magnitude beyond the required interval for one of the significant constants in our world. It is something about the narrowness of the band of actually permissible values that drives our intuition that it is extraordinarily fortuitous that our world had what it takes. But consider that the 'improbability' of our finely tuned world against an open-ended sea of possibilities can be no different than it would be for such a 'coarsely tuned' factor: in both cases, we must judge their chance likelihood (in our informal sense) to be *zero*.[23] The argument proves too much!

However, here it is the critic who has been led astray by faulty reasoning in the treacherous waters of infinity,[24] It is true that few would be tempted to make the coarse-tuning inference, but we ought to ask *why* that is the case. Resistance is partly fed, perhaps, by doubt that the constants might have taken *any* finite value whatever. This doubt may or may not be reasonable, but set it aside. Once we manage to screen off doubt on that score, it is hard not to conclude that the 'coarse-tuning' is no *reductio* at all. Consider again a series of lottery scenarios. Suppose you hold 10^{100} lottery tickets. In the first, there are one hundred times as many total tickets. Odds are against you, but there is reason to hope. In the second case, the number of tickets is one hundred times that in the first scenario. After ten iterations, we reasonably judge that you are *very* unlikely to win, despite the fact that you hold a 'large' number of tickets. When we go to the limit of God's infinite lottery, you clearly should think that you have no chance at all, despite all those tickets you have. Likewise with the 'coarsely tuned' laws case. Offhand, it doesn't seem terribly surprising that a chance universe should fall within the required parameters, given *that* fat of a target. But when we gaze steadily at the (stipulated) unbounded set of alternatives and recognize that the seemingly large permissible interval is as nothing in comparison, it should indeed evoke a judgment that it was overwhelmingly likely (in some sense certain) not to occur by chance. The coarse-tuning rejoinder fails.

The above objection assumes that we would weight each possibility equally. Our final objection questions whether we are in any position to assert either that the presumed possibilities are in fact equiprobable or that they are not. Suppose skepticism on this matter is well grounded. If the possibilities are *not* equiprobable, then even granting that we can motivate a restriction of the relevant space of possibility to a space of large but finite measure (and so avoid the first objection), all bets are off concerning the supposed great improbability that the values of the constants should have happened 'by chance' to fall within the life-permitting ranges. For all we know, life-preserving possibilities are intrinsically much more probable than others, so that it is not very surprising that one of them should have obtained, even though they take up a comparatively small proportion of the space of possibilities. Unless we can motivate the imposition of a uniform measure on the space of possibilities, then, the fine-tuning argument will run aground.[25]

I am unable to credit skepticism on this score. The legitimacy of particular probability measures is of course a serious question when probability considerations are invoked in physical theories such as statistical mechanics. These are attempts to gauge aggregate, large-scale patterns over myriad local interactions of immense complexity. These particular interactions are governed by physical law, and so are not truly 'chance' occurrences. But in the case at hand we are considering possible scenarios (the origins of universes) that are indeed provisionally assumed to be chance occurrences in the strongest sense of entirely uncaused brute facts. And it is hard to see how chance possibilities of this sort could be intrinsically weighted. So the only real question concerns whether all of the possible values for the constants correspond to real possibilities. Perhaps there are hidden constraints from features of the truly fundamental laws, which are presently unknown. But in the absence of such information, it is most reasonable to treat all values equally – precisely the sort of assumption we make in everyday contexts where we lack comprehensive information.

A rival inference from fine tuning: many universes

Another response to the design argument contends that there is a better way to account for fine tuning. It is indeed vastly improbable that your poker opponent should deal himself three straight royal flushes by chance, to an extent that the cheating hypothesis is far more reasonable. But were this the outcome at the end of a *very* long series of hands (long enough, alas, as to be unrealizable within the span of your lifetime), it would not be so surprising and hence would not demand special explanation. Just so, if our universe is but one of a very large number of universes, which in the aggregate roughly correspond to a sufficiently large and random selection from the space of possibilities defined by this universe's fine-tuned contingencies, no causal, purposive explanation of this universe's fine-tuned character seems required. The *totality* of contingent fact (precious few fine-tuned universes in a sea of life-precluding ones) accords with what we should expect on the chance hypothesis. There is, then, a rival, many-universe explanation of contingent fine-tuning. Recall the suggestion above that there is an observer 'selection effect' in what we observe (were our universe not fine-tuned, we would not be here to observe the universe's unhappy features). While earlier we correctly dismissed the significance of this to the explanation for fine-tuning in a one-universe picture of reality, it is entirely apropos in the context of a hypothesis that there are many universes whose distribution accords with the chance hypothesis.

Is there reason to prefer either the design or the many-universe hypothesis? There are, in truth, a variety of many-universe hypotheses, and when comparing them in general terms with the design hypothesis, we should distinguish two broad groups.

The first group are hypotheses associated with physical theories (however speculative their basis at present) which posit universe-generating mechanisms. One of the earliest hypotheses of this group was that of an *oscillating cosmos*, involving an ongoing sequence of Big Bangs followed by a Big Crunch and back to a Big Bang (Wheeler, Misner, & Thorne 1973: ch. 44). More recently, theorists have floated ideas involving *quantum fluctuations* (giving rise to discrete universes) in a preexisting space or space-time 'foam', akin to the spontaneous formation of surface bubbles in a soap-saturated liquid (Tryon 1973), or the *birth of universes within black holes*, through the tearing of the fabric of space-time (Smolin 1997). And of course, there is the *'many-worlds' interpretation of quantum mechanics*, on which each indeterministic, quantum-mechanical 'measurement event' is realized in a proportionate branching of reality (Everett 1957: 454–62).[26] Perhaps the most plausible of going ideas on current evidence is *chaotic inflationary* cosmology (Guth 1981; Linde 1983).[27] It hypothesizes that the origin of our universe is an extremely small space that underwent rapid expansion. The expansion caused the temperature of the space to decrease, resulting in droplet universes, analogous to the effect of the cooling of water vapor on expansion. These universes in turn underwent expansion of the sort described by standard Big Bang cosmology.

One thing that is made plain by the very recent proliferation of such ideas is that judgments about the viability of any them to serve as effective counters to a design hypothesis must be quite tentative. Still, the design argument resolutely ties *its* fortunes to empirical evidence, allowing for future empirical rebuttal, and we standardly make tentative judgments about the relative plausibility of theories despite their being open to revision in the light of further evidence. However, there are a couple substantial reasons to doubt the viability of these empirical theories to deliver the goods desired by the many-universe opponent to the argument from design. First, theories such as chaotic inflationary cosmology appear to draw upon deeper background features of the universe-generating mechanism that in some cases are no less fine-tuned than those of the visible universe. (It requires, e.g., that the original small space giving rise to the droplet universes conform to Einstein's equation of general relativity and have a high energy density in its inflaton field, and it presupposes other framework physical principles that structure the theory.) Secondly, there is not currently a lot of empirical reason to think that there will be *enough* universes, of the right aggregate distribution, to conform to the chance + observer – selection explanation for fine-tuning.[28]

Let us consider, then, a more metaphysical approach to the many-universes idea. On this view, there are a great many *wholly causally isolated* universes. (If empirical theory favors a picture of the reality we inhabit as much larger than that which stems from the Big Bang, this will still count as but one of the universes posited by our metaphysician.) The advantage of this approach is that it neatly overcomes both of the empirical problems for the first approach.[29] The metaphysical many-universe hypothesis requires no mechanism for world generation (which might itself appear fine-tuned) and posits precisely the number of worlds needed to make unsurprising the fact that at least one of them (ours) should be fine-tuned.

How does this compare with the design hypothesis? The first consideration that is likely to come to mind is theoretical economy. The design hypothesis posits a single entity, albeit one that is quite remarkable. Plausibly, the design hypothesis is stronger when made maximally ambitious in certain respects, as infinite power and knowledge are more natural, less arbitrary, than power and knowledge in some specific, finite measure.[30] The many-universes hypothesis, by contrast, posits many and diverse entities. Granted, none are as remarkable from a strictly empirical point of view as a transcendent, infinite designer, but taken collectively they seem far less simple. However, just as the hypothesis of an infinitely powerful being is simpler, or less arbitrary, than one of finite measure, so, we may argue, is the hypothesis of a plenitude of universes over that of a single, fine-tuned one. It may still be less simple than theism, but perhaps not as much so as simple counting of its basic posits might suggest at first glance. And we should also note that the existence of a fine-tuned universe on the many-universe hypothesis has a probability at or approaching unity, whereas the conditional probability on the design hypothesis is less obvious. (Although the argument of the section in Chapter 5, "Necessary Being and the Many Necessary Truths," I think, gives substantial reason to think it fairly high.)

But here is a consideration that seems to counter the ability of the many-universe hypothesis to effectively render unsurprising the existence of a fine-tuned universe. The many-universes possibility is but one of many 'totality' possibilities (which encompass both single and variably many universe totalities), and it is *still* one of only a few that contain intelligent life. Grant that it is less surprising that there are a few fine-tuned universes among a great many that are not than that there is a simply a single fine-tuned universe, or one among just a few others. But the many-universe hypothesis is itself surprising as the ultimate story on contingent reality, since it is one of comparatively few 'random possibilities' that involve any life at all. (Recall Parfit on 'global possibilities', which I discussed in the section in Chapter 3, "Two Objections to the Traditional Answer.") And since it is *compatible* with the design hypothesis (see Chapter 5, the section "How Many Universes Would Perfection Realize?"), it may thus itself be an appropriate candidate for further explanation.

The central weakness of the fine tuning argument

Thus far, the design inference from fine-tuning has fared reasonably well. However, we have yet to consider what I regard as the main objection to it, which is that its candidate for ultimate reality *also* looks to be highly improbable and seemingly 'fine-tuned'. What we have just observed in relation to the many-universe hypothesis applies to the hypothesis of design. Ultimately it presents itself as a chance hypothesis: in this case, that the fount of the one natural reality there happens to be is an intelligent, powerful being. Bringing supernatural agents into account threatens to upset the neatly defined character of our possibility space, of course, but it seems we may fairly judge this hypothesis as being intrinsically highly improbable. (We make this judgment against the assumption, contrary to the rest of this book, that whatever is ultimately real will be so as a 'result of chance.' This assumption underlies the present form of argument.) And it is not just improbable, but it is the kind of fact that cries out for explanation: how surprising that the ultimate fount of all else should *happen* to be the sort of entity whose structure permits the choice and execution of a world design!

I believe this objection is well taken. One possible response will seek to show that theism is made more probable than an uncaused fine-tuned universe by other factors that the existence of God would also contingently explain well. As this response no longer treats the design inference as a stand-alone argument, I will not assess prospects for this strategy here. At this point, assessment of the design argument will descend into cloudy debate about the relative intrinsic simplicity of the thesis of a contingent, supernatural designer and the thesis of a contingent, uncaused universe such as ours, and then about the bearing of comparative simplicity on intrinsic probability.[31] I don't dismiss the possible import of such debate altogether. But I do think the evident difficulty of assessing such matters renders the design argument less than probative as an independent argument for an intelligent designer.

From Necessary Being to God, II: *Logos,* Not *Random Chaos*

Some may reasonably judge the argument from fine-tuning to have a bit of force, but it is not compelling absent an account of the existence of the posited designer itself. But we may also consider it as sub-argument within the identification stage of the cosmological argument.[32] Against the background assumption of a transcendent, world-generating NB, the *Logos* view is more plausible than *Random Chaos* on the fine-tuning data. Suppose each of the hypotheses as having roughly equal prior likelihood. The outcome we observe – a world that is exquisitely fine-tuned for intelligent life – is far more likely given the *Logos* hypothesis than the *Chaos* alternative. While we cannot reasonably assume that the conditional probability of a fine-tuned universe on the *Logos* hypothesis is high, it seems that we can reasonably judge it to be not very low. The existence of intelligent life is presumably *a* good that an intelligent designer would contemplate, and it is not inconsistent with any other good of which we know. By contrast, the conditional probability of what we observe, given the *Chaos* hypothesis and our best current theory, is indeed very low. It is reasonable, then, to conditionalize on this information and prefer the *Logos* hypothesis. Again, we are already assuming that our universe is an outcome of an impersonal world-generator triggered to action by an internal randomizing device or of a world-generating purposive agent, and we judge these hypotheses to be equally likely apart from the fine-tuning data. So our fine-tuned universe is either the very unlikely outcome of a randomizing device or the not terribly unlikely outcome of a deliberate choice. We conclude that the latter better fits the data and so is more likely.

It may be objected that talk of relative likelihoods is out of place in this context. Since both hypotheses concern the activity of a putatively necessary being, the objective probability is either 0 or 1 in either case. Hence, a judgment of comparative plausibility based on the varying conditional probabilities of the observed outcome on the two causal source hypotheses relies on a notion of epistemic probability that is not grounded in objective probability. Furthermore, the appearance of greater 'plausibility' on the fine-tuning data seems to trade on the nonintuitive, purely theoretical nature of our grasp of the property of necessary existence. If *Immutable Chaos*, which I criticized earlier, is in fact true and we were to cognize its dynamical nature in something like the way we cognize certain overall features of middle-sized material objects, then we would 'see' the inevitability of its acting just as it does in generating our universe. Far from seeming implausible, it would seem inevitable!

While these considerations seem to me to be correct, the conclusion does not follow. There is an applicable notion of epistemic probability that is unconstrained by objective probability, and it governs reasonable belief concerning candidate necessary truths where formal proof is lacking – not just the existence and nature of a necessary being and other philosophical hypotheses concerning metaphysical necessities, but even unproven mathematical claims (such as Goldbach's Conjecture). The evidence we go on in such matters, whatever our verdicts, inevitably involves considerations of theoretical adequacy that do not seem amenable to objective probability assignment. (I suggest the same is true of judgments concerning contingent theoretical hypotheses in science.)[33]

Given the likelihood that there is a single, transcendent necessary being who is the source of the natural world and any other contingencies, the highly fine-tuned character of its product strongly suggests intelligent planning. Given that it is necessary being, we do not have to accept a result (a contingently existing, fine-tuned system which is the designer) similar in kind to the observed circumstance needing explanation in the first place. Finally, the premise of a unified necessary being, if justified by the cosmological argument, also gives a basis for a decisive response to the many universes alternative to the design inference. Positing many varied universes only adds to the explanandum of the cosmological argument, that is, contingent reality. (Note, as others have observed, that many-universe pictures, whether physical or metaphysical, are consistent with an ultimate hypothesis of a necessarily existing designer. Scientific cosmological reasoning is neither here nor there from the present vantage point.)

I conclude that the reflections of the past two chapters provide a significant reason to believe that contingent being has its explanatory ground in necessary being and that the *Logos* model of necessary being is the correct one. Philosophical arguments on fundamental metaphysical theses rarely if ever settle the matter, and the present line of argument is no exception. I do contend, however, that the considerations adduced are weighty enough to warrant some serious conceptual development by the philosopher inclined towards a rival metaphysical vision.

5 | The Scope of Contingency

I have argued that contingent beings plausibly find the ultimate explanation for their existence in *Logos*, a necessary being who transcends the natural world and wills its acts in accordance with reasons. I have not argued that *Logos* would have perfect power. Still less have I argued in more general, Anselmian fashion that *Logos* is perfect in every respect. I do believe that, given what has been argued, Anselmian theism is more plausible than limited-deity pictures. For one thing, the interconnectedness of essential attributes thesis exploited in the last chapter seems more congruent with the view that Logos has 'pure', unqualified attributes as opposed to ones of a particular finite magnitude. (A particular but limited degree of power necessarily linked to a particular, limited degree of knowledge, and so forth for other attributes – surely this smacks of contingency.) And Anselmian theism also seems better to account for the range of human religious experience, partly recorded in various texts that purport to be revealed by God. *Given* the existence of a transcendent and purposive necessary being, such experiences plausibly have greater evidential value than they do apart from prior acceptance of such a thesis.

But I will not try to develop these sorts of considerations here. Instead, I will merely take it as a provisional hypothesis that *Logos* is indeed absolutely perfect – in a word, *God* – and then consider the implications of this assumption for the scope of contingency. I will begin by contending that if God exists, it is likely that contingent reality is vastly greater than what current scientific theory or even speculation fancies.

How Many Universes Would Perfection Realize?

In classical philosophical as well as religious theology, God is a personal being perfect in every way: absolutely independent of everything, such that nothing exists apart from God's willing it to be so; unlimited in power and knowledge; perfectly blissful, lacking in nothing needed or desired; morally perfect. If such a being were to create, on what basis would He choose?

Since there is a universe, we know that God did not in fact opt not to create anything at all. But was it really an open possibility that He might have done so? There is a strong case to be made that a perfect being would create something or other, though it is open to Him to create any of a number of contingent orders. Norman Kretzmann makes this case within the context of Aquinas's theological system (1997: 220–5). The central reason is that there is no plausible account of how an absolutely perfect God might have a *resistible* motivation – one consideration among other, competing considerations – for creating something rather than nothing. The most plausible understanding of God's being motivated to create at all (one which in places Aquinas himself comes very close to endorsing) is to see it as reflecting the fact that God's very being, which is goodness, necessarily diffuses itself. Perfect goodness will naturally communicate itself outwardly; God who is perfect goodness will naturally create, generating a dependent reality that imperfectly reflects that goodness.[1]

If one rejects this 'Dionysian Principle', however, it is difficult to envision a coherent scenario in which God eternally chooses not to create. On the Logos model of agency sketched in Chapter 3, for example, God's positively willing *not* to create requires His having some reason for not doing so. What kind of reason could that be?[2] (Note that God could not Himself benefit from that choice.) One might suggest that rather than positively choosing not to create, God might have simply refrained from deciding one way or other. This is a familiar circumstance for human beings, who often have a motivation to uncover more relevant information, and sometimes stall in the hope that the choice will be "taken from their hands." But there can be no analogous factors in God.

Some Christian thinkers will resist our suggestion at this point by appealing to the doctrine of the Trinity, on which God the Father necessarily originates God the Son, and through or with the Son originates the Holy Spirit. The perfect, interpenetrating relations of love between the divine persons would suffice as a response to any natural impetus to communicatively express God's perfect goodness.[3] The reflection driving this response is suggestive, enough so that there is some force to an argument going back at least to Richard of St Victor's twelfth-century *De Trinitate* that if God exists, something like the Christian doctrine of Trinity is apt to be true.[4] Nevertheless, it is equally plausible that a natural impetus towards *inward* expression of divine goodness would be matched by an impetus to outward sharing of goodness with nondivine creatures. And, in any case, the oddity in God's acting on an entirely resistible motivation to create at all is not alleviated by acceptance of intra-Trinitarian generation and love.

Perhaps it is inevitable, then, that a perfect God would create. But what? Let us assume (as perfect being theologians generally do) that there is an objective, degreed property of intrinsic goodness, such that every possible object is intrinsically good to some degree. We need not assume that this property generates a linear ordering in the sense that every object is comparable to every other, such that for every pair of objects a, b, the value of a is greater than, less than, or equal to the value of b. We assume only that objects are 'partially ordered' in the sense that every object belongs to one or another linear ordering of objects and has less goodness than God Himself. We thus replace the image of a linear 'great chain of being' with that of a branching structure whose branches reconnect only at their limit, which is God. And let us further suppose that whole systems of objects and their total histories – that is, possible universes – are likewise partially ordered by their intrinsic goodness.

Now, if one or more of these creative options on each of the branches are of maximal overall value, it appears inevitable that God would choose one of them. It would be passing strange that God would opt for less than the best when creating the best involves no cost at all! It is implausible that a perfect being should have idiosyncratic preferences for certain kinds of universes, quite apart from their value.

But, on further reflection, it appears anyways unlikely that there is a finite upper bound on possible universes ordered by their intrinsic goodness, if for no other reason than that there is no finite limit to the number of good things one can have or to the space needed to comfortably house them. For every universe, there is a better, with no finite upper bound on the ranked series. Here, matters are *more* puzzling. It appears that no matter which option God might choose (a universe, whose value is, say, 10^{100} sgu [standard goodness units]), He must do so in the knowledge that there are options of arbitrarily greater value. Seems like an odd constraint for a perfect being to have to live with, does it not?

William Rowe (2004) sees here the makings of a serious dilemma for the theist.[5] The central premise of the argument is that a perfectly good God necessarily would create the best world that He can. As he notes, if we accept this thesis, we must either deny that God exists or heroically maintain that there is a best possible world (or equally good set of worlds) and that God has created it (or one of them).

One reply to the argument comes from Robert Adams, who contends that there is no moral obligation to create the best and that a choice of less than the best can be adequately accounted for in terms of divine grace, a disposition to love independent of the value or merit of that which is loved (1972: 317–32). Rowe counters that perfect goodness is not a function simply of meeting one's obligations: it also reflects the disposition to achieve as much good as one can. God's being both perfectly good in this manner and also gracious in His attitudes towards imperfect creatures are not inconsistent; they merely entail that His creative choice would be motivated by something other than love alone. (And what is a more natural candidate motivation than a desire for the best?)

But what if (as I've already suggested) choosing the best is not an option? Perhaps for every world, there is a better one. If that is so (and Rowe concedes that it well might be), it seems one could hardly fault God for choosing some very good world or other. Rowe, however, demurs, on the basis of the following claim: "If an omniscient being creates a world when there is a better world that it could have created, then it is possible that there exists a being morally better than it" (2004: 112).

Clearly, a perfectly good being would reject worlds that are on balance bad. But where would He set the minimum? Rowe thinks it evident that, other things being equal, a being whose minimum standards are higher than another's is a better being. Imagine a good, omniscient, and omnipotent creative being faced with a series of increasingly good possible worlds whose value has no upper bound. Being good, it wants to create something, and something very good. Perhaps it has to resort in the end to some arbitrary procedure for settling upon a particular world, subject to the constraint imposed by its judgment about an acceptable minimum level of goodness, n. Now imagine another being just like the first but for whom the minimum acceptable value in a world is twice n. Rowe believes it is clear that this second being is better, in virtue of its higher standards (95). Some will reply that this result is absurd in the context of options with no upper limit of value, since whatever standard such a being sets, there will be an arbitrarily higher one it might have set. How can one be faulted for failing to achieve the best if doing so is impossible (Howard-Snyder & Howard-Snyder 1994: 260–8)?

However, we need to be careful here, says Rowe. We must distinguish three claims:

(a) Failing to do the best one can is a defect only if doing the best one can is possible for one to do.
(b) Failing to do better than one did is a defect only if doing better than one did is possible for one to do.
(c) Failing to do *better than one did* is a defect only if doing *the best one can* is possible for one to do.

While a and b are true, Rowe argues that c is not. Otherwise, we should have to suppose that a being that opted to create a world that was just *barely* good on balance might be wholly above reproach. However one judges Rowe's fundamental intuition, this buttressing argument is less than compelling. Might not one coherently suppose that goodness entails the creation of a world that is *very* good, on balance, while denying that degree of goodness in general is a function of the degree of goodness one is willing to settle for, given that one is inevitably going to have to settle for something suboptimal?

One should not be quick to dismiss out of hand Rowe's thesis that facts about the structure of possibility space have direct implications concerning the possibility of an infinitely perfect being. We cannot take it as axiomatic that the notion of an absolutely perfect being is a coherent one. Although some challenges to this notion's coherence are purely internal ones, others concern the very possibility of certain omni-attributes, given seeming facts about the structure of facts over which the attributes range (e.g., there are challenges to omniscience from the structure of knowable facts). And since it is less than evident whether or not there is a best possible world, one who is committed to the possible existence of a perfect being may infer that there is, after all, a best possible world.

What, then, are we to make of the issue Rowe presses? One needn't agree with Rowe that moral *goodness* necessarily tracks one's minimum standard for result acceptability in order to find unsatisfactory, or at least highly peculiar, the picture of God arbitrarily selecting one very good option, at the price of rejecting an infinity of alternatives which are of surpassingly greater value.[6] It suggests an inevitable frustration of what, goodness aside, looks to be a natural aspiration (overall value maximization) of a perfect Creator. And yet the claim that our universe is a prominent component of this world's being the best of all possible worlds seems unduly bold.

So the philosophical theologian will naturally seek a different way of framing the matter, one that may lend itself to a better option. I suggest we start by questioning the common assumption that in deciding what to create, God contemplates *possible worlds*, conceived as total ways things might have been, maximal propositions that encompass *all* the facts, including facts about God and his acts of creation. If God were to create a particular universe that unfolded by indeterministic processes, then plausibly His creation decision could not be informed by comprehensive knowledge of which particular world would eventually be actualized as a result of His creative activity.[7] God's evaluation of the options might focus accordingly on the degree of goodness of the indeterministic universe *type* that His activity directly ensures, independent of the particulars of how this is realized in its details.

Perhaps we should think of a universe type as a massively branching structure, each complete branch of which represents one possible total way that world might unfold if the type is selected. And then the value of a universe-type might be thought of as some sort of function from the values of the individual branches, weighted to reflect their particular probability. (I will not here consider the issue of how to assign values for universe types with infinitely many branches, each of which would have probability zero on standard assumptions.) It would be a mistake to assume that in a universe-type that incorporates pervasive indeterministic activity, the values of the specific branches will sharply vary, leaving the value of the determinate universe that results hostage to fortune. Plausibly, the value of a determinate outcome is heavily determined by global features that will be invariant across the branches. Granted, the specific choices of human and other responsible agents is a relevant feature. But it is one among many others, including the very fact of there being agents given some measure of control over their destiny, which is independent of how they choose to exercise that control. A second point to bear in mind is that God might well plan to orchestrate large-scale outcomes for humans, channeling human choices towards optimal overall results. (Think here of Geach's 'chess Grandmaster' analogy.)[8] Finally, a universe-type is perhaps incomplete in a more subtle respect: prior to an individual object's coming to be, there are only facts about its possible qualitative nature, a nature that could be instanced more than once by exactly similar yet distinct constituent objects. God could conceive you, for example, only in qualitative terms prior to your coming to be. Your irreducible particularity – your being the very individual that you are – is not an eternally existing quality, but is instead inseparable from you yourself, and so could not have pre-dated your coming to be. Or so I believe.[9] Nonetheless, for expository simplicity, I will speak of God's considering this or that 'universe'.

Let a 'single universe' be a concrete totality whose components are causally connected to each other but to nothing else save God. A universe is a relatively causally isolated part of the one actual world. Let us say that a 'super-universe' is a collection of one or more totalities that are mutually disconnected save for their common origin within God's creative choice. Clearly, God's choice isn't between the single universes, but between the super universes. A perfect being would be capable of creating more than one universe, and should God choose to create only one particular universe, there is a super-universe having it as its sole member.

How might thinking of things this way help with our puzzle of creation by a perfect Creator? Here is a first pass at a line of thought that seems to me to have considerable plausibility. We have supposed that no single universe has maximal value (as much as or more than that of any other universe). And it is plausible that God, intending to create, would not wish to settle for a universe than which there are an infinity of better universes, whose increase in value over our universe stretches without limit as we go up the series. What is more, since the value of universes is likely not fully commensurate – there is not a linear ordering of the possibilities, given the wide diversity of types – a perfect Creator would be disposed to create universes from among every significant type. So God has reason not to settle for creating a super-universe that has only one universe as member. Nor will it help for God to create a two- or three-membered super-universe, or, in fact, an n-membered super-universe, for any finite value n. But it would appear to help if God were to create an infinitely membered super-universe, provided there is no finite upper limit on the value of its members. For example, God could simply bring about the entire, partially ordered hierarchy of single universes (that super-universe containing all possible universes). On reflection, this simple option appears unsatisfactory, since presumably there is some goodness threshold τ below which God would not create.[10] More likely, then, is that God would elect to create that super-universe containing every single universe at or above τ. But notice that he could also avoid the unwanted consequence by creating every other universe, or every third universe, or every n-th universe, for all finite values of n. So, at least as far as our puzzle is concerned, God retains an infinity of adequate choices among the super-universes. Any of these choices would have the same aggregate value of infinity.

Against this simple, initial line of argument, there is the following natural objection: Will super-universes not also be ordered in a hierarchy according to value, with the result that there is no best super-universe? In that case, would a perfect Creator who contemplates all possible super-universes not confront the same problem as one who merely confined his attention to single universes?

In reply, notice that we go up the scale of super-universes (unlike universes), eventually the values become infinite, in such a way that the hierarchy seems to "flatten out." The super-universe God creates is one of these equally top-valued members, the choice between them to be decided on grounds *in addition to* objective value. To defend this response, I need to explore the formal properties of the value had by possible universes.

It seems that the value of a single universe is measurable in at least three different ways:

1. The *intensive* value of each of its basic objects, reflecting both the value of its kind and its degree of perfection as an exemplar of its kind.[11]

2. The *extensive, or aggregate*, value of those objects taken collectively.
3. The *organic* value of the universe as a whole, and perhaps of its sub-regions. Aesthetic, moral, and other kinds of objective value all attach to situations or complexes partly in virtue of their relational structure. For example, it has been supposed (by Leibniz and many others) that rich complexity achieved through elegant, simple laws governing simple basic elements is an arrangement of great metaphysical goodness and beauty. Still better and more beautiful, *ceteris peribus*, are nested structures or processes, whereby the manifestation of complexity through underlying simplicity is repeated at stages of resolution (as with fractals or living organisms). However precisely we conceive its determinants, the organic value of a universe seems analogous to the intensive value of a natural object. It will be a function both of the value of its constituents objects and their qualitative states and of the relational structure they embody.

Earlier, I suggested that it is plausible to suppose that simple universes may not have 'maximal' value. It would seem that a universe could have infinite value (of cardinality aleph-null only?) *extensively* simply in virtue of its having infinitely many natural objects, all possessing some finite value. But, plausibly, a finite created object could not have infinite intensive value and a universe, however well ordered, could not have infinite organic value. The limit case, if attainable at all, could be reflected only by that which is perfect goodness itself – God Himself. If there is an absolutely perfect being, by the argument of the previous chapter it is one for whom nature and existence are not separable. When such a being creates, it cannot convey one of its essential attributes to its creation, so inevitably any candidate creation will be less than maximally perfect. (I am assuming that a natural assignment of units will assign aleph-null, or countable infinity, as the maximum for organic unity.)

The total value of a universe appears, then, to be a point in a three-space. Given that none of a universe's objects may have infinite intensive value, its value in this regard – perhaps measured as the average momentary value of its basic objects – will typically not be infinite. (The exceptional case is where a universe instances an infinite number of basic object types whose value can be ordered without a finite upper bound. Note, however, that universes meeting this condition might necessarily be constrained in organic value.) And, crucially, a universe's organic value will always be less than maximal. Even allowing for infinite aggregate value, then, no single universe will be of maximal value – the highest possible value along all three dimensions. Hence, there is a natural impetus for a perfect being to create an infinitely membered super-universe, whose members are ordered by value without an upper bound.

One might worry that these three measures of value vary inversely, at least once values get high enough, as might be the case when it comes to mean intensive value and organic value. In that case, were these equal inputs to the value of a universe – something I will dispute below – it could be that the product of all three measures has a maximum, so that there really is a best possible simple universe. But while I cannot show that this is not so, it does not strike me as plausible. Why should the organic value of a certain arrangement be diminished if each of its elements were themselves realized by multiplicities of arbitrary size?

Now let us return to the value of super-universes. Recall the objection that they also might be ordered in a hierarchy according to value, without a maximal value. At first glance, it seems that if a perfect Creator would be dissatisfied creating a single universe, knowing that there are an abundance of alternatives whose additional value is arbitrarily large, a similar dilemma would arise when considering the range of super-universes. In reply we have said that it may be that there is a maximal aggregate value of super-universes, one shared by all infinitely membered super-universes meeting certain constraints on the value of each of their members. (There does not seem to be anything analogous to organic value for super-universes, however, given their disconnectedness in all respects save their point of origin.)

But now we must confront a substantial complication: there is no highest transfinite cardinal. (There is the infinity of the natural numbers – countable infinity – a still greater infinity of the real numbers, and greater infinities still, without end.) Thus, a strategy that concedes that God would opt for *unlimited* aggregate goodness requires us either to assume that there is an intrinsic upper limit, inscrutable to us, to the size of super-universes omnipotence may create (a limit measured by a particular infinite cardinal) or to suppose that God may create a proper class of universes, one that simply has no measure at all. The latter option would not have sat well with George Cantor, the great nineteenth century mathematician who first unveiled the limitless structure of the infinite. A devout Lutheran, Cantor thought that God alone (the "Absolute Infinite") is beyond the limitless hierarchy of transfinite cardinals.

There is a better response, however. It is doubtful that a perfect being would desire to pursue maximal aggregate value at all. Why should a master artisan, even one of maximal goodness and without limitations, pursue mere duplication, much less unlimited duplication, of similar objects and systems?[12] What clearly will be of concern, it seems to me, is not to place arbitrary limits on the intensive value of whatever natural objects, and organic value of whatever overall systems, He contemplates. We've already seen that, plausibly, neither of these could attain infinite value. (God alone, who is uncreated independent being and the source of every possibility, is an infinitely valuable individual.) If both these claims are right, then the worry about finding an upper limit on the cardinality of the value of super-universes is circumvented. The natural object of a perfect Creator's consideration will be any infinitely membered, partially ordered super-universe for which there is no finite upper bound on the organic value of its members (and perhaps intensive value of its member's constituent objects), all of which exceed threshold τ. However, we may need to add one further condition. Imagine two infinite super-universes, SU_1 and SU_2, the members of which can be ordered similarly, such that the first member of each is of the same organic kind, O_1, and so on for each successive pair of members. Now suppose that the SU_2 universe is always a more valuable instance of the relevant kind than the SU_1 universe. If this is possible, then, plausibly, a perfect Creator would opt for SU_2. But equally plausibly, for reasons similar to before, there will not always be a finite upper bound on the values that can be reached by universes that are instances of some organic kind. If this is right, it seems natural to extend our reasoning by supposing that God will select a super-universe in which there is no upper bound on the values taken by the set of universes of value type O_i, for every value-type O_i.[13]

I have argued that all the possibilities deemed creation-worthy by a perfect Creator would conform to a rich structure. Even so, an infinity of options satisfies these constraints, and there is no reason yet uncovered to suppose that any highly particular sort of universe will be deemed necessary. Hence, for all we've seen, the extent of alternatives open to a perfect Creator may be quite wide indeed.

Some will suppose that a perfect being would naturally opt for a *plenitude*, creating as many valuable things as he can. If this were so, it would seem that the existence of every possible universe (recall that I here am speaking of universe types, as described above) is inevitable. I believe this supposition is on a par with the thought that a perfect being would be concerned with mere aggregate value. And so my reply is similar as well: this assumption is far less plausible than the more limited thesis that perfection would opt to realize every basic *kind* of valuable thing, incommensurate with the other basic kinds. (Suppose the theist *does* make the stronger assumption. Rowe would object that doing so is to endorse, in the end, the Leibnizian claim that this is the best, or one of infinitely many equally best, of all possible worlds, and this is incredible. But the theist who endorses plenitude may reply that once we recognize that his thesis implies nothing about the organic goodness of our particular universe, we should regard the judgment of its incredibility as totally unfounded.)

Perfection and Freedom

I have argued that the theist has reason to believe that it is inevitable both that God create something or other and that He create at least a countable infinity of universes (in the broad sense of causally connected and effectively isolated totalities or systems). Both of these conclusions were rejected by most traditional philosophical theologians on the grounds that they compromise God's perfect freedom. This line of thought assumes that freedom is necessarily proportionate to the range of alternative possibilities open to the agent. I suggest that this belief, while natural enough, results from a hasty generalization from particularities of our own case as finite, conditioned agents.

It is plausible that the core metaphysical feature of freedom is being the *ultimate source*, or originator, of one's choices, and that being able to do otherwise is *for us* closely connected to this feature.[14] For human beings or any created persons who owe their existence to factors outside themselves, the only way their actions could find their ultimate origin in themselves is for such acts not to be wholly determined by their character and circumstances. For if all my actions were wholly determined, then if we were to trace my causal history back far enough, we would ultimately arrive at external factors that gave rise to me, with my particular genetic dispositions. My motives at the time would not be the ultimate source of my willings, only the most proximate ones. Thus, only by there being less than deterministic connections between external influences and choices – and so my having alternative possibilities open to me in the final analysis – is it possible for me to be an ultimate source of my activity, concerning which I may truly say, "The buck stops here."

However, the conditions for freedom in the divine and human cases differ in a way that reflects the difference in ontological status between an absolutely independent Creator and a dependent, causally conditioned creature. God's choices reflect His character – and His character alone. He was not *given* a nature, nor does He act in an environment that influences the development of individualizing traits. If His character precludes His undertaking various options that are within the scope of his power, this fact cannot be attributed in the final analysis to something else. (And we may note that most of those theologians who hold that there was a real possibility that God not have created anything or have created something other than an infinite creation, also suppose that God is perfectly good, an essential, not acquired, attribute. God cannot lie or be in any way immoral in His dealings with His creatures. Unless we take the minority position on which this is a trivial claim, on which whatever God does *definitionally* counts as good, this is a substantive limit on the range of open alternatives.) Therefore, the impossibility of His undertaking such options is solely and finally attributable to Him.[15] Anselm had it right: although God is certain to act with perfect goodness (and, we have added, with a kind of maximal creative ambition), it is not true that God is good out of an 'inevitable necessity'. Instead, his perfect goodness and freedom are both attributes he has 'in Himself', for all eternity (1998: 327).

Some Applications of the Many-Universe-Creation Hypothesis

The problem of evil

My contention that a perfect Creator would opt for an infinite number of universes, ordered without a finite upper bound, appears to have some relevance to the problem of evil, which in its various versions raises the question of whether the existence, quantity, and/or distribution of human and animal suffering, or of certain horrific instances of such suffering, render the existence of God unlikely (cf. Turner 2003).[16] To put the point crudely, if the question is, Why didn't God create a realm much like ours in its having significant positive respects, yet without its seemingly avoidable horrific kinds of evil, or without the quantity and distribution of suffering therein? the answer made possible by the present perspective is, He did – lots of them!

Objection 1
This suggestion is flagrantly ad hoc. You are vastly inflating our ontological commitment in order to avoid a straightforward conclusion from the data that we have.

Reply
This objection might be apt if we were positing that God has created a vast plurality of universes in order to respond to some version or another of the problem of evil. But we have argued that this thesis is independently motivated.

Objection 2
A morally perfect being would desire to prevent unnecessary suffering. No doubt there are valuable universes that contain intense, prolonged suffering, and perhaps for all we know the suffering in our universe often or always leads in the end to goods of various kinds. But consider the choice between a super-universe that contains this sort of suffering, and one of *equal* value that contains no suffering at all. Why would God choose a super-universe with suffering (even suffering that leads to good) when he could have chosen a super-universe of equal value that contains no suffering?

Reply
It is not my purpose here to so much as hint at a full-blown theodicy. But I do wish to point out that the present view has an advantage in replying to this kind of question, which is just a version of a question that is standardly posed to theodicies of all kinds. In common with typical theodicies, I suggest that certain moral goods entail the real possibility or outright existence of significant suffering. These include the creaturely goods of heroism, perseverance, and trust.[17] A Christian theist may also plausibly contend that suffering is integrally connected to the great goods of divine incarnation and atonement.[18] The sole point I wish to make here is that, given our multiverse theism, we needn't claim that these suffering-entailing or suffering-risking goods are the *greatest* goods, or such that some possible universes that contain these goods as well as significant suffering are on balance better than any possible universe that lacks them. I have argued that a perfect Creator would desire so to act that

(a)   there would not be an arbitrary upper bound to the goodness of the universe(s) that He creates, such that He might have created a universe that was better to an arbitrary degree than any that He did create; and
(b)   every significant kind of goodness capable of creaturely realization would be instantiated somewhere or other in the created order.

    If these contentions are correct, then on plausible assumptions, God will in fact have compelling reasons to create a universe in which significant suffering is permitted to occur *even if the goods that require suffering are not the greatest goods, or if the universe in which they occur does not belong to a class of supremely valuable realms.* All that is required is that the suffering-risking universes satisfy a minimum threshold of goodness. Since it is plausible that the one-universe theist is rationally committed to something along the lines of the stronger claim along these lines – it is another matter altogether whether the rational theist must suppose himself to be able *to show* that our universe plausibly falls into this special class – the present view has the advantage that it can get by with weaker assumptions in responding to the problem of evil.

The argument from fine-tuning

Consider again the design argument from fine-tuning, *taken in its usual form as a stand-alone argument.* We suggested in the previous chapter that, apart from the prior commitment to a transcendent necessary being as defended in the present work, the choice between the design hypothesis and its multiverse rival (on which there are a vast abundance of chance-occurring universes, only a small band of which are life-sustaining) will turn on a judgment of theoretical simplicity. Some defenders of the argument are happy to leave the matter there, confident that the hypothesis of a single powerful and intelligent designer is far simpler in the relevant sense than the hypothesis of a vast array of systematically varying universes.

But the argument of the section above "How Many Universes Would Perfection Realize?" if accepted threatens to undercut this contention. On the present view, theism, properly unpacked, predicts an equally plenitudinous reality. Set aside for the moment our conception of God as *inter alia* necessary being. We begin with the discovery that our universe is finely tuned for life. We consider three possible ways of accounting for this fact. One way is to posit a powerful yet limited designer, one who is either not capable of generating an infinitely membered super-universe or lacks the moral attribute that would motivate him to do so. Another way is to posit a contingent, but infinitely perfect being who has generated an infinitely membered super-universe which includes this universe. The final way is to suppose that there is a vast realm of universes corresponding to a sizeable random sampling from among the possibilities that involve variations in the values of the fundamental constants of our universe. On this last approach, we do not *explain* the existence of our universe (its existence is a brute fact); instead, we make a large ontological commitment that renders it unsurprising, and so not requiring special explanation.

The first approach is obviously not attractive to one who seeks to make an argument for classical theism. And some defenders of the fine-tuning argument (most emphatically, Richard Swinburne) will in any case see it as less simple than the theistic alternative, since finite limits to theoretical posits are more arbitrary, less plausible a priori, than ones whose posits always take the values of either zero or infinity. So let us set aside the first approach.

Two approaches remain, each of which predicts that our universe is but a small fraction of reality, one element of a highly structured set of universes. On the first view, there are at least aleph-null universes, all of which are created and sustained by an infinitely perfect purposive being. Though their intrinsic character probably varies enormously, all of these universes are very good on balance and they collectively conform to an ascending, unbounded ordering on their overall goodness. The other approach posits a very large, but possibly finite set of universes, all of which instantiate the same generic law-structure and feature the same types of basic elements, and all of which exist by brute chance. The universes differ only in the values that the constants take in the laws and initial conditions.

Now we ask, Does either view have the advantage of greater theoretical simplicity? The fan of the argument from fine-tuning might argue that the answer is yes, despite the likelihood of infinitely many universes on theism. He might reason as follows: It may be true *for other reasons* that theism predicts that created reality extends far beyond our universe. But when we focus solely on the data of fine-tuning and what is needed to account for them, we properly ignore this implication. We are simply to consider what must directly be posited to account for the data in question, and here (I contend) theism has the advantage, as infinite perfect designer is simpler than is the multiverse alternative.

However, this reply is uncompelling, it seems to me. The contingent-theism explanation of fine-tuning appeals to the fittingness of a finely tuned universe as a candidate for an intelligent world-designer. But as we probe this 'theoretical derivation', we come to see intelligent life as but one of many desirable features that it is plausible to suppose a perfect designer would want to achieve. It comes as part of a larger package of considerations, such that the act of creating our universe is not independent of the (possibly simultaneous) creation of infinitely many others. And as these other universes are not among the observables for which we seek explanation, they are probably accounted as part of the designer theory's theoretical commitments. As a result, the perfect-designer hypothesis does not seem well positioned to win the match on points via appeal to greater simplicity.

Necessary Being and the Scope of Possibility

In Chapter 2, in the section "The Spheres of Possibility," I briefly considered the impact that significant, less than obvious constraints on absolute possibility have on our ability to acquire modal knowledge. Given the views defended in the chapters that followed, this question may have renewed urgency for some of my readers. According to our account, the range of the ways things might have been, absolutely speaking, spans those *formally* possible, maximal propositions[19] that satisfy at least the following constraints:

(a)   the existence of necessary being on which all contingent being depends;

(b)   the constraint of natures on contingent being, including:
　　(i)   internal relations of inclusion/exclusion among properties,
　　(ii)   necessities of identity for at least ontologically basic entities,
　　(iii)   there being an objective basis for the putative possibility in the necessary being's power; and

(c)   the exclusion of *apparent* possibilities that are within the scope of the necessary being's power but for which there is *sufficient* reason for it not to generate.

Note the kind of priority of actuality over possibility that Aquinas and other medieval metaphysicians stressed. The apparently opposing intuitions of (i) states of affairs as (im)possible in and of themselves and of (ii) the actual as explanatorily prior to the possible are reconcilable when one takes the former in relation to formal *logical* consistency (or some other restricted aspect of metaphysical possibility) and the latter in relation to genuine *metaphysical* possibility.

This view of the matter runs contrary to much current thought regarding the metaphysical modality. For according to the present view, it is easier to establish a *necessity* claim than a possibility claim. (Conceivability, however this is to be understood, is not by itself a reliable guide to metaphysical possibility.) But this is less surprising once we recognize the point argued earlier that claims concerning the metaphysical modality are best accepted for definite *explanatory* purposes, and explanation often involves necessary connections. Philosophers who recognize the existence and importance of the metaphysical modality insist that one cannot rest at the superficial level of pretheoretical concepts in order to establish a genuine possibility (though that will suffice in some cases to establish a genuine, though trivial, *necessity*). One must "see the proposed scenario through," which requires grasping the natures of the entities involved and taking due notice of relations of inclusion and exclusion among them. (How thorough a grasp on the natures is requires will depend on the possibility claim involved.) What I am suggesting, in effect, is that the existence question forces us to recognize a further level to this procedure of seeing a putative unactualized possibility through, namely, seeing through to the ground of its possibility in necessary being.[20]

Having said that, there remains an epistemological worry that is naturally suggested by this nonstandard conception of the metaphysical modality (viewed from the vantage point of contemporary analytical metaphysics). Baldly put, it is that following this route lands us in the bog of skepticism about what is and is not possible. For if a transcendent necessary being – even one with a capacity to generate a broad range of effects – is the delimiter of metaphysical possibility, who knows what perfectly coherent scenarios might nonetheless fall outside the scope of its power, for whatever reason? Even if we accept the transcendent, free Creator conception of necessary being that I have defended, we must countenance the possibility, for example, of moral and aesthetic constraints on its choices, as well as other, unenvisionable specific constraints. More generally, we might wonder how many jars there are in God's kitchen. That is, given that such a being has a capacity to generate physical objects with certain basic properties (we know this much because the actual world exists), how many varieties of 'alien' features (features entirely absent from our world) and of alternative spatiotemporal frameworks fall within the scope of his power?[21]

The fact that we may be unable to say much to answer such questions need not lead us to reject altogether the reliability of modal reasoning, however. Recall that we have urged thinking of modality in terms of the *concentric* spheres of absolute possibility: with formally consistent descriptions (at the outermost), then descriptions also consistent with the natures of the hypothesized entities, considered in and of themselves, and finally, full metaphysical possibility at the core, which further requires a basis for putative possibilities in the nature of necessary being. As I suggested previously, what a philosopher is able to grasp in suitably constrained 'modal thought experiments' are second-sphere 'possibilities', concerning contingent natures in and of themselves, abstracted from the ground of their possibility (or lack thereof). There can be reliable reasoning concerning such possibilities, provided one takes due account (as is now widely appreciated) of the constraints of hidden structure and the like on conceptions involving natural kinds, for example. But what of alien kinds, to which we have no empirical access? Here I think a fairly robust sort of agnosticism is entirely appropriate, and for reasons having nothing whatever to do with our added constraint on putative possibilities, concerning the power of necessary being. Once we abandon the Humean view that 'anything can cause anything', we must recognize that the conceivability of superficially imagined objects behaving in all sorts of fashion is no guide at all to whether there *could* be objects of the imagined sort behaving in such a manner. And *even the Humean* who takes intrinsic properties (and the objects that have them) to be complete in themselves apart from any dispositional constraints at all must allow that he has no idea what the *extent* of such intrinsically inert alien properties and objects is. Whether or not there is anyone minding the storehouse of possibility, there's just no saying by us how many jars it contains.[22]

Necessary Being and the Many Necessary Truths

A related issue that a full treatment of our topic would need to address is the relationship of *Logos* to logical and mathematical necessities. I have argued that there could be but *one* kind of being that exists necessarily *a se* (of itself, rather than having its necessity rest in a connection to something else that necessarily exists). But there is a plurality of necessary truths that apparently require necessarily existing *truthmakers* (propositions, sets, etc.). How precisely should one think of this within the present perspective?

The best available strategy of which I am aware is that suggested by Leibniz: such truths are necessary because necessarily thought by God. This conception would integrate the formal and metaphysical modal spheres. But there are deep and subtle issues lurking here, perhaps the most important of which is captured in Bertrand Russell's objection to Leibniz on this score:

> without the law of identity or contradiction, as Leibniz truly says, there would be no difference between truth and falsehood. Therefore, without this law, it could not be true, rather than false, that God exists. Hence, though God's existence may depend upon the law of contradiction, this law cannot in turn depend upon God's existence. (1937: 180)

Robert Adams suggests that the best position to take in response to this objection (and this may well be Leibniz's own position) is to say that

> the *being* of necessary truths consists in their being recognized or accepted as true by God, though the *reason why* they are true (and hence accepted) rather than false (and hence rejected) is to be found in their *content* rather than in the divine acceptance as such. (1994: 191; emphasis added)

This is at best in the neighborhood of what we are after. We start by denying that there are self-subsisting Platonic entities that are the ground of logical truths. The being of such truths consists, rather, in the intellectual activity of the necessarily unique necessary being (the only being that exists *of itself*). This activity does not result from an act of contingent *will* on God's part (in which case they might not have existed, a position that would indeed seem to fall afoul of something like the charge Russell made). It is instead a product of God's unchanging *understanding*. But understanding of what? Given the wider view, the answer evidently is, the divine nature itself – more specifically, *the range of God's power*. Our epistemic access to the nature of God's power is by thinking of it as the ability to produce all that is possible. But the *metaphysics* of divine power and possibility run in the reverse direction: God's power is the ultimate truthmaker for all possibility. The response to Russell, then, is that, just as God could not exist without understanding logical truths, so those truths could not exist without being understood by God. But in each case, the hypothesis is an impossible one. They are, as Adams puts it, "two sides of a single fact" (1994: 185) – and, we might add, one that is metaphysically bedrock.[23]

While it would take some doing to fully make out this idea, one should not overlook that the general project of bringing modality within a unified framework is also sought by contemporary philosophical naturalists who have given the matter thought, and rightly so.[24] As Bob Hale has emphasized, it is profoundly unsatisfactory to have a disjointed account of the truthmakers for absolute necessities (1996: 93–117). Indeed, Leibniz himself puts forth the divine-thought conception as the basis for an *independent* argument for God's existence, as the only plausible way to steer a middle course between the excesses of Platonism and views which try, problematically, to tie the basis for logical truths to the nature of the human mind.

A further advantage is epistemological. Recall our discussion in Chapter 2 of the justification of our beliefs concerning general necessities, particularly those of logic and mathematics. I defended an account on which we start with a jumble of modal intuitions and proceed through a process of reflective equilibrium. However, we noted that it remained to show that our original acceptances are not 'accidental', evidentially unrelated to the truthmakers for the propositions believed. It is open to the theist (and our *Logos* hypothesis, while not identical to theism, is consistent with and has strong affinities to it) to suppose that it is a divine intention that human cognitive abilities are disposed to modalize reliably in accordance with modal fact. In this way, there can be a tie between modal fact and human modal judgments that plausibly accords with the proper function of human cognition while preserving the integrity of the purely natural causal processes generating such judgments.[25] Our typical naturalist will be scandalized at this Leibnizian solution, but can he do any better?

6 | The God of Abraham, Isaac, and *Anselm*?

In this chapter, I abruptly shift gears. My remarks are aimed less at philosophers than at theologians, and more particularly, Christian theologians. A major trend among Christian theologians of the century just concluded (one that shows no sign of abating) has been to sharply question the consonance of the type of natural theology displayed in Chapters 3–5 with biblical revelation. The chief villain is our guiding concept of *necessary being*, a being for whom existence and nature are inseparable. For many contemporary Christian theologians, even those of a traditional theological stripe, these modest a priori constraints on the concept of God are enough to raise red flags. For, they say, we all know the ultimate destination of taking *that* metaphysical conception as our first step in constructing a theology. The full-blown traditional schemes may vary in certain details, but the basic picture is invariably one of an immutable, utterly transcendent ground of being. A being that is usually taken, indeed, to have an utterly simple, and hence unchanging, nature (in a manner completely beyond our ken). And is not this picture sharply at odds with the God who has revealed Himself as a tripersonal reality, engaged with a specific people in human history, incarnate at a particular time and place as a human being, and so in some way subject to all the forms of constant change which that last fact immediately implies? Say our theologians: away with such *onto-theology*![1]

Christian philosopher-theologians from Augustine onwards who subscribed to the picture delivered by natural theology were quite keenly aware of this prima facie incompatibility. Their attempts to show that the incompatibility was prima facie only were elaborate and highly sophisticated. But clearly they did not settle the matter, as the intensive labors of their modern-day heirs attests. Moreover, whatever degree of success one may judge them to have had in working out a consistent framework fitting together natural and revealed theological claims, they did not address at all, or with the same depth, certain other, characteristically modern theological criticisms of the enterprise. First, these frameworks inevitably *modify* (or even implicitly discard) the face-value claims of revealed theology concerning God's nature. Second, by giving pride of place to natural theology (as embodied in Aquinas's *Summa Theologiae*), the overall systems give distorted *emphasis* to the alleged metaphysical attributes while consigning to the periphery what God has revealed to be central to His nature: His tripersonal nature and His passionate, sacrificial love for and involvement with His people. And third, they distort the *epistemology* of religious belief, by implying that a defense of the reasonableness of accepting and committing oneself to the basic tenets of traditional Christianity (at least for the intellectual authorities of the tradition) must proceed by way of a defense of 'bare theism' – a defense that is completely independent of revelation in the history of God's people and preeminently in the person and life of Jesus, and independent also of our experiences in response to the narration of these events in the Church, communally and individually. The contemporary Catholic theologian Michael Buckley scornfully remarks that the widely differing forms of Christian apologetic in the seventeenth and eighteenth centuries held in common that "the Christian God was to be justified without Christ" (1987: 346).

As one who is both a philosopher and a Christian, I naturally have an interest in these criticisms of natural theology from both sides of the fence. Hence, the present chapter. In my own view, the proper verdict on the reconcilability of the content of Christian revelation with the full-blown natural theological concept of God found in the works of classical theologians is much less clear than many contemporary theologians would have it. The peremptory dismissal of this project by some theologians is made in apparent ignorance or lack of serious regard of the flowering of philosophical work on this subject in the last three decades (both friendly to and critical of aspects of classical natural theology). Nonetheless, I am partially sympathetic to the conceptual worries embodied in the first objection above. The good news, I will argue, is that one can reasonably accept the philosophical concept of God as necessary being while rejecting the more problematic notions of immutability and simplicity. In consequence, theologians should be discriminating in their suspicions of traditional natural theology. The fuller story on how one might rethink the relationship of philosophical reflection and revelation, as well as incorporating lessons from the epistemology of science, is one that I cannot tell here.[2]

However, there is also bad news for the uncompromisingly 'de-Helleniz-ing' theologians. Natural theological reflection cannot be neatly separated from unphilosophical religious belief. Specifically, the concept of God implicit in certain claims at the heart of the Biblical revelation themselves *require* articulation in the metaphysical terms of necessary being.

The Unity of the Divine Nature and Its Consequences

Natural theology consists of many strands of thought, so let us remind ourselves just which strands we have selected within the previous chapters. Our starting point was the existence of contingent reality and our goal was the form of its possible explanation. We argued that the world we inhabit need not have existed – nothing about its constituents and basic dynamical principles are, as best we can tell, absolutely necessary – and that the only possible form of an ultimate *explanation* of why it does exist points to the causal efficacy of necessary being. In reflecting on this notion of necessary being, we inferred that its *essential* features must form a tight unity – they must be so bound up with one another that any one could not exist in the absence of the others. While there may be any number of distinct features, it is only by an abstraction, based on an incomplete understanding, that one may conceive of one of them as existing apart from the others. A fully adequate grasp of such a being's nature would involve a recognition of the intimate interdependency or interconnectedness of these attributes in broadly the way we recognize the internal connection between triangularity and trilaterality in two-dimensional Euclidean geometry, or the one-way entailment of spatiality by greenness. The reason we must suppose this in the case of necessary being turns on its peculiar status as the ultimate locus of explanation. Were its fundamental properties only contingently con-nected, so that omnipotence, say, might have existed in the absence of omniscience, there could be no explanation of how these properties came to coexist in this particular being.

Thus was our reasoning concerning the nature of necessary being. It is actually difficult to be sure just how far short of the medievals' doctrine of simplicity our unity-of-essential-features claim actually is, when one consid-ers the simplicity doctrine in a form restricted to a consideration of God's *essential* properties. It is noteworthy that the most common formulations of simplicity-based claims were negative in form, for example, that 'omnip-otence is *not other than* omniscience', and that 'God is not other than His omnipotent power'. That is, careful statements of simplicity theses tended to shy away from bald assertions of strict, logical identity, as would be the case in the claim 'omnipotence *is* omniscience'. Expressing their theses in this way may reflect an intention to capture something logically weaker, akin to the logical or metaphysical interconnectedness indicated in the previous paragraph. Duns Scotus asserted outright that simplicity was compatible with saying that the divine attributes were 'formally distinct' (in a technical sense), though 'really the same'.

But even if my own view with respect to the core, essential attributes of necessary being is similar to that of some of the medievals, I would sharply differ with them on the claim that this conception of the divine unity is (demonstrably) incompatible with *in*essential *change*. Let us briefly consider a common reason for denying the possibility of change within a necessary being. It was standard to follow Aristotle in supposing that 'whatever is moved is moved by another'. And this thesis was, of course, the basis for a rather different cosmological argument from the argument from contingency. It was argued that the observed sequence of changes that in turn give rise to other changes must have a first element. This first element would have to be an unmoved mover. But ignoring the justification for that argument as a whole, and focusing solely on the *concept* of an entity that is unmoved with respect to its activity of moving the immediately posterior element in a causal series, why should it be evident that such an entity must *remain* unmoved? Indeed, why cannot its first action be that of *self*-movement? Or even if the first 'movement' is taken to be outwardly directed, involving the generation of another being or group of beings, why cannot those beings in turn act on the one who generated and sustains them?

To elaborate: We agree that God's essential, defining nature forms a tight unity. Among the interconnected cluster of attributes, it is further agreed, are ones embodying causal *capacities*. This would seem to imply that among the 'ground-floor' attributes is a tendency toward activity (as is reflected in the Dionysian Principle that 'Goodness is diffusive of itself'). These divine capacities are in important respects quite different in kind from ours, of course: For example, they are capacities to generate and sustain objects in existence, qualified in certain ways, rather than merely to *modify* things which exist independently. But suppose, contrary to simplicity theorists, there are causally *receptive* attributes in His nature as well. Guided by more specific reasons known only to Him, God directly gives being to this very world. And He has so constructed this world that its pattern of development consequently 'registers' in His awareness, which at times prompts focused responses from Him in turn, as in the call of Abraham to leave his people and go where God should lead him.

Now the question is, where is the inconsistency in this very simple picture of how God not only acts on His creation, but allows Himself to *be acted on* by it as well? I believe the most impressive challenge to this picture comes from those who argue that an absolutely perfect being cannot have a 'time-like' mode of existence. Such theorists argue, to the contrary, that God exists in a timeless eternity, which is to be thought of as a seamless plenum that is ever present to each event occurring in the temporal unfolding of our world.[3] God timelessly is present to Moses at the burning bush, just as He is present to you as you read this page in the temporal present, and He timelessly is present to each of us at the future moment of our deaths. The changeless present of eternity is distinct from the ever-changing present of temporality, and yet it encompasses it.

It is difficult to assess with any confidence the coherence of the thesis of God's timeless eternity per se, not least because of the inescapable temporality of our own perspective. If one accepts (as some eternity theorists do) a dynamical conception of our own world, the price of the eternity thesis is an irreducibly perspectival view of being and truth. (Consider the future event of your death. On the dynamical view of the world's becoming, there *is* no such event, though there will be. On the timeless eternity thesis, however, that event is already determined and out *there-then* from *God's* eternal vantage point, being eternally simultaneous with God's unchanging eternity. So the eternity theorist who is also a dynamicist must hold that your death both really does not exist, from the temporal perspective, and really is occurring from the perspective of, or in, God's eternity.)

If God *is* timeless in this way, His immutability follows. There are numerous arguments for the timeless eternity thesis, and I cannot attempt to reply to them all here.[4] The questionable coherence of the thesis itself gives some reason to question arguments on its behalf. Here I want to point out that even if we grant the coherence of the intended view of God's eternity and of its relationship to time, it is very doubtful that it is consistent with God's special *activity* in history, in accordance with biblical revelation. The eternity theorist says that God eternally performs a *single*, indivisible act, an act whose *effects* are nonetheless scattered throughout time. God's creation of the world is bound up in the same act as His speaking to Moses on Mt Sinai. In his timeless act of creating the world, we might say, God 'builds in' his responses to human beings at particular moments and other such special forms of engaging the world beyond generally conserving it in being.

It is at just this point that a clear difficulty arises. If, as would appear to be the case, the temporal evolution of the world is not 'programmed' (in rigorous, deterministic fashion) into its earliest state or states, precisely how it will unfold would seem to be *unknowable* in advance. In reply, it will be suggested that the whole matter of knowing or not knowing temporal events 'in advance' is inapplicable here, since we are of course supposing God to be outside time altogether. (Just as God's *action* is a single indivisible act, so God's *cognition* of the world is indivisible and unchanging.) Granted, there is no *temporal* priority in God's knowledge, on the picture. But eternity theorists allow that we can (and must) speak in terms of a *logical* priority of 'moments' or 'phases' to God's creation, given that it was a *free* creation (as Christian theology requires) and not a necessary emanation from God's nature. That is, though God eternally *is* acting in sustaining our world in existence, He *might* instead have sustained another world; and had He done so, He would have been guided by different *specific* considerations (though the same ultimate general end). In thinking about what actually and eternally occurs on God's side of the equation, we cannot suppose that all the contingent features of how our world unfolds are contained in the 'store of information' *guiding* God's creative act. What clearly is included are the *necessary* truths concerning His nature, logic, mathematics, and the like. But in this 'logically prior moment' of having information on which to act, there *are* no truths about what our world is like, as that is precisely what is to be *decided*.

Fair enough, you might say, but provided God knows, logically prior to creating, how things *would* in fact unfold, relative to the *first* moment of the world, for *any* possible world under consideration, then He has knowledge enough. For presumably He would also then know how *He* would want to respond to each such stage of its unfolding, which response would be plugged into the 'divine model' of that world. And He would also know how things would *then* occur, given that very response and the vast array of other factors at work that He sustains. And so on. The result is that 'logically prior' to creating our world, God knows all the possible options *including His interactions with us*, whose actions are not preprogrammed. He need not 'wait and see' how things unfold before responding. Knowing how things *would* act in *any* specific situation He might bring about (and how He would want to respond, and so on), in the 'logical moment' of deciding which world to create, He could build in His 'responses' within the single eternal act of creation.

Perhaps the first philosopher-theologian to make fully explicit this picture of God's act of creation was the sixteenth-century Spanish theologian, Luis de Molina. Molina coined the term "middle knowledge" for this knowledge he ascribed to God of how things *would* develop, as a contingent matter of fact, out of any possible prior circumstance that God might cause to be and allow to unfold of its own accord (1988). Such knowledge is 'midway', we might say, between God's knowledge of *necessary* truths and His knowledge of how things actually *are* in the contingent order. (The knowledge informing God's decision of which world to create cannot, as we said earlier, be thought to include knowledge of what the nature of the world *is*, as that is precisely what is to be determined, but it includes the so-called "middle knowledge" of how things *would* develop subsequent to any circumstance He *might* bring about.)

The allure of Molina's view is that it is a way of having your cake and eating it, too.[5] The problem with Molina's view is that it is a way of having your cake and eating it, too! There are actually two fundamental problems here. First and foremost is that Molinism posits a breathtaking number of contingent truths without any truthmakers. The items in question are a special subset of the set of subjunctive conditionals, many of which are counterfactuals, propositions about what would have happened under purely hypothetical circumstances. The truth of some counterfactuals is entirely unproblematic. Consider the counterfactual *If I were to hold out the pen in my pocket and then let go (and no extraordinary force were to be brought to bear), it would fall to the ground*. This is obviously true and knowable by us, let alone an omniscient being. Why? Because it has a *basis* in certain facts about gravitational force, how physical forces in general interact, and facts about the pen. None of us may know all the details, but we know enough in a general sort of way to know that this counterfactual is true.

Now think about counterfactuals about how we would *freely* act under specific hypothetical circumstances. There undoubtedly are relative *tendencies* in us to act in certain ways rather than others, and in some cases, the outcome of a hypothetical scenario approaches certainty. But if we have a significant measure of freedom, it is entirely in doubt how we would act in certain *other* scenarios. In many actual scenarios, it is, within a fixed range of possibility, up to us *at the time of the action* to determine what we will do. But how is this consistent with supposing that, prior to our action (and indeed, prior to our *existence*) there already was a definite fact of the matter about how we would act? What could be the basis of these supposed purely counterfactual truths that are the objects of divine middle knowledge? Not facts about what our characters would be in the hypothetical situations, since these, by hypothesis, do not make *inevitable* what we would do. (At most, they make certain actions more probable than others.) And no plausible alternative basis appears to be in the offing. It seems our Molinist offers us truths without truthmakers.[6]

The second problem with Molinism is independent of the first. Stipulate some ontological basis for the counterfactuals of freedom that are true logically prior to God's creation decision. Some of these concern what we would do under conditions that actually come to pass. It now seems that our actions under these circumstances cannot be free, since there is a truth-maker for what we will do prior to our doing it – a truthmaker that does not reside in *us*, since it obtained prior to our existence. The existence of these truthmakers is beyond our control; they are necessary for us in the way that features of the past are necessary for us. From these truths, fur-thermore, our actions logically follow. But Jonathan Edwards was surely right that "those things that are indissolubly connected with other things that are necessary, are themselves necessary." In other words, Molinism is (contrary to intention) most naturally taken as a covert form of the doctrine that our actions are predetermined, rather than freely undertaken.[7] The theologian who is happy to accept this consequence should pause once he recognizes that the same argument applied to God's alleged middle knowl-edge of His own actions. (Molina denied that God has middle knowledge of his own free actions, perhaps for just this reason. But how can this asym-metry be sustained in a principled way?)

The standard Molinist reply is to insist that this *logical* necessitation (from contingent counterfactuals of freedom and God's creation decision) of ostensibly free action is harmless, unlike views on which our actions are one and all *causally* necessitated (whether by natural physical and psycho-logical facts or by God's volition). The distinction the Molinist wishes to draw here is not wholly clear, especially given that these counterfactuals of freedom manifestly *are* at least a causal condition (via God's middle knowl-edge) on the action's occurring. But note a further oddity of the view, a direct result of the lack of middle known truthmakers, on its standard ver-sions. We imagine God contemplating the creation of a contingent reality and having to take account of a vast array of already given contingent truths, the counterfactuals of freedom. Since they are contingent, they might have been false (and others of similar form that are actually false, true). And had that been so, it would not have been because of *anything* else's being different at all! True counterfactuals of freedom are basic, brute truths, most of which concern individuals that will forever remain mere possibilities. They are, so to speak, a cosmic hand that God is dealt from nowhere, not foreordained somehow, but as a matter of sheer chance. For myself, I experience a kind of intellectual vertigo when I ruminate on this suggestion. Certainly, it flies in the face of a commitment to anything like ultimate explanation, even of our softer-than-sufficient-reason variety.

The usual Molinist takes himself to be committed to such an extraordi-nary thesis because to suppose that the counterfactuals of freedom are absolutely necessary is apparently to abandon the freedom of the actions so prefigured – they would no longer properly be called "counterfactuals of *freedom*." To say that one acts freely is to say that one could have done otherwise. And, sensibly enough, the Molinist takes as a minimal condition on being able to do otherwise that there is a possible world in which one does do otherwise, where the causal preconditions on one's action are, until at least some prior time, exactly the same. This may be sensible, but it does not follow that giving it up is the least attractive move in defending the view. And we've noted that they are already on shaky ground on that score by virtue of the fact that counterfactuals of freedom are at least part of a causally necessary condition on the action. My counsel to the Molinist is to remove the vertigo induced by commitments to vast arrays of brute primordial truths and allow that they are in some way necessary after all. This will require a change in one's view about the semantics of "could have done otherwise" and allied notions, but that, while also a cost, hardly seems worse. Consider that the Molinist has at hand the distinction between 'harmless' logical necessitation and freedom-negating causal determination. It is open to him to say that free agents are not causally necessitated to act as they do, even though they do so act in every possible world with the same prior history. Their necessity of the counterfactuals of freedom flows, perhaps, from certain necessary truths about how agents with a given determinate psychology will respond to his circumstances. Something like this view may be just what Leibniz is after (in certain places in his mature philosophy) with his distinction between moral and metaphysical necessity.[8] The resultant view may be a lot closer to traditionally deterministic conceptions of freedom than the Molinist would like, but it does not obviously collapse into one more species thereof.

I will mention one alternative for the eternity theorist who does not wish to embrace the problematic doctrine of middle knowledge. We may suppose that in eternally willing the creation, God wills only disjunctive facts concerning human actions, since there are no facts concerning what a creature would or will freely choose to do prior to his acting, and God also wills that certain outcomes would follow upon on any of the disjuncts. In effect, God is building in conditional responses to all the possibilities open to the agent in question. Brian Leftow (1991: 262–5) has developed an account along these lines. Similarly, in discussing the way in which a timelessly eternal God might respond to petitionary prayer, Peter Forrest has suggested that God directly produces (material) conditional situations, with it being left to the agent to determine whether the antecedent is false or the consequent is true (1998: 41–51). Let us suppose that one of these views can be made out. Nevertheless, a serious problem remains. The knowledge of what contingently occurs as a result of causally undetermined actions is, on the picture, explanatorily/ontologically posterior to the knowledge that informs the willing of creation. How does this not entail a real change in

God (which would require temporality)? Leftow suggests that though God's willing would not be informed by *knowledge* of what free creatures would do (there being no facts to be known), it might be consistent with a perfectly certain "*prediction,*" based on his maximal insight into the agent's character and circumstances (1991: 264). This suggestion does not strike me as very plausible. It is akin to Suarez's notion that God's middle knowledge involves a "supercomprehension" of the nature of creatures. The problem is that calling such predictive belief "knowledge" requires there to be a basis in reality. If all the ordinary empirical facts concerning an agent makes it only 40 percent objectively probable that he will do an action, and he in fact does it, then God's certain prediction would have to be tracking something deeper. We can deny that it is a 'fact', but then it is a shadow fact, like ordinary facts in all but name. And such facts, as with the ordinary middle knowledge view, raise the specter of predetermination that is inconsistent with freedom.

Our discussion of Molina's problematic notion of middle knowledge was a brief side road en route to assessing the timeless eternity theorist's conception of God's knowledge of and actions in response to the world. I have argued that the eternity thesis is committed to the doctrine of middle knowledge (or, as with Leftow's alternative, something very much like it), ands have tried to persuade the reader that this constitutes something of a *reductio* of the eternity thesis. In so doing, I am supporting *critics* of natural theology that some degree of real *mutability* in God's nature may be required to elucidate all that we want to say in the context of Christian theology. Surely it would be a sham for God to predetermine our every response to Him – such putative dialogue would in reality be a very complicated monologue that He was carrying on with Himself. Since the timeless eternity thesis does not appear to allow for genuinely responsive, *un*determined dialogue and other activity between God and ourselves, it may well be at loggerheads with Christian revelation.

Assuming the case for timeless eternity is not unanswerable, then, we have ample reason to try to develop the alternative picture I sketched above, on which God has a tightly unified essential nature consistent with His undergoing change in response to the activity of His creation. This does not make Him *dependent* on His creation – it is He who freely gives it being moment to moment, such that were He for one moment to cease from His activity of intending that the created order continue, it would vanish, as a dream evaporates on the waking of the dreamer. And it is He who freely chooses to fashion parts of it 'in His own image' as knowing, self-determining beings, providing the space for uncompelled, loving engagement of those creatures with the omnipotent Creator on whom they utterly depend.

Mutability, then, does not entail a problematic notion of dependence of Creator on creature. Furthermore, such a less constricted conception of God's nature also provides more theoretical room to maneuver in articulating an understanding of the trinitarian persons of the Godhead, and of the incarnate nature of Christ. I won't explore these matters here, as they famously raise all by themselves extremely difficult conceptual issues, which have been explored at great length by Christian philosophers past and present.[9] But clearly the more moderate view of God's unity suggests the possibility, for example, of a more adequate understanding of the suffering of Christ as not being entirely insulated from his divine nature, as classical theologians had it.[10] And it also suggests the possibility of a more adequate picture of loving interpersonal relationships within the Godhead. We must also acknowledge that there are challenges specifically to a temporal conception of God's life, such as the question Augustine raised about what God was doing in the infinite time before the moment of creation, and the related question of why God chose to create when he did, and not at some earlier or later time.[11]

I'm going to shift gears again. Thus far, I have taken a conciliatory line on theological criticisms of *certain* aspects of traditional natural theology. I want now to lay down a forthright challenge to those theologians who look askance on the role of philosophy in articulating *any* general aspects of the content of Christian faith. Specifically, I will try to show that the coherence of the very concept of God is threatened when it is cut loose from the natural theological notion of necessary being.

Natural Theology in the Understanding of Revealed Theology

Consider the conception of God's independent existence held by one who denies (or does not affirm) the 'Hellenistic', philosophical thesis that God is necessary being. Presumably, the de-Hellenizing theologian will suppose that God is causally immune from destruction, that is, no existing thing or collection of things have the capacity indirectly or directly to destroy Him. What is disavowed is the stronger thesis that God is an *absolutely necessary* being, one who exists in any possible world. Now let us ask ourselves: is this a stable position for the ordinary religious theist? According to it, God just happens to exist. But in that case, it seems, He could sensibly feel *fortunate* that He happens to exist, even though He owes His existence to no existing thing. And that appears to be inadequate, clearly at odds with how ordinary theists implicitly regard God's ontological status.[12] I say that our de-Hellenizer owes us a way of understanding this matter which makes this consequence appear less jarring. And in attempting this, he is going to be doing (*malgré lui*) a bit of natural theology or philosophy.

In any case, the de-Hellenizing thesis has a much deeper problem. Consider the concept of omnipotence, which has its subtleties, but which in a rough and ready way is the concept of being able within oneself to realize any truly possible state of affairs. That is, an omnipotent being does not need the assistance of another to realize His aims, at least insofar as those aims do not include the uncoerced cooperation of another. (If it is God's aim only that I act in kindness to my neighbor, He can bring that to pass without depending on cooperation from me. He can simply bring it to pass that I do it, even with the illusion that it is I who freely do it. But if it is His aim that I *freely* act in kindness to my neighbor, then plausibly He must depend on my cooperation, even if He acts in some way to entice it.)[13] Let us ignore this sort of complication and just focus on the question of God's power in relation to states of affairs that do *not* involve free response on the part of other persons. (The continued supporting of the ceiling of the room in which you read this chapter, say.) If God is not a necessary being, if He might not have existed, then it is *possible* that there is a being which neither owes its existence to Him nor derives its power from Him. From this it follows that, possibly, there is a being over which God has no causal control. But if this last is so, then whether our world, the actual world, contains such a being (or indeed, an arbitrary plurality of such beings) is an entirely contingent fact, and more particularly, one whose obtaining God has not controlled. And this would seem to call into question God's sovereignty on even a hazy, untheoretical grasp of this notion, let alone strict omnipotence.

You may be tempted to reply, "Not so fast! We are supposing only that there is no need to give a Hellenistic metaphysical spin to the idea that God is the source of everything that *actually* is. That is, we see no need to buy into the idea that God is necessary being in a quasi-logical sense. There might have been, in an absolute, broadly logical sense, a world in which God was not. So what? That's not the way things *are*. How does this 'concession' get us into the quandary of supposing that anything goes in the *actual* world? Why cannot we in consistency say that nothing *can* happen in the actual world save that God either directly brings it to pass or permits it to happen?"

You may be tempted to say that, but I defy you to follow out that idea in a consistent, plausible manner. Use disparaging labels such as 'Hellenistic metaphysics', if you like, but the denial that God exists of absolute necessity just is to say that God is not the ultimate delimiter of what *might* have been. It *directly* follows that God exists in some absolutely possible worlds (including, as it happens, the actual one), but not in others. Now, the objector's idea seems to be this: Should there have *been*, instead of our world, one of those worlds in which God did not exist, then He of course would have had no control over what went on in it, owing to the rather severe handicap of nonexistence. But nothing can happen beyond His power in a world in which He *does* exist, because He is, after all, *omnipotent*. But there are subtleties here connected to the notion of possibility and necessity of which the objector is failing to take account. (Unsurprisingly, given that he is a de-Hellenizer.)

To see the problem, consider first an analogy. Imagine a world much as an educated atheist believes our world to be: an orderly world, describable by deep causal regularities, such that everything that occurs in it is a consequence of some prior conditions, and yet a world that just happens to exist, without explanation. Call that world 'Alpha'. Now imagine a second world exactly like Alpha until some time *t*, at which point a tree suddenly materializes outside the counterpart of your bedroom window without any cause whatsoever – a brute, inexplicable fact. Call this latter world 'Beta'. Now, there is clearly nothing about the objects in the unremarkable world Alpha before time *t* that sufficed to *guarantee* that the tree materialization would not happen in it. That is to say, if there truly could have been an Alpha world, and there could have been a Beta world, then given the *uncaused* nature of the distinguishing event, there's nothing about the hypothetical constituents of Alpha that would ensure that such an event not occur. If Alpha were to have existed, it would just *happen* to be true that it didn't involve an inexplicable tree materialization; nothing about any of its constituents would be *responsible* for the failure of such an event to occur.[14]

An analogous point holds on the assumption that God exists only contingently. If this is so, it may turn out to be the case that the only objects ever to appear on the scene are those to which He gives being. But if it *does* so turn out, that is a contingent fact whose truth He did not (and could not) ensure. Because once you give up the assumption (leading to the concept of necessary being) that the existence of anything requires an explanation, as a matter of metaphysical necessity, there is no principled basis for maintaining that *in those possible worlds (including the actual one) in which God exists there must always be an explanation for every existing thing, in terms of God's power*.[15] To say this last is to say that while there is no *ultimate* explanation for the existence of things (God's existence, on this view, has no such explanation, not even internal to His nature), it is metaphysically *necessary* that any world in which God exists cannot contain any other object that does not owe its existence to Him. But what could be the *basis* for this more limited necessity? The de-Hellenizing objector has conceded that, as a *general* matter, there *could* have been objects other than God who do not owe their existence to anything, who just 'happen' to exist. So how could it be that God's nature nonetheless *prevents* them from inconveniently appearing in His *own* backyard, so to speak, that is, in a world in which He does exist? It is as if the objector were positing a divine modal force field, that keeps away *uncaused* occurrences that are otherwise perfectly possible. To borrow a phrase from Leibniz, it is a mythology somewhat ill conceived.

Given this basic point that the denial of God's absolutely necessary existence impugns His sovereignty, we could draw out all sorts of particular, ever more absurd consequences flowing from it. (It might even turn out to be a contingent fact that something not appear that could cause God to cease to exist.) But the unacceptability of this should already be plain. The upshot is that any minimally acceptable understanding of God's sovereign control over what happens in the world implicitly requires the concept of necessary being.

Coda

It has been a long and at times wild ride. Though I promised at the outset not to arbitrarily dismiss our cab when it arrived at an agreeable location, no doubt even the most patient of my readers will agree that it is best to put it into park for a while. I have argued that the Existence Question can sensibly be posed, and if it is, we will see reason to posit necessary being at the heart of our metaphysics. Furthermore, there is good reason to suppose that this will transcend the natural world, and also some reason to suppose that it will conform to our generic 'Logos' model, instead of 'Chaos'. But unlike both John Duns Scotus and Samuel Clarke, the two most direct influences on the present line of argument, I would take pains once again to deflate the quasi-mathematical rhetoric of 'demonstration'. It is, I believe, a plausible line of thought that adds to the attractiveness of traditional theistic metaphysics. As such, it merits careful response by those contemporary philosophers (whose name is legion) who take themselves to have seen through its illusory promise – a much more careful response, alas, than is fashionable in these days of breezily dogmatic adherence to philosophical naturalism.

The argument is a contribution to the classical project in natural theology, a project that has its roots in a deep philosophical tradition stemming back to the ancient Greek philosopher Parmenides, and which was incorporated into standard Christian theology from Augustine onwards. Some strands of modern Christian theology have overreacted to the excessive and quite possibly distorting ambition of natural theologians. I suggest that a more reasonable course involves a measured friendliness to the basic enterprise while rejecting the self-understanding of that project by many of its most notable architects. They may have seen the full-blown picture as akin to a seamless garment, such that to attempt to remove any unwanted aspect of it is to irrevocably destroy the whole. But this is far less evident than has been claimed. The metaphor I favor instead is one I learned from my teacher, Norman Kretzmann: reflective Christian theology, of which natural theology and philosophical reflection more generally is properly a part, is an ongoing project of building a bridge of understanding to the absolutely perfect reality which is God. When we engage in this project, we are, as Nicholas of Cusa said, like night owls, trying to look at the sun. We may recognize the need to repair or perhaps jettison altogether certain pillars laid by earlier laborers, but it would be sheer folly to start from scratch and suppose ourselves to see so much more clearly than they the materials needed for forging ahead.

Notes

1. Modality and Explanation

1 *Necessary* and *possible* are 'modes' of truth. The term "modal" has come to apply to all claims about what might have been or must be, including, e.g., assertions about the essential features of objects and their dispositions.

2 "Robust" because certain of the opposing views (see section "Rosen and Sider" below) endorse a limited form of modal realism.

3 A similar worry, directed at Platonism in the philosophy of mathematics, was forcefully developed by Benacerraf (1973: 661–79). ('Platonism' is here a label for any view that holds that our mathematical statements refer to abstract, non-spatiotemporal objects.)

4 For discussion of whether the strategy of positing a global "that's all" fact will even do the job, see Cox (1997: 45–62, esp. 56–60). On Armstrong's difficulty in handling nonmodal truths concerning properties and individuals that are the elements of states of affairs, see Lewis (2001: 275–80). For a deeper worry concerning modal claims about the elements, see MacBride (1999: 471–501). (I discuss MacBride's point below, when I consider the main contours of Armstrong's theory of modality.) I believe that the view to be elaborated in this work allows us to uphold a version of the Truthmaker Doctrine that circumvents these difficulties. On this modified version, to every truth, there is a fact *or nature* that is its truthmaker. But it is a move that is unavailable to Armstrong, given his commitment to reducing modality (as I discuss below).

5 I take it that this claim should stand even for the mind–body dualist. The most plausible form of dualism will maintain that the human mind is ontologically emergent from and dependent upon a properly functioning brain and nervous system. It is highly implausible that the brain could generate a mind having a primitive capacity to detect modal properties that is not grounded in some kind of psychophysical causal process.

6   At the end of Chapter 2, I consider a quite different sort of causal/perceptual model (offered by Koons) than the sort criticized in the text. This alternative model depends on the unusual thesis that modal facts are embedded in the natural world.

7   See his classic essay (1961: 20–46).

8   In the next chapter, I will question whether Quine and others are right to suppose that a priority and unrevisability are so tightly linked. In the text of this chapter, I endorse a criticism only of the extreme claim that *all* theses traditionally deemed a priori are in fact revisable, depending on the nature of our empirical evidence.

9   Quine's epistemological views are set out in several places (e.g., 1969: 69–90; and with Ullian 1970).

10 One much-debated matter is whether his 'coherentist' epistemology is adequate to the justification of uncontroversially empirical beliefs, quite apart from how one thinks of the justification of logic, mathematics, and other 'formal' principles.

11 A theist has the option of going occasionalist on the patterns in the natural world, but doing so simply pushes our basic problem back one step, as we will need to resort, in the end, to modal theses concerning God's continued existence and enduring intentions. The more recent suggestion (available to theist and naturalist alike) that we posit a 'contingent necessity' view of causation will be taken up and criticized in the next chapter.

12 The foregoing claims are directed in the first instance at contexts where the most plausible theoretical inferences involve the activity of causal mechanisms. There are special contexts where one might, e.g., infer the purposive actions of an agent. Since these are mediated by causal mechanisms, the point about presuming underlying necessity stands, though the way it enters into the explanation is less direct than cases where the patterns themselves reflect a causal necessity.

13 It is natural to read Quine himself as simply giving up on epistemological normativity altogether (1969: 19, 24).

14 Most references in the text are to his more recent (unpublished) "Reflections on Consequence" (RC) paper, which helpfully clarifies his position in several ways, but see also his 1995: 49.

15 Etchemendy, as it happens, also thinks that e-Tarski's particular way of developing model-theoretic semantics is extensionally inadequate for special reasons, having to do with contingent facts about the cardinality of objects in our universe. I will not consider here this additional claim or the proposal that theorists should (or in fact do) work within an alternative, "representational" semantics, on which we hold fixed the meanings of all terms, logical and nonlogical alike, and systematically 'vary the worlds' from one interpretation to the next. For critical discussion of Etchemendy's interpretation of Tarski and his interpretational/representational dichotomy, see Sher (1996: 652–86) and Shapiro (1998: 131–56).

16 David Robb offered this suggestion to me in correspondence.
17 MacBride makes this point (1999: 471–501).
18 See the discussion in Lewis (1986: 184–9).
19 The claim that all we need to do to effect the reduction is to believe in 'more of what we already believe in' is nonsense. On any reasonable comparisons of commitments to theoretical entities, Lewis's debt is unfathomably large: elves, fairies, dragons, and Greek gods are just the tip of the iceberg.
20 Plantinga (1987) makes a similar criticism of Lewis's candidate modal truthmakers.
21 I say "it" for convenience, although there will be a plurality of sentences satisfying his account. Sider notes (2002: 295 n. 27) that this will be harmless provided they are logically equivalent, as intended.
22 For a careful comparison, see section V of Sider (2002).
23 Cf. the objection posed to Rosen: Why suppose that there is some *one* fiction whose content is the object of our disagreement?
24 A similarly conventionalist line run on behalf of a different view of the modality of identity statements is found in Gibbard's "Contingent Identity" (1975: 187–222).
25 Perhaps there is room for the barest supposition of a real causal connection linking quantities of the world-stuff, as a referee suggests. However, this will still be inadequate to underwrite the laws we use that quantify over conventional kinds.
26 And mere bits of stuff cannot do the job, either. Convention-imposing thinking and speaking could not themselves be conventional. Such activities, therefore, imply the existence of thinkers with objective persistence condition.
27 It appears to be committed to rejecting S5, which plausibly accords with the structure of ordinary modal thinking.
28 Sympathy for the broader view that modality is to be understood in noncognitivist fashion is expressed by Wright (1980: ch. 23; 1989). See also Craig (1985).
29 Field defends a nonfactualist, 'evaluativist' view of the reasonableness of our adopting the a priori rules of inference that we do (2001: ch. 13). In his review of Field's book, Koons (2003: 119–26) effectively makes the point that Field's attempt to rebut the charge that his position leads to rank relativism concerning epistemic standards is plausible only to the extent that he presupposes a notion of objective propensity. Koons's observation illustrates the bulge-in-the-carpet problem that is inherent in deflationary strategies concerning modality and a priori knowledge.

2. Modal Knowledge

1 Van Inwagen makes this point in assessing Yablo's account (1998: 67–84).
2 For a more careful statement of this idea, see Lewis (1986: 87–9).
3 Yablo recognizes these worries without attempting to address them. He suggests that such questions are apt to lead us to reconsider "either the nature of

the target facts or the nature of our access to them," citing in a note recent work with a strongly conceptualist flavor, including Sidelle (1989). I argued in Chapter 1 that such strategies are quite unpromising, and it is hard to see what other sort of strategy could be followed to bolster our confidence in the imagination-based account Yablo sets before us.

4   See also the symposium on his book (2002b: 636–79), all of which centers on Peacocke's account of modality.

5   I discuss this conception below.

6   Peacocke at one point suggests that the Principle-based conception is not undermined even if it is true that the very notion of a concept involves the notion of metaphysical necessity. (Cf. my discussion in Chapter 1, in the section "Modal Reductionism and Deflationism.") He points to the object- vs. meta-level distinction, saying that a theorist's own modal understanding need not infect his characterization of another thinker's mastery of modal concepts (159–60). This is true enough, but if the claim about the identity conditions of concepts stands, it shows that reductionist ambitions for Peacocke's project cannot be achieved.

7   Fine urges us to replace a modal characterization of essence with one that answer's to Aristotle's notion of 'real definition' (1994: 1–16). But this, if accepted, does not lend aid to a thoroughgoing reductionist program, partly for just the reason indicated in the text: our grasping of essences, so construed, is rooted in counterfactual reasoning that presupposes objective modal facts.

8   Compare the criticism of Sider's and Rosen's metaphysical views in Chapter 1.

9   Another unsatisfying aspect of Peacocke's project, typical of deflationary strategies, is its inability to provide a place for possibilities involving fundamentally 'alien' properties (properties not instantiated in the actual world). All nonactual possibilities must, on his picture, "be constructed from the materials of the actual world" (153). In his symposium response (2002: 676), Peacocke acknowledges the need to generalize the account to nonactual kinds, while not offering any suggestions concerning how this might be done. It seems that the resources of his theory can at best underwrite kinds consisting of novel combinations of actual world properties.

10 This is revealed *inter alia* in our persistent inclination to raise modal questions about the surrogate items featured in deflationary and thinker-dependent theories of modality. And note that the thesis that items in the world have a modal character must be distinguished from a mere functional-role view of our *concepts* that denies or is neutral on the metaphysical thesis. The latter view holds that it is essential to our *classifying* something as an electron that it exhibit a characteristic pattern of behavior associated with the terms "negative charge," "mass," and "spin," but allows that an actual electron might have behaved entirely differently, in which case it would not be an electron. Ellis and Lierse (1994: 27–45) reject this view for much the same reason as I do. Mumford (1998: 232–8) criticizes their argument by defending the plausibility of combining an essentialism about dispositions with the view that objects belong to the

dispositionally determined kinds that they do only contingently. I briefly discuss the question of kind essentialism in the section "Objectual modal judgments" later in this chapter.

11 Here I agree with Bealer, who argues that any view that denies that a priori 'intuitions' count as 'basic evidence' is incoherent (1999: 29–55). We will consider later the question of the connection between such modal beliefs and the facts known.

I will not undertake an analysis of Bealer's own intricate theory of a priori justification set out in a series of papers that includes the one just cited. Instead, I simply note a basic disagreement underlying our respective pictures. He proposes that the reason that our basic intuitions reliably modally track the modal facts is that *determinate concept possession* (an idealized state to which we can sometimes approximate) entails that there is such a tie, that the subject would have a given intuition if and only if it is true. I see little to recommend such a strong claim, unless, perhaps, one is already committed to the transparency of modal truths to ideal inquirers. I am animated instead by the belief that theoretical explanations properly often invoke or tacitly assume necessities that are not transparent even given an idealized grasp of the relevant concepts. Nonetheless, we agree that (as I will go on to suggest in the text) reflective equilibrium governs the process of revising a priori beliefs even while it remains autonomous with respect to empirical inquiry.

12 See the brief discussion in Boyer (1991: 545–6).

13 See the summary of some of this process in Kitcher (1984: ch. 10). However, Kitcher himself draws the wrong lesson from this developmental process, rejecting the a priority of mathematical knowledge. His cardinal error lies in wedding the notion of a priority to infallibility. But for his response to this and other criticisms of his thesis, see Kitcher (2000: 65–91).

14 There is now a clear trend away from the infallibilist thesis. See, e.g., Plantinga (1993: 110–13), Goldman (1999: 1–28 [5]), Bonjour (1998: 111–13), and Bealer (1999: 29–55).

15 Whether there is a distinctive phenomenology to our conscious believings of necessities is a difficult question. Bealer (1999: 30) and Bonjour (1998: 102) speak of 'intuitions' (or 'intellectual seemings') and 'rational insight', respectively, and maintain that these are instances of a distinctive propositional attitude that ordinarily occasion belief, much as sensory experiences are distinct from but generally occasion empirical beliefs. Plantinga (1993: 106) agrees with the view in the text that they are a certain kind of belief, while arguing that they have a distinctive phenomenal character. We may suppose in either case that such a distinctive quality of intellectual seeming is a necessary condition on the beliefs having a priori warrant. (I note that Goldman [1999: 9] claims that varieties of rational thinking generally often have phenomenal aspects but doubts that there is a single distinctive form.)

16 Plantinga is a contemporary philosopher who is admirably clear on this point (1993: 110ff.).

17   Hilary Putnam's wholesale repudiation of a priori knowledge in response to the development and successful application of non-Euclidean geometry probably reflects both of these reactions (1965).

18   See Sklar (1976: 14–15) and the appendix to Bonjour (1998).

19   The supervaluationist alternative of course shows that rejection of this law is not a *required* response to vagueness.

20   And so also our affirmations and denials that certain propositions are necessary truths.

21   Here I am indebted to a similar argument made by Railton, though he does not draw as firm a conclusion from it (2000: 174). A referee suggests that we take the reasoning of the critic as a kind of reductio of classical logic, undermining it from within. But this fails to appreciate the point that our ability to *grasp* the rules of the nonclassical logic that is supposedly shown to be preferable requires us to reason classically and is thus dependent on the normative status of such reasoning.

22   Another kind of case where certain beliefs may receive *both* a priori and a posteriori justification is this: There are empirical results that are deeply puzzling, conceptually, in the context of well-confirmed empirical theories. On reflection, we are able to accommodate these results within an improved physical theory without abandoning any formal or philosophical commitments that had vaguely seemed 'threatened' by those results. Here, the successful accommodation seems to properly augment our confidence that we haven't made some sort of mistake within the a priori chain of thought leading to those commitments. Depending on how strongly we characterize a priori justification, a simpler instance of the same phenomenon may occur when my confidence in the belief in the necessity of a theorem increases upon my getting the same result after checking a complicated proof, or in having my proof confirmed by an expert referee.

23   Epistemic possibility might be thought of as consistency with what one confidently believes (or perhaps believed consistency with what one believes, for a still more agent-relative notion).

24   Armstrong is equating an unmanifested disposition with a one-sided *relation* attached to the dispositional circumstance on one end and nothing on the other. The proper reply is that this assimilation of dispositions to relations reflects a failure to keep firmly in mind the distinction between the dispositional and qualitative aspect of things. Dispositions are intrinsic and 'complete' entities quite apart from their manifestations.

25   To make matters worse, Armstrong has to give back the (spurious) advantage of the type-based account when dealing with probabilistic causality (1997: 237ff.). In such cases, he suggests, "the first state-of-affairs type will give a certain objective probability . . . that an instance of the second state-of-affairs type will be caused to exist in suitable relation to the first state of affairs" (237).

So the type-level fact is only a propensity – a propensity for a first-level instance of causation, which in some cases will not occur (such a 'misfiring' has a nonzero probability of occurring).

Tooley's response to the same problem of showing the relevance of second-order causal laws to first-order sequences of events is different from Armstrong's. He posits unusual features in the mereology of transcendent universals. If it is a law of nature that all things having property P have property Q, then we might suppose that P "exists only as part of the conjunctive universal, P and Q" (1987: 125). It would then follow that any time P is instantiated, Q is as well. But this response puts pressure on the official view that the second-order relations by means of which we specify the causal relation are only contingently associated with it. What more than the obtaining of N (P, Q) can be meant by Tooley's claim, if not that it is part of P's nature to be bound up in the second-order fact? (And, like Armstrong, Tooley cannot extend this suggestion to the case of probabilistic causation. See Tooley 1987: 148ff.)

Both Tooley and Armstrong are driven into the original difficulty precisely because of their insistence, in opposition to the causal powers account, that the nomic structure among universals is merely contingent.

26   It would take us too far afield to consider an alternative 'pure dispositionalist' view, as defended, for example, in Shoemaker (1980: 109–35). Either view would serve my argumentative purposes in this chapter.

27   Ellis emphasizes this point in arguing for the dispositional conception of properties (2000: 329–51; 2001).

28   This point has been made recently by several authors, including Armstrong (1978, 1983) and Swoyer (1999: 100–31).

29   There are any number of other macroscopic patterns that human beings are not wired to be sensitive to. But it would be absurd to claim that one has fully characterized the world only when one has taken notice of every such supervening pattern. I discuss this matter more fully in "What Kim Should Have Said," currently unpublished.

30   This at least will characterize the *onset* of emergent states within a system. Since the initial emergent states will themselves help to determine similar subsequent states – possibly resulting in a complex, stratified range of such states in some systems – the microphysics alone will not determine these later states. Furthermore, emergent states will work in tandem with the underling micro-states to determine later micro-states, manifesting a sort of 'downward causation'. I discuss the concept of ontological emergence at length in O'Connor (2000a: 105–17) and O'Connor and Wong (2005: 659–79).

31   We shall still have to contemplate cases in which there are layers of emergent features, along a spectrum from those in which there is a single baseline feature accompanied by ephemeral accoutrements which that baseline feature partly sustains to those in which secondary and tertiary emergents are more robust and radically reconfigure the causal capacities of the system. See O'Connor and Jacobs (2003: 540–55).

32   I regard as quite plausible the claim that mental phenomena are emergent in this sense. See O'Connor (2000b: ch. 6).

33   Happily, a few recent thinkers have also begun to question this orthodoxy. (See, e.g., Shoemaker 1998: 59–77.) The reader who takes the standard view

of distinct kinds of possibility to be just obvious is urged to consider Peter van Inwagen's (1998) amusing and instructive analogy to someone who posits a distinctively 'cartographic' variety of uninhabitability: uninhabitability that is indicated by an imagined infallible Standard Atlas, which marks certain islands as uninhabitable, none as inhabitable, and does not claim to be complete in this matter (71).

34 Chalmers criticizes the acceptance of nontransparent necessities (which he dubs "strong metaphysical necessities") on the grounds that it leads to *modal dualism*, with the two wholly distinct modal primitives of logical and metaphysical possibility (1999: 473–96; 2002: 145–200.) The present view posits no such dualism, as the notion of 'narrow' logical possibility is here conceived as an abstraction resulting from restricting one's focus to the essential properties of the logical constants. Furthermore, the arguments of Chapters 1–2 imply the untenability of his own monist position, 'modal rationalism', which posits a notion of logical possibility defined in terms of a notion of ideal conceivability. (See also Jackson 1998.) Rather than seek to ground metaphysical possibility in an allegedly independent notion of logical possibility, we have seen reason to reverse this procedure.

3.   Ultimate Explanation and Necessary Being: The Existence Stage of the Cosmological Argument

1 J. J. C. Smart, who evinces a great deal of sympathy for the Existence Question while regarding it as inherently unanswerable, is quite explicit that his rejection of the cosmological argument from contingency is based precisely on his failure to grasp any absolute modality other than that exhausted by formal logic. See his and John Haldane's contribution to the debate in Smart and Haldane (1996: esp. 180–3).

2 And whatever the ultimate merits of such objections in relation to Aquinas and Scotus, Leibniz's metaphysics is of course clearly beset with this problem, though for a very different reason, connected to his understanding of the conditions for adequate explanation.

3 Of course, Kant is correct that anyone who accepts the existence of a necessary being that has other traditional perfections must also accept that there is a sound version of the ontological argument – valid in form and with all true premises. But that is not the same as accepting that the ontological argument has independent force as an argument for the existence of a necessary being. (Cf. the atheist's position with respect to the following argument: [1] Everything is red or God does not exist. [2] Not everything is red. Therefore: God does not exist.) Cf. Forgie (2003: 364–70).

4 Walker alleges that the simple appeal to necessary existence is not even formally satisfactory in providing an ultimate stopping point of explanation (1997: 109–23). He writes, "Sugar is necessarily soluble, in the sense that to be soluble is part of its essence, but it is still reasonable to ask why it is; in that case we

are in a position to ask the question, by explaining how molecules of different forms interact. So we do not stop the demand for explanations by observing that sugar is necessarily soluble, and for the same reason we do not stop the demand for explanations why God exists by observing that existence is part of his essence" (115).

His argument fails. Consider first the case of sugar's necessary solubility. *Part* of its explanation appeals to its molecular structure and the characteristic forms of interaction of certain kinds of molecules. Solubility is not a fundamental physical disposition, but depends on molecular and even more fundamental dispositions at a basic physical level. But the causal dispositions of entities at the fundamental level will not be further explainable in this way. Secondly, and more importantly, further *necessity* claims are needed to support the explanandum: that sugar is necessarily constituted by the structure it has in the actual world and that such structures have their causal dispositions of necessity. As for necessary existence, I will argue later that necessary existence cannot be a derived attribute of a being, but must instead be fundamental.

5   I here agree with many that S5 is the correct logic of absolute necessity. While a few philosophers dispute this, it would take us too far afield to consider their arguments here.

6   On scientific reasons for interpreting Big Bang cosmology as yielding a finite but unbounded totality, see Hartle and Hawking (1983: 2960–75) and Hawking (1982: 563–72). For arguments that an implication of this picture is that it leaves no 'explanatory loose ends' for theism to fill, see Hawking (1988: 136–41) and Smith (1993).

7   Thus my response is different from that of Rowe (1992: 142–57). Rowe allows that contingent events within the universe are fully explainable, in principle, by citing their natural causes, while contending that the universe as a whole may still require additional explanation.

8   For further discussions of Hume's contention, see Gale (1991: 254–5) Campbell (1996: 159–73), Forrest (1996: 92), and Pruss (1998: 149–65).

9   For more recent and concise statements, see Leslie 1997: 218–31; 2001.

10 Cf. Lewis's quip in another connection (1986: 111).

11 I here assume actualism – the thesis that everything that is, actually exists.

12 This formulation of the objection closely follows that given by van Inwagen (1996: 95–110; see 97–9). See also Rowe (1984: 357–69).

13 Pruss (2006: 148–59) suggests a couple ways to reconcile contingency with the PSR. One is to insist that if one explains P noncontrastively, there is nothing further to be explained having the form of *that P rather than Q*. In my judgment, he does not make a convincing case for this surprising thesis. The alternative strategem is to restrict the intended scope of PSR. The restriction can be motivated, and indeed results in a position much like I will go on to defend, though it is arguably at odds with the spirit of PSR as intended by rationalist proponents such as Leibniz.

14   E.g. van Inwagen (1996) implies that the *only* superficially plausible argument
      for there being a necessary being is the one involving PSR (and since that must
      be rejected owing to the absurd consequence just shown, there can be no cogent
      argument for this conclusion). Similarly, Sobel contends that the only way to
      achieve a 'complete' reason for the existence of contingent facts would be to
      provide a necessitating reason, thereby undercutting their contingent status
      (2004: 222–4).
15   I defend this account in O'Connor 2000b.
16   I consider this question in O'Connor 1999: 405–12.
17   I discuss a somewhat different account of intentional explanation in O'Connor
      2000b: ch. 5. I there draw upon central elements of the account of Ginet, *On
      Action* (1990: ch. 5), although Ginet deploys it in the context of a wholly
      noncausal theory of the genesis of an action. In O'Connor 2005: 207–27, I
      modify the account in a way that is reflected in the text.
18   See, e.g., van Fraassen (1980: 126–9) and the essays by van Fraasen, Lipton,
      and Woodward in Ruben (1993).
19   I thank a 1997 audience at Western Washington University, and Hud Hudson
      in particular, for a discussion of this point.
20   This example was introduced to philosophers by Scriven (1959: 443–75). For
      discussion of issues concerning the bearing of indeterminism and relative prob-
      abilities of possible outcomes on causal explanation, the reader may consult
      the articles found in Ruben (1993).

4.   The Identification Stage

 1   See, e.g., Scotus 1966: ch. 4. I discuss the existence stage of Scotus's argument
      (corresponding to Chapter 2 of the present work) in O'Connor 1993: 17–32,
      and the identification stage (corresponding to the present chapter) in O'Connor
      1996. The general thrust of some of what I argue here is foreshadowed in the
      latter paper, though the details are necessarily different in important points,
      owing to my differences with Scotus on how best to make the case as well as
      on matters of basic metaphysics. Much of the present chapter is taken from
      O'Connor 2004: 417–35.
          There are, of course, similarities with other important historical figures.
      Among the more striking, yet often unnoticed, parallels is Samuel Clarke in
      his enormously influential 1704 Boyle lectures, *A Demonstration of the Being
      and Attributes of God, More Particularly in Answer to Mr. Hobbs, Spinoza
      and their Followers.*
 2   I did not explicitly consider this possibility in O'Connor 2004. Wes Morriston
      raised it in correspondence.
 3   Adams provides a good overview of some prominent medieval views on sim-
      plicity (1987: ch. 21). For a discussion of Scotus's formal distinction in applica-
      tion to the problem of universals, see King (1992: 50–76).
 4   Hawking flirts with this idea (1988).

5 Here it is tempting to consider the actual views of Spinoza himself, for whom 'God or Nature' is explanatorily prior to its finite modes. Tempting, but a temptation to be resisted, as the meaning of Spinoza in this connection is notoriously difficult. I will say only this: If (as is commonly supposed) Spinoza's God is identical with the whole of Nature, the totality of physical things, then I simply cannot make sense of the claim that it has finite 'modes' which are explanatorily posterior to it. On the other hand, if (as Curley suggests [1988]), God is instead identical with his infinite attributes, conceived as a system of laws of nature, then (as Curley himself holds) Spinoza's metaphysic is not one of a truly necessary being in the sense being explored in this work, and so it is of no relevance, despite appearances, to the Existence Question.

6 This is widely accepted, but as with all metaphysical theses, it has been disputed. I will not try to consider opposing arguments here.

7 Remember, my term "necessary being" is meant to apply only to entities that have necessary existence *a se*, or from themselves. We might (and indeed later I will) entertain the idea that a necessary being might necessarily cause there to be some further object. The latter would exist necessarily, but it would not be a necessary being in my sense.

8 *On the other hand*: if we adopt a strong truthmaker principle for basic facts, on which for every truth, there is some state of affairs *in re* that necessitates the truth, it is not true that the global fact of how many NBs there are 'falls out' of those individual facts. (Recall the discussion of this in Chapter 1.) Suppose there are ten turtles on the road. Now consider the state of affairs involving just five of those. This, obviously enough, is not a truthmaker for the false proposition, *There are exactly five turtles on the road*. Likewise, the state of affairs consisting in the ten turtles on the road does not suffice for the true proposition that *there are exactly ten turtles on the road*. What is needed beyond the positive states of affairs involving the ten turtles is a negative, global state of affairs entailing that *that is all there are*. Now it is hard to see wherein such a necessary 'that's all' fact would reside, were there a plurality of necessary beings. If, necessarily, there were uniquely one such necessary being, and this truth supervened on that being's nature, no such 'that's all' truthmaker, external to necessary being, would be needed.

9 These cover all the possibilities for which I am able to conceive a coherent model. While hybrid versions could be developed, as I note below in the text, this fact does not bear on the cogency of my argument. For both *Logos* and *Chaos*, I ignore the issue of whether the fount of being acts temporally or timelessly, as this issue seems to me to be orthogonal to issues of concern here.

10 Bill Hasker suggested this route to me.

11 I thank Brian Leftow for urging me to consider this possibility.

12 The name you favor, of course, depends on which side of the singularity you are situated on. This idea is associated with John Wheeler. See Misner, Thorne, and Wheeler (1973: ch. 44).

13   An extended defense of the argument is given by Leslie (1989); a variety of assessments may be found in Manson (2003).

14   Brandon Carter first called attention to this data (1974: 291–8). For an accessible summary, see Leslie (1989: ch. 2); for a comprehensive treatment, see Barrow and Tippler (1986).

15   On the latter, see Guth (1997).

16   Collins develops this point (2005b: 654–66).

17   They present a short summary of the possible alternatives to carbon-based life that they envision (1998: 254–61).

18   Here I closely follow Neil Manson's presentation (Manson 2003: 7).

19   These objections are discussed in Leslie (1989), and the analogies I employ in response are his.

20   This sort of objection is mentioned by several authors, beginning with Leslie (1989) himself.

21   For an excellent development of this objection, see McGrew, McGrew, and Vestrup (2003: 200–8). See also Colyvan, Garfield, and Priest (2005: 325–38).

22   Both Pruss (2005: 405–24) and Collins (2005a: 385–404) make this point in a symposium devoted to this issue. Colyvan, Garfield, and Priest (2005) contend, implausibly, that the argument simply collapses once one abandons the attempt to represent the reasoning in terms of a consistent probability theory.

23   Here I ignore the option of appealing to the nonstandard theory of infinitesimals, on which there are numbers greater than zero but less than every positive real.

24   In thinking about the 'coarse-grained' *reductio* argument, I have been helped by reading Pruss (2005) and Koperski (2005: 303–19), both of whom take the same general line as I do in the text. (Obviously, they are not responsible for my way of formulating the response.)

25   Here again see McGrew, McGrew, and Vestrup (2003: 205).

26   An updated statement is found in Everett 1973.

27   For an accessible discussion of these theories, see Guth 1997.

28   Collins develops these points (2005b: 654–66).

29   The disadvantage is that it has the form of a rival hypothesis invoked solely for the purpose of explaining the fine-tuning. So we must then compare its intrinsic merits with the design hypothesis. The physical versions of the many-universe story, by contrast, hold out the hope of an independently verified account which makes unnecessary nonempirical hypothesizing.

30   See the argument on this point in Swinburne (1996: ch. 3).

31   Swinburne argues for the comparative simplicity of theism and its consequently greater (though still small) intrinsic probability (2005: 641–53).

32   As Koons notes (1997: 193–211).

33   For further discussion of the concept of epistemic possibility, see Plantinga (1993: chs. 8–9).

5. The Scope of Contingency

1 This picture is reflected in the fifth-century neo-Platonist, Pseudo-Dionysius (1980), which influenced later medieval thinkers, including Aquinas, who wrote a commentary on it. For discussion of Aquinas's ambivalence regarding this principle, see Kretzmann (1988).

2 A Blackwell referee makes the interesting suggestion that one possible motivation for not creating might be the preservation of maximal unity in what is. I am skeptical of this on the grounds that it is implausible to conceive God as looking at Creator plus a contemplated creation possibility as a totality with a kind of organic value. God's maximal unity is in no ways compromised by creating a contingent reality, and while any creation would be wholly dependent on the Creator, the ontological gulf between the two seems too stark to think of them as jointly having interesting systemic properties.

3 Aquinas points to this response in his *Scriptum super libros Sententiarum* (1253–6: I, d. 2, q. 1, a. 4, s.c), but does not repeat it in either of his two later major treatises, *Summa Contra Gentiles* (1259–65) and *Summa Theologiae* (1266–73).

4 *Three* persons because perfect love requires not only mutual love between two persons of equal worth but also the sharing of the delight in the love received from the one with another. See Chapters 14–20 of the excerpt from Richard of St Victor's *De Trinitate* (1979). For modern discussion, see Swinburne (1994: 190–1).

5 Rowe first set out his argument in his 1993 work. A more recent and thorough treatment is given in 2004.

6 In a 2006 lecture held June 25 in Alexandra, VA, Dean Zimmerman persuasively criticized Rowe's claim that a omniscient and omnipotent who creates a world less good than one it is capable of creating is less than perfectly good. Zimmerman pointed out that one who accepts this claim and the ensuing argument ought to accept a parallel claim that if an ideal gambler is willing to bet n dollars on a horse x but could have bet more, then it is possible for someone to be more certain that x would win. So in a scenario where there is no finite limit to the sum the gambler could bet, we should conclude, whatever the sum the gambler bets, that he was less than maximally certain, yet this seems an unwarranted inference.

Note, however, that we may plausibly modify the principle such that the conclusion of the gambler argument, also plausible, is that a maximally certain ideal gamble will inevitably be frustrated in his aim of value maximization. Likewise, in the scenario Rowe envisions, it is plausible to conclude that a perfect Creator will inevitably be frustrated in His creative ambition. Unlike Rowe's argument, this is not a threat to theism, but it does motivate the theist to consider whether there was, after all, a way around making a less-than-optimal choice. If so, it is plausible that God would take it. In what follows in the text, I suggest just such a way.

7   We will revisit this matter in Chapter 6.

8   "God is the supreme Grand Master who has everything under his control. Some of the players are consciously helping his plan, others trying to hinder it; whatever the finite players do, God's plan will be executed; though various lines of God's play will answer to various moves of the finite players. God cannot be surprised or thwarted or cheated or disappointed. God, like some grand master of chess, can carry out his plan even if he has announced it beforehand. 'On this square,' says the Grand Master, 'I will promote my pawn to Queen and deliver checkmate to my adversary': and it is even so. No line of play that finite players may think of can force God to improvise: his knowledge of the game already embraces all possible variants of play, theirs does not" (Geach 1977: 58).

9   Adams has defended this claim (1981: 3–41); Plantinga replies (1983: 1–20). Menzel tries to show the consistency of the claims that there are only general (qualitative) truths concerning nonactual possibilities and the unrealized future with the claim that God knew (e.g.) that Prior (the very individual) was to be a philosopher, through a novel analysis of the semantics of statements of the latter sort (1991: 475–507).

10 Perhaps it is a vague threshold, but if the subsequent reasoning in the text is correct, this will be of no significance.

11 Basic objects in the sense intended here will include both unstructured fundamental particulars, such as electrons might be, as well as composite objects which are true unities. See the discussion in Chapter 2 concerning emergence properties and individuals.

12 For a discussion of puzzles concerning value in infinite contexts where the value in question is assumed (unlike here) to be finitely additive, as with utilitarian theories of moral value, see Vallentyne and Kagan (1997: 5–26). E.g., one might be inclined to think that two universes having infinite aggregate value may nevertheless be ordered by value (as when one contains a duplicate of the other as a proper part). Vallentyne and Kagan defend such an intuition through use of the infinitesimals of nonstandard analysis.

13 Thanks to Ted Sider for helpful commentary on a paper I gave presenting some of this material and to the audience at Azusa Pacific University for discussion on this point.

14 See Kane (1996: ch. 6) for an extended defense of the primacy of ultimate origination to freedom of will.

15 Of course, this allows the possibility that God's reasons might lead him to conclusively favor the creation of one specific array of universes. (We have been bold enough to suppose that God's creative choice will be shaped by certain considerations. We are not so bold as to claim to know *all* such considerations.) So, for all that we have argued, it might be that God's creative choice was both certain to occur and yet free.

This might be at odds with certain official theological positions on God's freedom in creation. As Michael Rota has pointed out to me, for example, the

Roman Catholic First Vatican General Council (1870) condemns the position that "says that God created not by an act of will free from all necessity, but with the same necessity by which He necessarily loves Himself." However, it seems that one might draw the required distinction by maintaining that God's love of Himself is a different sort of activity than would be His 'necessary' choice in creation, if such it is. Plausibly, this self-love is not an intending (as is a creative choice), but is instead a kind of desire (or joint desire and affirmation).

16 I learned of Turner's article after developing the essential ideas of this chapter (Turner 2003). Turner argues that a perfect being would create *all* possible universes above some cut-off point, defined in terms of intrinsic goodness. One instantiation of each maximally specific type, since (he holds, contrary to the haecceitistic position I voiced earlier) qualitatively indiscernible worlds are identical. He uses this assumption in offering a limited response to the problem of evil from the vantage point of his thesis. Also see the related set of ideas developed in a fascinating way by Hudson (2006). This work appeared too late for me to engage with it directly here, but I hope to do so elsewhere.

17 Numerous authors develop this sort of point; e.g., Lewis (1940), Hick (1978), and Swinburne (1998).

18 Plantinga develops this point (2004: 1–25).

19 Formally possible propositions, in the sense intended here, are those consistent both formally and with the meaning of the constituent terms. Maximal propositions are ones which entail, for every proposition P, either P or its denial.

20 There is a similarity here to the claim of Leibniz that an "effect is conceived through its cause" and the claim of Spinoza that "the knowledge of the effect depends on the knowledge of the cause, and involves it." The similarity is superficial, however, if these other claims are interpreted in a strongly rationalist manner. See the brief discussion of the role of this claim in Leibniz's thinking by Adams (1994: 152ff.).

21 In discussing Anselm's ontological argument, Brian Leftow writes, "So the existence of God would have consequences for modal truths not involving the concept of God: God would have a modal footprint" (2005b: 96).

22 I also note that this perspective on modality undercuts Richard Gale's purported 'ontological disproof' of the cosmological argument. Gale notes that the *possibility* of morally unjustified evil is, given certain plausible assumptions, incompatible with God as traditionally conceived. And he then argues that the claim that there *could* have been such evil is more plausible than the claim that there is a *necessarily* existent God so conceived. (1991: 227–37, 281–4). Though I have not attempted in the present work to bring moral attributes into the argument, we could easily give a more general version of Gale's strategy in terms of any fairly 'simple' possibility that is nonetheless excluded by our necessary being's nature. The reply should be clear: Gale assumes a strong presumption in favor of possibility from apparent conceivability, and we have given reason to deny this. (Gale considers both a cosmological argument of the sort defended here and Plantinga's modal ontological argument from the

possibility of there being an 'unsurpassably great' being that, among other things, exists of necessity. Clearly, Gale has a stronger case against Plantinga, but he is mistaken to think it easily generalizes to the present sort of cosmological argument.)

23   The resulting view of the general ontological basis of modality is similar to the one defended by Pruss (2002: 317–33).

24   Fine has recently advanced a unified account of absolute modality within a framework of natures – including the natures of logical and nonlogical concepts as well as individuals (1994: 1–16; 1995: 269–89).

25   Here I am of course influenced by Plantinga's theistic account of belief warrant (1993).

6.   The God of Abraham, Isaac, and *Anselm*?

1   Among the many theologians expressing such antipathy to traditional philosophical theology, one might especially cite Jürgen Moltmann (e.g., 1993). One may also find broadly similar sentiments in religious philosophers influenced by twentieth-century trends in European continental philosophy, especially Heidegger's critique of 'onto-theology'. See Westphal (2001; 2005: 484ff.).

2   Various others have already made substantial contributions. I have in mind, among others, the writings of the scientist John Polkinghorne, the theologian Thomas Torrance, and the philosophers Richard Swinburne, Alvin Plantinga, William Alston, and Eleonore Stump, among many others.

3   See the seminal paper by Stump and Kretzmann (1981: 429–58), and the subsequent, splendid treatment of the topic, including discussion of select medieval accounts, in Leftow (1991).

4   See Leftow 1991, contributions to Ganssle and Woodruff 2002, and Leftow 2005a: 48–77.

5   Those succumbing to the allure include Plantinga (1974a), Feddoso (see his introduction to Molina 1988), and Flint (1998).

6   For criticisms of Molinism along these lines, see Adams (1977: 109–17).

7   Arguments along these lines are made by Adams (1991: 343–53), Hasker (1999: 291–7), and Koons (2002: 397–410).

8   For discussion of interpretative options here, see Murray (2005).

9   See, e.g., Senor (2002: 220–35), and in reply Leftow (2002: 273–301).

10   And thus allow for points of contact with the work of theologians such as Moltmann (1973).

11   A Blackwell referee notes that the thesis I defended in the previous chapter, on which God would inevitably create an infinite number of universes, provides the material for a partial answer to these questions: We may suppose that God has always been creating, bringing different universes into being at different times.

12   The referee mentioned in the previous note suggests similarly that the 'onto-theology' we are here developing plausibly fits well with the mystical experi-

ences of people such as Catherine of Siena, who claim to experience God as radically unlike the being of objects of experience.

13 Plantinga captures this limitation on God's creative activity by saying that God does not *strongly* actualize a possible world involving free creatures, but instead *weakly* actualizes it by directly bringing about certain states of affairs that will eventuate in the totality of contingent truth that determines which world is actual (1974b: 169–84).

14 A referee suggests one can consistently maintain that no events can occur which are ruled out by a law of nature, even though not every existing thing has an explanation. One might suppose that the laws of Alpha preclude an uncaused tree materialization, even if the existence of Alpha itself has no explanation. But I am unmoved. Laws of nature may rule out certain objects interacting in ways contrary to their natural dispositional profile, relative to contexts of a certain sort. Implicit in such context-relativity is the absence of any nonnatural factor that might interfere with the usual pattern of interactions. If events lacking ultimate explanation are impossible, as I maintain, no special proviso will be needed. Otherwise, we must suppose every law to be subject to the proviso, "absent any uncaused interfering factor." There need be no intrinsic difference between Alpha and Beta right up to the moment that the tree appears in Beta. The subsequent difference is solely owing to the contingent occurrence of an uncaused event in Beta, one which could have (but did not) occur in Alpha.

15 One may be tempted here to assert that there is an eminently principled basis for maintaining this claim: we are speaking of *God*, after all, and the claim simply *follows* from an understanding of who God is supposed to be. But this definitional move is inappropriate in the present context, where it is essentially in doubt that a contingently existing being could satisfy the concept of God in this respect.

Bibliography

Adams, Marilyn (1987) *William Ockham*, vol. 2, Notre Dame: University of Notre Dame Press.

Adams, Robert (1972) Must God create the best? *Philosophical Review* 81, 317–32.

Adams, Robert (1977) Middle knowledge and the problem of evil. *American Philosophical Quarterly* 14, 109–17.

Adams, Robert (1981) Actualism and thisness. *Synthese* 49, 3–41.

Adams, Robert (1991) An anti-molinist argument. In James Tomberlin (ed.), *Philosophical Perspectives 5: Philosophy of Religion*. Ridgeview: Atascadero, 343–53.

Adams, Robert (1994) *Leibniz: Determinist, Theist, and Idealist*. New York: Oxford University Press.

Anselm, St (1998) Why God became man. In Brian Davies and G. R. Evans (eds.), *Anselm of Canterbury: The Major Works*. Oxford: Oxford University Press, 275.

Aquinas, Thomas (1253–6) *Scriptum super libros Sententiarum*.

Aquinas, Thomas (1259–65) *Summa Contra Gentiles*.

Aquinas, Thomas (1266–73) *Summa Theologiae*.

Armstrong, David (1978) *Universals and Scientific Realism*, vols. 1–2. Cambridge: Cambridge University Press.

Armstrong, David (1983) *What Is a Law of Nature?* Cambridge: Cambridge University Press.

Armstrong, David (1997) *A World of States of Affairs*. Cambridge: Cambridge University Press.

Barrow, J. D., and Tippler, F. J. (1986) *The Anthropic Cosmological Principle*. Oxford: Clarendon Press.

Bealer, George (1999) A theory of the a priori. *Philosophical Perspectives* 13, 29–55.

Benacerraf, Paul (1973) Mathematical truth. *Journal of Philosophy* 70, 661–79.

Blackburn, Simon (1986) Morals and modals. In G. Macdonald and C. Wright (eds.), *Fact, Science, and Morality*. Oxford: Basil Blackwell, 119–41.

Boghossian, P., and Peacocke, C. (eds.) (2000) *New Essays on the A Priori*. Oxford: Oxford University Press.

Bonjour, Laurence (1998) *In Defense of Pure Reason*. Cambridge: Cambridge University Press.

Boyer, Carl (1991) *A History of Mathematics*, 2nd ed. New York: John Wiley & Sons.

Buckley, Michael (1987) *At The Origins of Modern Atheism*. New Haven: Yale University Press.

Burnett, Keith, Julienne, Paul, Lett, Paul, Tiesinga, Eite, and Williams, Carl (2002) Quantum encounters of the cold kind. *Nature* 416, 225–32.

Campbell, Joseph (1996) Hume's refutation of the cosmological argument. *International Journal for the Philosophy of Religion* 40, 159–73.

Carter, Brandon (1974) Large number coincidences and the anthropic principle in cosmology. In M. S. Longair (ed.), *Confrontation of Cosmological Theories with Observational Data*. Dordrecht: D. Reidel, 291–8.

Chalmers, David (1999) Materialism and the metaphysics of modality. *Philosophy and Phenomenological Research* 59, 473–96.

Chalmers, David (2002) Does conceivability entail possibility? In T. Gendler and J. Hawthorne (eds.), *Conceivability and Possibility*. New York: Oxford University Press, 145–200.

Chihara, Charles (1998) *The Worlds of Possibility*. Oxford: Clarendon Press.

Clarke, Samuel (1704) *A Demonstration of the Being and Attributes of God, More Particularly in Answer to Mr. Hobbs, Spinoza and their Followers*.

Collins, Robin (2005a) Fine-tuning arguments and the problem of the comparison range. *Philosophia Christi* 7, 385–404.

Collins, Robin (2005b) The many-worlds hypothesis as an explanation of cosmic fine-tuning: an alternative to design? *Faith and Philosophy* 22 (2005), 654–66.

Colyvan, Mark, Garfield, Jay, and Priest, Graham (2005) Problems with the argument from fine-tuning. *Synthese* 145, 325–38.

Cox, Damian (1997) The trouble with truthmakers. *Pacific Philosophical Quarterly* 78, 45–62.

Craig, Edward (1985) Arithmetic and fact. In, I. Hacking (ed.), *Exercises in Analysis*. New York: Cambridge University Press, 52–74.

Curley, Edwin (1988) *Behind the Geometrical Method*. Princeton: Princeton University Press.

de Molina, Luis (1988) *On Divine Foreknowledge: Part IV of The Concordia*, tr. Alfred J. Freddoso. Ithaca: Cornell University Press.

Dodd, Julian (2001) Is truth supervenient on being? *Proceedings of the Aristotelian Society* 102, 69–86.

Ellis, Brian (2000) Causal laws and singular causation. *Philosophy and Phenomenological Research* 61, 329–51.

Ellis, Brian (2001) *Scientific Essentialism*. Cambridge: Cambridge University Press.

Ellis, Brian, and Lierse, Carolyn (1994) Dispositional essentialism. *Australasian Journal of Philosophy* 72, 27–45.

Etchemendy, John (1990) *The Concept of Logical Consequence*. Cambridge: Harvard University Press, 1990.

Everett, H. (1957) Relative State formulation of quantum mechanics. *Review of Modern Physics* 29, 454–62.

Everett, H. (1973) The theory of the universal wave function. In B. De Witt and N. Graham (eds.), *The Many-Worlds Interpretation of Quantum Mechanics*. Princeton: Princeton University Press, 3–140.

Feinberg, Gerald, and Shapiro, Robert (1980) *Life Beyond Earth: The Intelligent Earthling's Guide to Life in the Universe*. New York: William Morrow.

Feinberg, Gerald, and Shapiro, Robert (1998) Possible forms of life in environments very different from the earth. In J. Leslie (ed.), *Modern Cosmology and Philosophy*. New York: Prometheus Books, 254–61.

Field, Hartry (2001) *Truth and the Absence of Fact*. Oxford: Clarendon Press, 2001.

Fine, Kit (1994) Essence and modality. In J. Tomberlin (ed.), *Philosophical Perspectives, 8: Logic and Language*. Cambridge, MA: Blackwell, 1–16.

Fine, Kit (1995) Ontological dependence. *Proceedings of the Aristotelian Society*, 269–89.

Flint, Thomas (1998) *Divine Providence*. Ithaca: Cornell University Press.

Foley, Stephen, Tiepolo, Massimo, and Vannucci, Riccardo (2002) Growth of early continental crust controlled by melting of amphibolite in subduction zones. Letter to *Nature* 417, 837–40.

Forgie, J. William (2003) The alleged dependency of the cosmological argument on the ontological. *Faith and Philosophy* 20, 364–70.

Forrest, Peter (1996) *God without the Supernatural: A Defense of Scientific Theism*. Ithaca: Cornell University Press.

Forrest, Peter (1998) Answers to prayer and conditional situations. *Faith and Philosophy* 15, 41–51.

Friedman, Michael (2001) *Dynamics of Reason*. Stanford: CSLI Publications.

Gale, Richard (1991) *On the Nature and Existence of God*. Cambridge: Cambridge University Press.

Ganssle, Gregory, and Woodruff, David (eds.) (2002) *God and Time: Essays on the Divine Nature*. Oxford: Oxford University Press.

Geach, Peter (1977) *Providence and Evil*. Cambridge: Cambridge University Press.

Geeves, Michael A. (2002) Molecular motors: stretching the lever-arm theory. *Nature* 415, 129–31.

Gibbard, Allan (1975) Contingent identity. *Journal of Philosophical Logic* 4, 187–222.

Ginet, Carl (1990) *On Action*. Cambridge: Cambridge University Press.

Goldman, Alvin (1999) A priori warrant and naturalistic epistemology. In J. Tomberlin (ed.) *Philosophical Perspectives 13: Epistemology*, 1–28.

Guth, Alan (1981) The inflationary universe: a possible solution to the horizon and flatness problems. *Physical Review D* 23, 347–56.

Guth, Alan (1997) *The Inflationary Universe*. Reading, Mass.: Addison-Wesley.

Hale, Bob (1996) Absolute necessities. In J. Tomberlin (ed.) *Philosophical Perspectives, 10: Metaphysics*. Cambridge, MA: Blackwell, 93–117.

Hale, Bob (1997) Modality. In B. Hale and C. Wright (eds.), *A Companion to the Philosophy of Language*. Oxford: Blackwell Publishing, 487–514.

Hale, Bob (2003) Knowledge of possibility and of necessity. *Proceedings of the Aristotelian Society* 103, 1–20.

Hartle, J., and Hawking, S. (1983) Wave function of the universe. *Physical Review D* 28, 2960–75.

Hasker, William (1999) A new anti-molinist argument. *Religious Studies* 35, 291–7.

Hawking, Stephen (1982) The boundary condition of the universe. In H. A. Brück, G. V. Coyne, and M. S. Longair (eds.), *Astrophysical Cosmology*. Vatican City: Pontifical Academy of Science, 563–72.

Hawking, Stephen (1988) *A Brief History of Time*. New York: Bantam Books.

Hick, John (1978) *Evil and the God of Love*, rev. ed. New York: Harper & Row.

Horner, Philip J., and Gage, Fred H. (2000) Regenerating the damaged central nervous system. *Nature* 407, 26 October, 963–70.

Howard-Snyder, Daniel, and Howard-Snyder, Frances (1994) How an unsurpassable being can create a surpassable world. *Faith and Philosophy* 11, 260–8.

Hudson, Hud (2006) *The Metaphysics of Hyperspace*. Oxford: Oxford University Press.

Hume, David (1935) *Dialogue Concerning Natural Religion*, ed. Norman Kemp Smith. Oxford: Oxford University Press.

Jackson, Frank (1998) *From Metaphysics to Ethics*. Oxford: Clarendon Press.

James, William (1987) A pluralistic universe. In *William James: Writings 1902–1910*. New York: Library Classics of the United States, 625–781.

James, William (1998) The problem of being. In *Some Problems of Philosophy*. New York: Longmans, Green, 1911; reprinted in Peter van Inwagen and Dean Zimmerman (eds.), *Metaphysics: The Big Questions*. Malden, MA: Blackwell Publishing, 415–18.

Kane, Robert (1996) *The Significance of Free Will*. New York: Oxford University Press.

Katz, Bernard, and Kremer, Elmer (1997) The cosmological argument without the principle of sufficient reason. *Faith and Philosophy* 14, 62–70.

King, Peter (1992) Duns Scotus on the common nature and the individual differentia. *Philosophical Topics* 20, 50–76.

Kitcher, Philip (1984) *The Nature of Mathematical Knowledge*. New York: Oxford University Press.

Kitcher, Philip (2000) A priori knowledge revisited. In P. Boghossian and C. Peacocke (eds.), *New Essays on the A Priori*. Oxford: Clarendon Press, 65–91.

Koons, Robert (1997) A new look at the cosmological argument. *American Philosophical Quarterly* 34, 193–211.

Koons, Robert (2000) *Realism Regained*. New York: Oxford University Press.

Koons, Robert (2001) Defeasible reasoning, special pleading and the cosmological argument: a reply to Oppy. *Faith and Philosophy* 18, 192–203.

Koons, Robert (2002) Dual agency: a thomistic account of divine providence and human freedom. *Philosophia Christi* 4, 397–410.

Koons, Robert (2003) Review of *Truth and the Absence of Fact*. *Mind* 112, 119–26.

Koperski, Jeffrey (2005) Should we care about fine-tuning? *British Journal for the Philosophy of Science* 56, 303–19.

Kraay, Klaas (2005) William Rowe's *a priori* argument for atheism. *Faith and Philosophy* 22, 211–34.

Kretzmann, Norman (1988) A general problem of creation: why would God create anything at all? In Scott MacDonald (ed.), *Being and Goodness*. Ithaca: Cornell University Press, 208–28.

Kretzmann, Norman (1997) *The Metaphysics of Theism: Aquinas's Natural Theology in* Summa Contra Gentiles *I*. Oxford: Clarendon Press.

Leftow, Brian (1991) *Time and Eternity*. Ithaca: Cornell University Press.

Leftow, Brian (2002) A timeless God incarnate. In Stephen Davis, Daniel Kendall, and Gerald O'Collins (eds.), *The Incarnation*. New York: Oxford University Press, 273–301.

Leftow, Brian (2005a) Eternity and immutability. In William Mann (ed.), *The Blackwell Guide to the Philosophy of Religion*. Oxford: Blackwell, 48–77.

Leftow, Brian (2005b) The ontological argument. In William J. Wainwright (ed.), *The Oxford Handbook of Philosophy of Religion*. Oxford: Oxford University Press, 80–115.

Leslie, John (1979) *Value and Existence*. Oxford: Blackwell.

Leslie, John (1989) *Universes*. London: Routledge.

Leslie, John (1997) A neoplatonist's pantheism. *Monist* 80 (2), 218–31.

Leslie, John (2001) *Infinite Minds*. Oxford: Clarendon Press.

Lewis, C. S. (1940) *The Problem of Pain*. London: Macmillan.

Lewis, David (1986) *On the Plurality of Worlds*. Oxford: Blackwell.

Lewis, David (1999a) A world of truthmakers? In *Papers in Metaphysics and Epistemology*. Cambridge: Cambridge University Press, 215–20.

Lewis, David (1999b) New work for a theory of universals. In *Papers in Metaphysics and Epistemology*. Cambridge: Cambridge University Press, 8–55.

Lewis, David (2001) Forget about the "correspondence theory of truth." *Analysis* 61, 275–80.

Linde, Andrei (1983) Chaotic inflation. *Physics Letters* 129B, 177–81.

Linde, Andrei (1986) Eternal chaotic inflation. *Modern Physics Letters* A1, 81.

Loewer, Barry (1996) Humean supervenience. *Philosophical Topics* 24 (1), 101–27.

MacBride, Frasier (1999) Could Armstrong have been a universal? *Mind* 108, 471–501.

Manson, Neil (ed.) (2003) *God and Design.* London: Routledge.

Martin, C. B. (1980) Substance substantiated. *Australasian Journal of Philosophy* 1–10.

McGrew, Timothy, McGrew, Lydia, and Vestrup, Eric (2003) Probabilities and the fine-tuning argument: a skeptical view. In Manson (2003), 200–8.

Menzel, Christopher (1991) Temporal actualism and singular foreknowledge. In James Tomberlin (ed.), *Philosophical Perspectives, 5: Philosophy of Religion.* Atascadero CA: Ridgeview, 475–507.

Misner, C. W., Thorne, K. S., and Wheeler, J. A. (1973) *Gravitation.* San Francisco: W. H. Freeman.

Moderation in all things (1999) *Nature* Science Update (May 6).

Molnar, George (2003) *Powers.* Oxford: Oxford University Press.

Moltmann, Jürgen (1973) *The Crucified God: The Cross of Christ As the Foundation and Criticism of Christian Theology.* London: SCM Press.

Moltmann, Jürgen (1993) *The Trinity and the Kingdom: The Doctrine of God.* Minneapolis: Augsburg Fortress.

Morris, Thomas V. (1987) *Anselmian Explorations.* Notre Dame, IN: University of Notre Dame Press.

Mumford, Stephen (1998) *Dispositions.* Oxford: Oxford University Press.

Murray, Michael (2005) Leibniz on the problem of evil. *Stanford Encyclopedia of Philosophy,* http://plato.stanford.edu/entries/leibniz-evil/.

Netland, Harold (2004) Natural theology and religious diversity. *Faith and Philosophy* 21, 503–18.

O'Connor, Timothy (1993) Scotus on the existence of a first efficient cause. *International Journal for the Philosophy of Religion* 33, 17–32.

O'Connor, Timothy (1996) From first efficient cause to God: Scotus on the identification stage of the cosmological argument. In L. Honnefelder, R. Wood, and M. Dreyer (eds.), *John Duns Scotus: Metaphysics and Ethics.* Leiden: E. J. Brill, 435–54.

O'Connor, Timothy (1999) Simplicity and creation. *Faith and Philosophy* 16 (3), 405–12.

O'Connor, Timothy (2000a) Causality, mind, and free will. *Philosophical Perspectives 14: Action and Freedom,* 105–17.

O'Connor, Timothy (2000b) *Persons and Causes: The Metaphysics of Free Will.* New York: Oxford University Press.

O'Connor, Timothy (2004) "And this all men call God." *Faith and Philosophy* 21 (4), 417–35.

O'Connor, Timothy (2005) Freedom with a human face. *Midwest Studies in Philosophy* 29, 207–27.

O'Connor, Timothy (2008) Theism and the scope of contingency. *Oxford Studies in Philosophy of Religion* 1, 134–219.

O'Connor, Timothy, and Jacobs, Jon (2003) Emergent individuals. *Philosophical Quarterly* 53 (October), 540–55.

O'Connor, Timothy, and Wong, Hong Yu (2005) The metaphysics of emergence. *Noûs* 39 (4), 659–79.

Oppy, Graham (1999) Koons' cosmological argument. *Faith and Philosophy* 16, 378–89.

Oppy, Graham (2004) Faulty reasoning about default principles in cosmological arguments. *Faith and Philosophy* 21, 242–9.

Parfit, Derek (1998) The puzzle of reality: why does the universe exist? In Peter van Inwagen and Dean Zimmerman (eds.), *Metaphysics: The Big Questions.* Cambridge, MA: Blackwell, 418–27.

Peacocke, Christopher (1999) *Being Known.* Oxford: Clarendon Press.

Peacocke, Christopher (2002a) Précis of *Being Known. Philosophy and Phenomenological Research* 64, 636–40.

Peacocke, Christopher (2002b) Replies to critics. *Philosophy and Phenomenological Research* 64, 663–79.

Plantinga, Alvin (1974a) *God, Freedom, and Evil.* New York: Harper Torchbook.

Plantinga, Alvin (1974b) *The Nature of Necessity.* Oxford: Clarendon Press.

Plantinga, Alvin (1983) On existentialism. *Philosophical Studies* 44, 1–20.

Plantinga, Alvin (1987) Two concepts of modality: modal realism and modal reductionism. In James Tomberlin (ed.), *Philosophical Perspectives.* Atascadero, CA: Ridgeview, 189–231.

Plantinga, Alvin (1993) *Warrant and Proper Function.* New York: Oxford University Press.

Plantinga, Alvin (2004) Supralapsarianism, or "o felix culpa." In Peter van Inwagen (ed.), *Christian Faith and the Problem of Evil.* Grand Rapids, Mich.: Eeerdmans, 1–25.

Priest, Graham (1999) Perceiving contradictions. *Australasian Journal of Philosophy* 77 (4), 439–46.

Pruss, Alexander (1998) The Hume-Edwards principle and the cosmological argument. *International Journal for the Philosophy of Religion* 43, 149–65.

Pruss, Alexander (2002) The actual and the possible. In Richard Gale (ed.), *The Blackwell Guide to Metaphysics.* Oxford: Blackwell, 317–33.

Pruss, Alexander (2005) Fine- and coarse-tuning, normalizability, and probabilistic reasoning. *Philosophia Christi* 7, 405–24.

Pruss, Alexander (2006) *The Principle of Sufficient Reason.* Cambridge: Cambridge University Press.

Pseudo-Dionysius (1980) *The Divine Names and Mystical Theology*, tr. John D. Jones. Milwaukee: Marquette University Press.

Putnam, Hilary (1965) A philosopher looks at quantum mechanics. In Robert G. Colodny (ed.), *Beyond the Edge of Certainty: Essays in Contemporary Science and Philosophy.* Englewood Cliffs, N.J.: Prentice-Hall, 75–101.

Quine, Willard van Orman (1961) Two dogmas of empiricism. Reprinted in *From a Logical Point of View.* Cambridge MA: Harvard University Press, 20–46.

Quine, Willard van Orman (1969) Epistemology naturalized. In *Ontological Relativity and Other Essays*. New York: Columbia University Press, 69–90.

Quine, Willard van Orman, and Ullian, Joseph (1970) *The Web of Belief*. New York: Random House.

Quine, W.V.O. (1995) *From Stimulus to Science*. Cambridge, MA: Harvard University Press.

Railton, Peter (2000) A priori rules: Wittgenstein on the normativity of logic. In Boghossian and Peacocke (2000), 170–96.

Resnik, Michael (1997) *Mathematics as a Science of Patterns*. Oxford: Clarendon Press.

Richard of St Victor (1979) *De Trinitate*. In Grover Zinn (ed. and tr.), *The Twelve Patriarchs, The Mystical Ark, and Book Three of the Trinity*. New York: Paulist Press, 1979, 371–97.

Rosen, Gideon (1990) Modal fictionalism. *Mind* 99, 327–54.

Rosen, Gideon (2002) Peacocke on modality. *Philosophy and Phenomenological Research* 64, 641–8.

Rowe, William (1975) *The Cosmological Argument*. Princeton: Princeton University Press.

Rowe, William (1984) Rationalistic theology and some principles of explanation. *Faith and Philosophy* 1, 357–69.

Rowe, William (1992) Two criticisms of the cosmological argument. In Baruch Brody (ed.), *Readings in the Philosophy of Religion*, 2nd ed. Englewood Cliffs, NJ: Prentice-Hall, 142–57.

Rowe, William (1993) The problem of divine perfection and freedom. In Eleonore Stump (ed.), *Reasoned Faith*. Ithaca: Cornell University Press, 223–33.

Rowe, William (2004) *Can God Be Free?* New York: Oxford University Press.

Rowe, William (2005) Cosmological arguments. In William Mann (ed.), *The Blackwell Guide to the Philosophy of Religion*. Oxford: Blackwell, 103–16.

Ruben, David-Hillel (ed.) (1993) *Explanation*. Oxford: Oxford University Press.

Russell, Bertrand (1937) *A Critical Exposition of the Philosophy of Leibniz*. London: Allen & Unwin.

Scotus, Duns (1966) *Treatise on God as First Principle*, tr. and ed. Allen Wolter, 2nd ed. Chicago: Franciscan Herald Press.

Scriven, Michael (1959) Truisms as grounds for historical explanations. In P. Gardiner (ed.), *Theories of History*. New York: Free Press, 443–75.

Senor, Tom (2002) Incarnation, timelessness, and Leibniz's law problems. In Gregory Ganssle and David Woodruff (eds.), *God and Time: Essays on the Divine Nature*. Oxford: Oxford University Press, 220–35.

Shalkowski, Scott (2004) Logic and absolute necessity. *Journal of Philosophy* 100, 55–82.

Shapiro, Stewart (1998) Logical consequence: models and modality. In M. Schirn (ed.), *The Philosophy of Mathematics Today*. New York: Oxford University Press, 131–56.

Sher, Gila (1996) Did Tarski commit "Tarski's fallacy"? *Journal of Symbolic Logic* 61, 652–86.
Shoemaker, Sydney (1980) Causality and properties. In P. van Inwagen (ed.), *Time and Cause*. Dordrecht: D. Reidel, 109–35.
Shoemaker, Sydney (1998) Causal and metaphysical necessity. *Pacific Philosophical Quarterly* 79, 59–77.
Sidelle, Alan (1989) *Necessity, Essence, and Individuation*. Ithaca: Cornell University Press.
Sider, Ted (2002) The ersatz pluriverse. *Journal of Philosophy* 99, 279–315.
Sider, Ted (2003) Reductive theories of modality. In M. Loux and D. Zimmerman (eds.), *The Oxford Handbook of Metaphysics*. Oxford: Oxford University Press, 180–208.
Sklar, Lawrence (1976) *Space, Time, and Spacetime*. Berkeley: University of California Press.
Smart, J. J. C., and Haldane, John (1996) *Atheism and Theism*. Oxford: Basil Blackwell.
Smith, Quentin (1993) The uncaused beginning of the universe. In William Lane Craig and Quentin Smith, *Theism, Atheism and Big Bang Cosmology*. Oxford: Oxford University Press, 108–40.
Smolin, Lee (1997) *The Life of the Cosmos*. New York: Oxford University Press.
Sobel, Jordan Howard (2004) *Logic and Theism*. Cambridge: Cambridge University Press.
Strawson, Galen (1989) Realism and causation. *Philosophical Quarterly* 37, 253–77.
Stump, Eleonore, and Kretzmann, Norman (1981) Eternity. *Journal of Philosophy* 79, 429–58.
Swinburne, Richard (1994) *The Christian God*. Oxford: Clarendon Press.
Swinburne, Richard (1996) *Is There a God?* Oxford: Oxford University Press.
Swinburne, Richard (1998) *Providence and the Problem of Evil*. Oxford University Press.
Swinburne, Richard (2005) Prior probabilities in the argument from fine-tuning. *Faith and Philosophy* 22, 641–53.
Swoyer, Chris (1999) How ontology might be possible: explanation and inference in metaphysics. *Midwest Studies in Philosophy* 23, 100–31.
Tarski, Alfred (1983) On the concept of logical consequence. In Alfred Tarski, *Logic, Semantics, Metamathematics*, 2nd ed. Oxford: Oxford University Press, 409–20 (first published in Polish and German 1936).
Tooley, Michael (1987) *Causation: A Realist Approach*. Oxford: Clarendon Press.
Tryon, Edward (1973) Is the universe a vacuum fluctuation? *Nature* 246, 396–7.
Turner, Donald (2003) The many-universes solution to the problem of evil. In Alexander Pruss and Richard Gale (eds.), *The Existence of God*. Aldershot, UK: Ashgate Publishing, 143–59.
Vallentyne, Peter, and Kagan, Shelley (1997) Infinite value and finitely additive value theory. *Journal of Philosophy* 94, 5–26.

van Inwagen, Peter (1993) *Metaphysics*. Boulder: Westview Press.

van Inwagen, Peter (1996) Why is there anything at all? *Proceedings of the Aristotelian Society*, supp. vol. 70, 95–110.

van Inwagen, Peter (1998) Modal epistemology. *Philosophical Studies* 92, 67–84.

van Fraassen, Bas (1980) *The Scientific Image*. Oxford: Oxford University Press.

van Fraassen, Bas (1988) *Laws and Symmetry*. Oxford: Clarendon Press.

Walker, Ralph (1997) Sufficient reason. *Proceedings of the Aristotelian Society* 97, 109–23.

Westphal, Merold (2001) *Overcoming Onto-Theology: Towards a Postmodern Christian Faith*. New York: Fordham University Press.

Westphal, Merold (2005) Continental philosophy of religion. In William Wainwright (ed.), *The Oxford Handbook of Philosophy of Religion*. Oxford: Oxford University Press, 472–93.

Williams, Paul (2002) *The Unexpected Way: On Converting from Buddhism to Catholicism*. Edinburgh: T. & T. Clarke.

Williamson, Timothy (2002) Peacocke's Theory of Modality. *Philosophy and Phenomenological Research* 64, 649–54.

Wright, Crispin (1980) *Wittgenstein on the Foundations of Mathematics*. London: Duckworth.

Wright, Crispin (1986) Inventing logical necessity. In J. Butterfield (ed.), *Language, Mind, and Logic*. Cambridge: Cambridge University Press, 187–209.

Wright, Crispin (1989) Necessity, caution, and skepticism. *Proceedings of the Aristotelian Society Supplement* 63, 203–38.

Wright, Crispin (2002) On knowing what is necessary: three limitations of Peacocke's account. *Philosophy and Phenomenological Research* 64, 655–62.

Yablo, Stephen (1993) Is conceivability a guide to possibility? *Philosophy and Phenomenological Research* 53, 1–42.

Index

Printed and bound by CPI Group (UK) Ltd, Croydon, CR0 4YY

09/06/2025

14686120-0002